A Thousand Cuts

A Thousand Cuts

The Bizarre Underground World of Collectors
and Dealers Who Saved the Movies

Dennis Bartok and Jeff Joseph

University Press of Mississippi   Jackson

www.upress.state.ms.us

The University Press of Mississippi is a member
of the Association of American University Presses.

First printing 2016

Library of Congress Cataloging-in-Publication Data

Names: Bartok, Dennis, 1965– author. | Joseph, Jeff, 1953– author.
Title: A thousand cuts : the bizarre underground world of collectors and
    dealers who saved the movies / Dennis Bartok and Jeff Joseph.
Description: Jackson : University Press of Mississippi, 2016. | Includes
    bibliographical references and index.
Identifiers: LCCN 2016005823 (print) | LCCN 2016014403 (ebook) | ISBN
    9781496807731 (cloth : alk. paper) | ISBN 9781496808608 (ebook)
Subjects: LCSH: Motion pictures—Collectors and collecting—United States. |
    Motion pictures—United States—Societies, etc.
Classification: LCC PN1995.9.C54 B37 2016 (print) | LCC PN1995.9.C54 (ebook)
    | DDC 791.43/75
LC record available at http://lccn.loc.gov/2016005823

British Library Cataloging-in-Publication Data available

Contents

Contents

Introduction

This is a book about the death of Film. It's not, of course, about the death of the Movies, which are still in very good health, thank you, both commercially and creatively. Before you jump to the conclusion that what follows is one long, sad dirge for the passing of old-fashioned analog cinema, a last call at the bar before the cowboys ride into the sunset, it isn't. If anything, it's a sort of mad Irish wake for an underground subculture of often paranoid, secretive, eccentric, obsessive, and definitely *mad* film collectors and dealers, who made movies their own private religion.

Certainly the movies face far more competition in the twenty-first century from other forms of media: the video game industry may have caught up with motion pictures in terms of annual grosses, but it hasn't *replaced* the movies. If anything, there's a fascinating interchange going on between the movies, video games, and other media: my son Sandor watches the *Harry Potter* movies so he can better play his way through the *Harry Potter* video games, and then goes back and reads the *Harry Potter* books to enrich and fill in what he missed. This recombinant-DNA intermingling of media new and old reminds me of a unique phraseology that's recently popped up in Hollywood contracts: "*in any media, whether now known or hereafter devised, or in any form whether now known or hereafter devised, an unlimited number of times throughout the universe and forever.*"[1] But my son, and his, will *experience* the movies in a completely different way than I experienced them, and as the dozens of film collectors and dealers interviewed for this book experienced them. There will still be that magical "light coming out of the booth," as dealer Woody Wise remembers from his childhood at the Sylvia Theater in Franconia, Virginia, but that light will no longer be projected through a strip of film rattling through a Motiograph projector at twenty-four frames per second. And with that difference in experience, something in the relationship between audience and image, Man and the Movies, has changed forever.

Since it was introduced over one hundred years ago, 35mm motion picture film has proven to be one of the most durable, versatile, and well-loved formats in entertainment history. You can still, for example, take a multitinted, nitrate print of D. W. Griffith's 1915 *The Birth of a Nation* (to name one treasure that collector Marty Kearns once held in his trembling hands), and, as long as you have a variable-speed motor and the right aperture plates, run it properly on just about any modern 35mm projector. (You can even run it without the variable-speed motor and plates, but you'll get an image that's slightly cropped and, worse, comically sped up in the way that's made many silent films seem hokey by today's standards.) For a little comparison, try playing an Edison sound cylinder from 1921 on a modern record or CD player. (Or better yet, try a Blu-ray disc in your DVD player.)² There were numerous changes and improvements in motion picture technology since its inception, from silent to sound in the late 1920s, from nitrate film stock to safety stock two decades later, but the basic format of 35mm film has lasted for over a century.³ A tremendous achievement for *any* technology. But its time has drawn to a close: it's inexorably been replaced by digital formats, and there's nothing we can do about it. When George Lucas came to the American Cinematheque's Egyptian Theatre in Hollywood in 2003 for the opening night of an Industrial Light & Magic and Skywalker Sound tribute I'd organized there, I had a brief conversation with him in what passed for the "green room"—actually a cramped space outside the box office—about the impending change from film to digital. I mentioned a nitrate dye-transfer Technicolor print of Powell & Pressburger's art-house classic *The Red Shoes* (1948) that the Cinematheque had recently screened. Lucas listened calmly and thoughtfully as I described how beautiful the print was, how watching it was like literally stepping into a time machine and seeing the movie the way audiences had originally seen it. Finally the creator of *Star Wars* nodded his head: "I can do the same thing digitally," he replied. "I can add scratches and noise to the soundtrack. I can make it look like nitrate, like Technicolor, or whatever you want." At that point I knew the writing was on the wall. Film was dead. Long live Digital.

The industry trade paper *Hollywood Reporter*, in an April 15, 2013, article titled "CinemaCon: The End of Film Distribution in North America Is Almost Here," wrote, "By the end of this year, distributors might no longer deliver film prints to theaters in North America. Cans full of reels of celluloid will be a thing of the analog past." Fuji announced that same month that it had ceased production of motion picture film.[4] Eastman Kodak, at one time synonymous with still *and* motion picture film, filed for bankruptcy in 2012. These are, without a doubt, echoes of the death knell for film. Media changes. New media come in, old media become obsolete. But it's not only the technology that changes—lives and familiar habits are transformed too. We're living in an era when record stores and video rental stores have quickly become a thing of the past. So has film, and it's taking with it the bizarre network of collectors and dealers who obsessed, fought over, hoarded, and occasionally stole these precious images.

This book, then, is not just about the inevitable decay and death of the film medium itself, but it's also about the often strange, and strangely compelling, lives of film collectors and dealers, many of whom are dealing with their own issues of aging and mortality as they approach or reach retirement. More than a few collectors said they simply stopped projecting films because it was too physically exhausting to heft film cans or do changeovers; one die-hard collector, Latino graphic designer-turned-truck-driver Rik Lueras, uses his projection booth now to store his medical equipment. This book is about a post–WWII generation of (mostly) white, male collectors and dealers, many (although not all, by any means) of them gay men, who pursued their love for the movies with a glorious, unreasonable passion—a passion that may never quite be equaled, simply because they grew up in an era when *access to movies* was so limited. How many collectors were there at the height of the underground market? It's hard to say, but Donald Key, publisher of the collectors' "bible," *The Big Reel* magazine, says that subscriptions at their peak reached 4,800 in the late 1980s, which is a good guess for the number of collectors total at the time, at least in the United States.[5] Most of the collectors and dealers profiled in this book are American, with the largest concentrations around the film production and distribution centers in the Los Angeles and New York areas (although there were and still are active collecting scenes across the country, usually near distribution depots where there was easier access to prints). Britain had a small but very active collecting community, as Kevin Brownlow and Patrick Stanbury attest to in their chapter, as did France (see Serge Bromberg's chapter) and other countries—but the relatively smaller size of their national film industries also meant there were generally far fewer collectors overseas. It's worth pointing out that while there is a distinction between film collectors and dealers, the lines are often blurred. Many collectors backed into dealing part-time (or eventually full-time) to fund their habit. A good rule of thumb is that while not every film collector became a dealer, almost every dealer started out as a collector.

But why film collectors in particular? Or as *Gremlins* director Joe Dante bluntly asked me when I came to interview him, "So, what's your reason for writing this book?" Part of it is that film collectors are an endangered species. They are dying along with their obsession, and there is something particularly fascinating and moving about seeing them go down with their proverbial ship. Even in the age of the Kindle and e-books, hundreds of thousands of new books are still being printed on paper. Books and book collectors will be around long into the foreseeable future. The same goes for comic book, stamp, coin, baseball card, record, and almost every other kind of collector you can think of. But film stock is enormously expensive to make and process. Even for those directors dedicated to shooting on celluloid as long as it's available—and that's the key phrase, "as long as it's available"—like Quentin Tarantino, Christopher Nolan, Judd Apatow, and J. J. Abrams, getting access to raw film stock and the means to develop it is going to be increasingly difficult as laboratories and suppliers shut down their operations.[6] It's not only lack of access to new prints that's suffocating film collecting: the existing prints all carry the seeds of their own destruction inside them. The basic composition and processing of film slowly, inexorably eat away at the stock itself, producing a gripping odor and physical decay known as "vinegar syndrome," or film rot. As my writing partner Jeff (a former film dealer himself) explains it, "acetate plastic decomposes on its own over time; that produces the odor (acetic acid) that smells like vinegar. Things like unwashed chemicals, scratch-removal chemicals, and mostly heat and humidity all exacerbate a natural process." Properly stored, current film stocks should last for well over a century—but for older prints, the best guess is usually a smell test to see if there's a whiff of vinegar syndrome, which can hop from print to print like an airborne virus. (Some collectors put their vinegared prints in the freezer to try to slow the process, a habit that probably sits well with the non-film-collector partner.) An added problem is fading. Until the introduction of Eastmancolor LPP (low-fade positive print) stocks in 1982, prints generally fell into two broad camps: dye-transfer (or IB) Technicolor, which is highly resistant to fading, and Eastmancolor-derived stocks like 20th Century Fox's DeLuxe Color, Warner Bros.' WarnerColor, and others, which have turned anything from bright crimson to riotous purple as they've faded. Over the years desperate collectors have turned to all sorts of homemade fixes to restore color to faded prints. In his 1974 *16mm Filmland* catalogue, dealer Evan H. Foreman advertised a "Color Correction Kit" for five dollars, "designed to add blue tones to the film when projected by use of one or two blue filters in front of the projector lens." None of these fixes worked, despite the claims of many collectors to the contrary. Go into any used book shop (if you can find one these days), and it's relatively easy to pick up a title from the late nineteenth century for a few bucks, but finding a good film print from the dreaded Eastmancolor era of the 1970s is difficult. Almost all original 35mm copies of *Star Wars*, for example, are badly faded—except for one of the legendary British Technicolor prints of the film. Finding a pre-1948 nitrate print has also become a significant rarity, although not impossible, as several of the interviewees attest to.

Oddly, as the prints themselves become harder to find, their value has dropped, in stark contrast to other collectibles, like comic books. More than one collector I interviewed has wryly commented on the fact that vintage movie posters were once routinely available for one or two dollars, at a time when film prints cost hundreds. Now it's reversed, and those same posters are worth thousands or tens of thousands, while the value of the prints is negligible. *RoboCop* producer (and former Fillmore East theater projectionist) Jon Davison believes that this is a golden age for film collecting, because there's so little competition, but he's fairly alone in that enthusiastic judgment. Many of the interviewees for this book are *former* collectors or dealers. Some, like New Orleans native Mike Smith (or as he puts it in his infectious drawl, "New Oar-leunz"), changed heart when faced with the new technology: Smith decided on the spot to start selling his vast, expensive 16mm collection as soon as he saw a DVD of *His Girl Friday* projected at an audiovisual store in Baton Rouge. USC film school professor and screenwriter Tom Abrams recalls his excitement years ago at snagging a faded 16mm print of Roger Corman's *X: The Man with the X-*

Ray Eyes, which he'd loved as a child in the early 1960s; now, with the film easily available on DVD and the internet, he can't imagine anyone wanting to watch a beet-red print of the movie. Others, like vintage television collector Ronnie James, decided to hold on to their collections while the value and demand for the prints plummeted; Ronnie's fondest wish is that he could now travel back in time and warn his five-year-old self not to start collecting. There are still people paying decent money for good prints, and a handful of younger collectors pursuing treasures with the same passion as their elders. There are even collectors still willing to risk arrest and prosecution so they can "liberate" those last remaining prints: one man, who spoke on condition of anonymity, literally jumped up and down with uncontrollable excitement as he talked about reaching through a hole in a chain-link fence surrounding a film depot and grasping at odd reels of *Harry Potter and the Deathly Hallows: Part 1*, hoping to snatch enough to assemble a complete print. Not satisfied with that, later he and several friends broke into the depot and spent a long night huddled in a metal shed hiding from security—all for a few 35mm prints. But for the most part, film collecting is "a dying art," as Joe Dante puts it, and it will be even deader in ten or twenty years when there are no more new prints being struck, and no more theaters—apart from a handful of private screening rooms and cinematheques/museums—even capable of showing 16mm, 35mm, and 70mm. To underscore the grim reality, Atlanta-based projection consultant and film dealer Steve Newton (who throws the occasional, ingratiating "goodness gracious" and "oh gosh" into his conversation) sent me photos of dumpsters outside his Cinevision offices filled with hundreds of discarded 35mm projectors and metal Goldberg film cans.[7]

Yet another compelling reason to write this book is that film collectors and dealers found themselves, for a few relatively brief but panicked years in the 1970s, in the legal crosshairs of the FBI, the Justice Department, and the Motion Picture Association of America (MPAA) representing the major Hollywood studios. These formidable organizations harassed hundreds of collectors and dealers and even arrested a number of them on charges of copyright violation and receipt of stolen goods, their most high-profile target being *Planet of the Apes* actor Roddy McDowall. The legal rationale behind the FBI's and MPAA's actions is still hotly debated—my writing partner Jeff, who spent two months in prison on film-related charges, even suggests that the FBI was smarting from its public whipping in the Patty Hearst case and decided to go after a much easier target, namely, film dealers and collectors. Whether or not the inspiration for *Citizen Kane*'s granddaughter had anything to do with the so-called film busts of the 1970s, one thing is certain: collectors of film are almost unique in being targeted by the FBI for their hobby. Imagine being a rabid baseball card collector. You're sitting at home one afternoon, drooling over your Hank Aaron and Stan Musial rookie cards. Suddenly there's a knock at the door. You open it to find two federal agents standing there. They pepper you with questions: Where did you buy your baseball cards? Who else do you know that collects cards? Then they demand that you sign a blanket statement admitting your guilt and promising you'll never collect cards in the future. Before they leave, they seize your collection, claiming it violates copyright law and has been obtained illegally. This may sound incredible, but in fact this exact scenario happened to dozens of film collectors in the early 1970s. The picture that emerges of the FBI and the Justice Department is not a very flattering or overly intelligent one: two massive federal agencies essentially at the beck and call of the Hollywood studios, directing their formidable resources against an almost laughably easy target. There were real film pirates and bootleggers operating pretty much in the open, as is apparent from a number of the interviews that follow, but by the time the feds got around to them, the problem was quickly morphing into *video* piracy, and now the nearly unbeatable *digital* piracy. In retrospect, film piracy looks almost quaint, like those sweaty guys who used to sell bootleg cassettes of Springsteen concerts on St. Mark's Place in New York City. It was, as the MPAA's former head of antipiracy operations, James Bouras, describes it, "a frantic period," but one that the MPAA and studios might almost be nostalgic for, given the vast, untrackable digital landscape they now have to police.

We may be witnessing the final act (or the last reel) of movies-on-film, but the warning drums started sounding long ago. The introduction of VCRs and the laserdisc system in the mid-to-late 1970s was the opening shot. Suddenly, classic films from *The Maltese Falcon* to *The Pink Panther* that had been zealously pursued and fought over by a handful of private collectors were available almost everywhere, at a fraction of the cost of a good 16mm or 35mm print, and without having to own and operate a projector. Many collectors still defended their obsessive love for film, citing its far superior picture and audio as compared to prerecorded VHS tape. Not so once DVDs and, later, Blu-rays were introduced. As East Coast dealer and collector Dave Barnes laughingly puts it, "*The Mysterious Mr. M, Flash Gordon, Buck Rogers, The Great Alaskan Mystery*—I have them on DVD now. Cost me ten dollars for a DVD. Used to pay four hundred dollars for a serial years ago."

Then there are the lost treasures, the precious images that would have disappeared into the vastness of history—like most of Sophocles (of a reported 123 plays, only 7 survive), Leonardo da Vinci's lost painting *The Battle of Anghiari,* or John Barrymore's stage production of *Hamlet*—were it not for the possessive fingers of a handful of film collectors. I was amazed that almost *every* collector Jeff and I spoke with had at least one story of a unique film element that passed through his or her hands. For New Zealand exploitation buff and Incredibly Strange Film Festival creator Anthony Timpson, it was the sole surviving copy of an early 1960s *Doctor Who* episode entitled "The Lion." For noted French preservationist Serge Bromberg of Lobster Films and his partner, Eric Lange, it was a once-in-a-lifetime find of dozens of pre-1906 nitrate prints, including a number of lost Georges Méliès films, which they dubbed the "Treasures from a Chest." For dealer Bob DePietro it was a unique copy of legendary Russian director Sergei Eisenstein's very first film experiment, *Glumov's Diary,* a 1923 short Eisenstein shot for use in a stage production. *Glumov's Diary* was literally twice buried, hidden *inside* a newsreel by Soviet director Dziga Vertov, which had then been tossed into a dumpster in New Rochelle, New York, where it was plucked up by DePietro. For Philadelphia-area collector Wes Shank, it was realizing in a blinding flash that he'd laid his hands on four minutes of missing footage from the original 1933 production of *King Kong,* including censored images of Kong the ape toying erotically with Fay Wray's dress and stomping/munching on a handful of doomed natives. As Shank remembers the moment of the discovery, "I started unwinding the film and letting it go onto the floor. 'That's interesting . . . wait a minute. I don't remember any such scene in the film.' Then it hit me: '*invaluable*' . . . '*Kong.*' Could it be? I went down and put it on a pair of rewinds. Oh my god. *This is the lost footage.*" His sense of breathless excitement almost reminds me of the moment archaeologist Howard Carter first peered through a hole into the long-sealed tomb of Tutankhamun in the Valley of the Kings; when asked by Lord Carnarvon if he could see anything, Carter answered, "Yes, wonderful things." Not every collector, of course, found missing footage from *King Kong* or the lost stereo soundtrack elements to James Dean's *Rebel Without a Cause* (as did the Egyptian Theatre in Hollywood's head projectionist Paul Rayton), but almost every collector and dealer Jeff and I spoke with had found *something* rare and interesting. And "interesting" or "worthwhile" is truly in the eye of the beholder: sexploitation guru and Something Weird Video founder Mike Vraney spoke with the same sense of excitement about rooting through an antique shop in Everett, Washington, and discovering a treasure trove of softcore "nudie cuties" from the 1940s and 1950s, films that were so far off the radar screen that few people even knew they'd ever existed or were lost. One man's porn is another man's gem.

There was a social, or maybe I should call it "sociable," aspect that went hand-in-hand with collecting, and that was the basement or backyard screening. The image of setting up a 16mm Kodak Pageant and a portable white screen, and showing a slightly-less-than-legal print of *Goldfinger* for your family and neighbors—amazed that you could bring a touch of Hollywood magic, *the movies*, into suburbia—evokes a bygone era in American life, one that will never return. Some collectors went to extremes with their home theaters. Radio deejay Jim Zippo, something of a fanatic's fanatic, recalls his now-demolished private theater that boasted a handmade opera curtain controlled by electric motor. He and his former Dallas Cowboys cheerleader wife, Lori, would go all out, once hiring Russian musicians to accompany a screening of *Dr. Zhivago* in their home. More than one rabid collector cut holes in the walls to create a makeshift projection booth. Former film rejuvenator and 1960s garage-band drummer Bob Krasnow showed me the sad remnants of his former booth in his garage, pulling aside a set of curtains to reveal two glass portals. "I used to shoot out of these windows," he said wistfully, "but we got rid of all the projection equipment and converted it into a bathroom a while back." All that's left now are the two square glass "eyes" on the wall. Mark Punswick, at the time a Houston-area teenager in the early 1970s, recalled defying his parents' church-going habits to stay at home with his precious movies: "I said, 'I'm not renouncing your God, or God in general. I just have better things I want to do with my time.' One Sunday, I'm in my bedroom and there's a wall, and there's the living room. I realize if I cut a hole in my wall, my bedroom becomes the projection booth. So I do it. I get my dad's jigsaw and mark it out both sides. My parents came back from church, and I said, 'You wanna see what I did?'" He paused a moment, then added, "Of course, looking back, they should've killed me."

Sometimes you didn't even need a hole in the wall, or a basement screening room. Former New York–area projectionist Mike McKay fondly remembers snagging a 35mm print of *Jaws* while it was still playing in commercial theaters: "By this time it's four days into its run on Broadway—it's a huge hit. There's lines around the block. You can't get a ticket to save your life. I decided I was going to put my projector up to my window and show *Jaws* on the building front of my neighbor's house, across the street at 1876 Bleecker Street in Ridgewood, Queens. I dropped the speaker out, spliced in extra-long wire, put the speaker downstairs, and ran *Jaws* for my neighbors. Even the cops stopped." If there's one melancholy refrain that runs through nearly all the interviews that Jeff and I conducted, it's the loss of that communal feeling of film collecting: gathering friends and family around the cinematic campfire and watching a print of *Singin' in the Rain* or *Gone With the Wind*. (The tradition of backyard screenings isn't completely dead: editor/filmmaker Mike Williamson continues to show 16mm horror and sci-fi flicks like *The Lawnmower Man*, *Nightmare on Elm Street 4*, and *Piranha: The Ultimate Edition* in his leafy backyard in Burbank, California.)

For me, the most remarkable aspect of writing this book has been listening to the personal histories of the collectors and dealers Jeff and I interviewed. Many of their memories had nothing to do with film directly or revealed their connections only later on. Some memories floated by, evoking brief snippets of lost eras, like former film rejuvenator Allan Scott (the source for literally tens of thousands of prints in the collectors market), who recalled, "My dad had a bar, and he put bands on, on the weekend. He gave Big Jay McNeeley a start, and I believe Fats Domino played there, before Fats got started. We're going back more than fifty years, trying to remember this. It was rhythm & blues and rock & roll. The bar was at Broadway and Main . . . no, Main and Washington." A surprising number of collectors lost at least one parent at an early age. Mike McKay remembered his New York City policeman father buying him prints of *Godzilla* films out of a sense of guilt over the suicide of McKay's mother. Some of the most moving childhood memories came from Boris Zmijewsky, who was born in a refugee camp in Regensburg, Germany, to Ukrainian parents who'd been forced into slave labor by the Nazis. After immigrating to the United States, Zmijewsky recalled, "There used to be a movie theater called the Charles Theater on the Lower East Side, on Avenue B. That was my hangout, because my parents weren't around, so I used to spend a lot of time in the movies. At that time they used to show two movies with cartoons and everything, so that was like babysitting." When I asked if his parents were ever worried leaving him at the movie theater all by himself, he responded: "We used to be by ourselves in a wartime country, so being at the movies was safe. I felt safe. When you're talking about war-torn Europe, you're talking about buildings that were abandoned that we used to play in, so this was nothing." For these men the movies were obviously more than just a diversion or an entertainment. Many childhood memories were humorous or underscored cultural differences in postwar America: Michael Schlesinger, producer and former Sony Pictures executive, recalled that "the Victory Theater downtown in Dayton [Ohio] was the Disney house. So *101 Dalmatians* was opening on Christmas Day in 1961. Mom said the day before it opened, 'You should go tomorrow.' And I said, 'Mom, are you crazy? It's opening and the line's going to be around the block.' She said, 'No, that's the day to go, because the *goyim* will be home opening their presents!'" The more I heard, the more I realized that a lifelong passion for the movies has to come from *somewhere*, whether that's the tiny Sylvia Theater at Ward's Corner in Franconia, Virginia, during the Depression, or from a multiplex in Salinas, California, in the early 1980s, soaking up *Top Gun, Predator*, and *Ghostbusters*, as it did for soft-spoken horror and sci-fi collector Phil Blankenship. Many of those *somewheres*, theaters with such evocative names as the Ingomar, the RKO Missouri, the Yeadon, the Commodore, and even the western-themed the Hitching Post, are now as much a part of the past as the prints that screened there.

Writing this book offered a rare opportunity to visit many of the collectors in their own strange, wonderful, cluttered little "film worlds," whether that was former Broadway gypsy Tony Turano, surrounded by costumes from his beloved *The Ten Commandments* and clutching one of Marilyn

Monroe's sequined tops, or electrician and collector Peter Dyck in his truly maddening and mesmerizing House of Clocks, in Inglewood, California. Collector and former dealer Ken Kramer's office/theater/museum the Clip Joint sits hidden behind an unmarked door on a busy Burbank street, but inside the walls are covered with dazzling posters for *Some Like It Hot*, Mae West films, and the 1940s *Captain Marvel* serial. Movie memorabilia is scattered everywhere you look, including an original beanie-with-hand from *The 5,000 Fingers of Dr. T*, and through a door in back you catch a glimpse of Aladdin's cave: Ken's storage vault holding hundreds of rare 16mm and 35mm prints. Former projectionist Matt Spero has assembled a miniature movie palace in his Hollywood house, decorated with discarded bits and pieces from demolished theaters like the Imperial and the Brayton in Long Beach. Standing inside Matt's beautiful patchwork theater, with the constant rumble of cars passing nearby on the 101 freeway, is a haunting reminder of how collectors' obsessions with the movies literally molded and shaped their surroundings to reflect their uncontrollable love for these fleeting images. Sadly, with the passing of the collectors, their private cinema sanctums will also disappear, and with them, a fascinating part of film history, and the history of my city, Los Angeles.

I'll have to admit that part of my reason for writing this is purely personal. For a number of years I've been a screenwriter, film programmer, and distributor in Los Angeles, although I was never a film collector (records and movie posters are more to my taste, much to my ex-wife's exasperation). When I moved to Los Angeles in the early 1990s, film prints were far too expensive for my nonprofit salary—several hundred dollars for even common titles in 35mm—although I used to dream about what it would be like to own an original copy of one of my favorite movies, say, Mario Bava's phantasmagorical *Hercules in the Haunted World* (1961) or Budd Boetticher's lean, masterful *The Tall T* (1957). It is, strangely, a dream I still have. Over the years I've come to know and respect a number of collectors, men like Joe Dante, Ken Kramer, Bob DePietro, Mark Haggard, and Mike Hyatt, both for their enormous knowledge of the history of film and for what Mike describes in his interview as a "custodial" sense of responsibility to preserve their prints for future generations. For inspiration, I owe a debt of gratitude to author Nicholas Basbanes, whose captivating *A Gentle Madness* about ardent book collectors was my guiding light for wanting to set down this study of film collectors and their hunt for treasures hidden in rusted cans.

Finally, I should mention something about the collaborative process on this book. I use the first-person singular "I" throughout because I wrote the manuscript. My writing partner, Jeff, was both a subject and a collaborator, being an integral part of the dealing and collecting subculture for over forty years. All of the research and interviews for this book were conducted by the two of us, and without his guidance, expertise, and willingness to explore his own past and the vanishing world of film collecting, this couldn't have been written.

Dennis Bartok
Los Angeles, 2016

A Thousand Cuts

1.

Hollywood vs. Evan H. Foreman

The first real salvo in the protracted legal battle between the major film studios, on the one hand, and film dealers and collectors, on the other, was fired, oddly enough, not in Hollywood, but far, far away, in Mobile, Alabama. As described by Evan H. Foreman, owner of *16mm Filmland*, on the front page of his 1972 catalogue—a bulletin advertising used prints for sale—this is how it began:

> On August 19, 1971, four deputy U.S. Marshals, two film company attorneys and one film company private investigator entered my premises at 260 N. Jackson St., Mobile, Ala., and seized six of my film prints as called for by a Writ of Seizure issued by the U.S. District Court in Mobile, as part of seven simultaneous lawsuits brought against me, without notice by American-International Pictures, Inc., Columbia Pictures Industries, Inc., Metro-Goldwyn-Mayer, Inc., Twentieth Century-Fox Film Corporation, Walt Disney Productions, Universal City Studios, Inc., [and] United Artists Corporation. The Court also issued a temporary restraining order preventing me from dealing in any of the used film prints copyrighted by the plaintiffs.

Hollywood had declared war on Evan H. Foreman.
The civil case that arose came to be known as *American International*

Pictures, Inc. v. Foreman, and has been described by legal scholar Francis M. Nevins in the *Cleveland Law Review* as "the most important civil precedent with respect to the copyright aspects of the sale of film prints to collectors."[8] The Foreman case came nearly three years before the widely publicized film busts of 1974–1975, including the seizure of Roddy McDowall's collection. In many ways it anticipated the key issues that the FBI, the Justice Department, and the MPAA would bring to bear against dealers and collectors, namely, the right of the major studios to exercise their legal copyrights vs. the protections guaranteed to dealers and collectors under what is called the "first sale doctrine." This little-known but quite important principle of law was first established in a 1908 Supreme Court decision *Bobbs-Merrill Co. v. Straus.*[9] It guarantees that if you legally purchase a copy of, say, the latest Stephen King novel, once you read it you can sell it at a yard sale or on eBay, Amazon, and so on. You can also loan it, give it away, or destroy it if you choose: that particular copy is now *yours*, although you don't own the *copyright* to the book, and you aren't allowed to reproduce it. The first sale doctrine applies to just about any kind of media that can be copyrighted and sold: CDs, DVDs and Blu-rays, or—in the early 1970s—used 16mm film prints like those being offered for sale by Evan Foreman in his bare-bones, eight-page catalogue featuring such gems as *Law of the Range*, starring Johnny Mack Brown, *Thunder in the Pines*, with future Superman star George Reeves, and the delightfully alliterative sword-and-sandal flick *Hercules Against the Sons of the Sun*.

The man at the center of this lopsided David-vs.-Goliath struggle was an unlikely combatant. Born in 1928 in Atlanta, Georgia, and now well into his eighties, Foreman continues to send out e-mail broadsides to anyone who'll listen about copyright issues. His father served as a captain during World War I. "He couldn't see because of the poison gas," Foreman recalls. "It fogged up his goggles, so he took his gas mask off. He led his men across the river but at a high cost to himself." The price Foreman's father paid for his heroism was indeed severe: he spent over twenty years in Veterans Administration hospitals, leaving Foreman's mother to raise their son on her own. Foreman became fascinated with the movies at the age of eight, after a boyfriend of his mother's gave him a 16mm projector and a Bob Steele short in which the B-western star appeared through movie magic to catch a knife in mid-air. "I was living in Mobile, Alabama," he recalls, using the Deep South pronunciation "Moe-beel." "My allowance at the time was twenty-five cents a week, and I could get two streetcar tokens for fifteen cents or one for eight cents. I'd get on a streetcar and have a dime left over, and that car would take me four miles to the heart of downtown. I'd go to the movies at the Empire Theatre, and that dime would buy me a cowboy movie with Buck Jones, Gene Autry, and Roy Rogers."

After graduating from the Todd School for Boys in Woodstock, Illinois (whose most famous alumnus is Orson Welles), Foreman studied premed and psychology at UCLA in Los Angeles. He seems to have had a wandering spirit: after college he worked a colorful variety of jobs, including mining gypsum in the hot Nevada desert, installing Western Electric telephone equipment, and prospecting for gold in the Superstition Mountains in Arizona. He sounds a bit like Humphrey Bogart's Fred C. Dobbs character in *The Treasure of the Sierra Madre*.

In the mid-1960s Foreman began shooting his own amateur productions with a Bolex camera and soon after started *16mm Filmland*, rejuvenating beat-up prints that he purchased cheaply from other dealers like Gaines Sixteen Films Co. in Van Nuys and reselling them to collectors. "I got into it because I wanted to see movies," Foreman says now. "I was pretty limited in what I could find. There was a local film rental library—Mobile's the only port in Alabama. The library furnished films to merchant steamers while they were at sea." His prices ranged from $58 to $150: "The $58 films would be a B film in poor shape that had some pretty heavy cutting to fix the sprocket damage so it wouldn't flip out of the gate. One hundred fifty dollars would be a decent film in decent condition." By his own admission Foreman never sold new prints, and he never made illegal dupes like some other dealers.[10] Even by the standards of film dealers in the early 1970s, Foreman's was a tiny operation, far from the limelight of Hollywood.

But he's the man the studios chose to go after. In the complaint lodged against him, the studios asserted that "the defendant has offered to deal in specific motion pictures copyrighted by the respective plaintiffs and that he has sold prints of these pictures. These actions, according to the plaintiffs, constitute an infringement of their copyrights because they were without authority from the plaintiffs." Among the films he was charged with acquiring and reselling were *Secret Agent Fireball* (AIP), *The Devil at 4 O'Clock, The Gallant Blade,* and *Miami Exposé* (Columbia Pictures), *Anastasia* and *How to Marry a Millionaire* (20th Century Fox), *Big House U.S.A.* (United Artists), *Abbott and Costello Meet the Mummy* and *Bride of Frankenstein* (Universal), and *Emil and the Detectives* and *The Sword and the Rose* (Walt Disney). It's worth noting that the complaint filed against Foreman by the majors was a purely *civil* case, as opposed to later film busts like the "U.S. Indicts 16 in Movie, TV Film Pirating Case" in 1975, where *criminal* charges were leveled against my writing partner Jeff, Peter Dyck, Woody Wise, and other dealers.[11] Today, Foreman insists that the studios were trying to intimidate him with their tactics: "They just roll over you like they're using a tank and you've got a bow and arrow. Word gets around and people get scared. It's film Nazis, that's what I call 'em."

If the studios thought he would surrender quickly and admit guilt, they underestimated the man who had mined for gold at Weavers Needle in the Superstition Mountains. One of the most remarkable aspects of the case is the lengths to which Foreman went to fight the seven majors and their massive legal departments. Using the "first sale" defense, Foreman asserted that he had legally purchased used 16mm prints from a number of dealers, including the well-known Willoughby-Peerless Camera Store in New York City, which he then rejuvenated and resold. (To prove his point, during the trial Foreman asked a friend to surreptitiously purchase a used 16mm print from Willoughby-Peerless, which was entered as evidence.) More impressive than his legal defense, though, are the efforts he made to publicize the proceedings against him, to educate others about copyright law, and to warn other collectors and dealers that the same thing might soon happen to them. To that end he used every means at his disposal. In his own *16mm Filmland* bulletin, he published the headline "Legal Blitzkrieg Fails" and then asked fellow collectors and dealers,

> Who will be next? Surely not you? The film companies are now pushing for copyright law revisions which would give to the copyright owner of the film the right to prohibit "performances"—that is, projections—of the copyrighted film. So, you buy a film, and show it at home. How could that be a problem? Unless you write or otherwise secure permission

from the copyright owner, then conceivably you might find deputy U.S. Marshals, several film company private investigators and/or attorneys coming through your front door.

While this may seem paranoid at first, remember that *almost every film collector or dealer active in the 1970s* that Jeff and I spoke with was visited by the FBI at some point. A dozen years later, in the landmark 1984 *Sony Corp. of America v. Universal Studios, Inc.*, or "Betamax case," the major studios sued Sony to make all VCRs playback-only, insisting that recording shows off the air would be an infringement of copyright. Imagine the FBI banging on your door over that old episode of *Seinfeld* you recorded off the TV. Maybe Foreman wasn't being so paranoid after all.

In the same self-published essay, Foreman urged that "you should make certain your views as a film collector are known to your congressman" and included addresses to write to at the U.S. Department of Justice and Federal Trade Commission. Along with several other film dealers, he took out ads in *The Big Reel*, advising collectors what to do in case they were approached by the FBI. The warnings clearly had an impact. Former Thunderbird Films employee Kingsley Candler remembers when he was investigated: "The first thing this head [FBI] officer did: he gave me a sheet of paper and said, 'Would you please sign this?' I read through it very quickly and realized what it was and said, 'You cannot force me to sign this.' It was a waiver of rights. Thanks to *The Big Reel*: it was about a four-page spread in one issue, people like Evan Foreman, Woody Wise, Ray Atherton all contributed to this huge article about interrogation by the FBI, and they published a portion of a waiver of rights."

The *ne plus ultra* of Foreman's extraordinary one-man battle was his massive, self-published book *Copywrong*, which he advertised for sale for $99 in collectors' magazines:

At last! The film companies' legal tactics revealed! With the documents reproduced in this giant volume one, you and your attorney should be able to fully understand the legal issues involved in any phase of copyright litigation that you are likely to encounter as a film collector who buys and sells used film prints. . . . Your lawyer, if and when he needs it, will have untold thousands of dollars worth of information at his fingertips.

Copywrong was less a book than an obsessive compilation of the court actions directed against Foreman, and a "how-to guide" on defending yourself in case the FBI and the MPAA came knocking.[12]

The small-time 16mm dealer from Mobile, Alabama—who by now had become something of an expert and cause célèbre in copyright matters—was even invited to appear before the United States Senate Subcommittee on Patents, Trademarks, and Copyrights. On June 15, 1973, Foreman testified:

> Although I own several dozen copyrights on forms used in connection with a small family business,[13] I oppose this bill on the grounds that it drastically and unfairly extends the rights of copyright holders to the detriment of the public. . . . The Constitution, Article I, Section 8, Clause 8, provides that the Congress shall have the power 'to promote the progress of science and useful arts by securing for *limited time* to authors and inventors the exclusive rights to their respective writings.

He continued, in an eerie prediction of the current rampant extension and re-extension of copyright, that

> the intent of such copyright owners is amply demonstrated by a statement of Mr. E. Cardon Walker, president of Walt Disney Productions, quoted in the newspaper supplement *Parade*, March 18, 1973, page 4, "A large share of our product is timeless, which means that we can re-release our pictures generation by generation." This industry practice does violence to the constitutional mandate that copyrights shall be "for limited times" by insuring that *Snow White and the Seven Dwarfs* will never fall into the public domain and that our great-grandchildren and theirs as well, will perpetually be paying Mr. Walker's stockholders to enjoy it.

Whatever your feelings about Foreman or film dealers in general, you have to admire a guy who could gaze into the looking glass of the future and predict *exactly* what the major media companies have done in the four decades since his testimony, namely, push back the public's right to works entering the public domain, in favor of extending copyright protection again and again.

On August 7, 1975, Senior District Judge Daniel Holcombe Thomas—of the United States District Court for the Southern District of Alabama—ruled in the case of *American International Pictures, Inc. v. Foreman*. As summarized in the *Cleveland Law Review*,

> At trial the studios presented proof merely that they were or represented the holders of copyrights in the films at issue, and that Foreman had sold prints of those films without authorization. As for the "first sale" issue, each studio supplied a single employee who took the stand and testified that his studio never sold prints of any of its films. If this testimony was to be believed, it followed by deduction that the studios had never "first sold" prints of the particular films at issue. The defense discredited these witnesses, however, by establishing on cross-examination that they did not know enough about the practices of their own studios to be able to make such sweeping declarations under oath. Furthermore, Foreman's attorneys argued that over the years the plaintiff studios had transferred huge numbers of prints—not necessarily prints of the films at issue—to television stations, salvage dealers, and other parties under circumstances which made those transfers "first sales" under section 27. . . . The district judge agreed with Foreman, holding that the burden was on the plaintiff in such cases to establish by a preponderance of the evidence that no "first sales" of prints of the films at issue had occurred, and that the studios had failed to sustain that burden.[14]

The court found in his favor. In the lopsided battle against Hollywood, Foreman had, amazingly, won.

Or so it seemed. Loath to give up on such a well-publicized case—even against a dealer in Alabama who resold 16mm prints of *The Blonde Bandit* and *Curse of the Swamp Creature*—and with deep legal pockets, the studios appealed the Foreman case. On July 17, 1978, the United States Court of Appeals, Fifth Circuit, reversed the lower court's decision, essentially finding in the studios' favor by placing the burden *on Foreman* to prove that he'd acquired the films from someone who'd legally acquired them from the studios to begin with (and thus falling under the first sale doctrine). The court stated that "the person claiming authority to . . . vend generally must show that his authority to do so flows from the copyright holder," and that Foreman's mere possession of the film prints wasn't enough to meet the burden. Francis M. Nevins later pointed out, "Despite the murkiness of the language, the Fifth Circuit decision clearly requires a defendant in a civil right-to-vend case to show *something* about how he obtained *the particular film prints* for which sale he has been sued." [15]

If the case of *American International Pictures, Inc. v. Foreman* were a Hollywood movie, then the plucky, embattled film dealer from the Deep South, the self-educated copyright expert who waged a lopsided battle against big business, would win out in the end.

In real life, Evan H. Foreman was put out of business and *16mm Filmland* closed down immediately as a direct result of the Fifth Circuit ruling.

To this day, the feisty Foreman continues his efforts to educate others about copyright law, but now instead of the flimsy eight-page film catalogue he sent out in the 1970s, he uses e-mail. Recent articles forwarded by him include "How Intellectual Property Distorts Big Business, Science, and Creativity" and "Lawyers, Film, and Money: Copyrighting the First Movies." I ask Foreman if he knows how much he spent in legal bills fighting the studios, and he simply shrugs: "I don't remember. I'll say this, the film industry spent a whole hell of a lot more." He still loves the movies, and even after thirty-five years have passed, he still loves raising hell against the big media companies. "They're not interested in art, they're interested in squeezing the last nickel out of the film," he says with righteous fervor. "They're stealing from the American public. That's the real piracy. You see, the copyright law is not written for business or profit. It's written for the people of the United States."

When I ask if he has any regrets about his struggles with the Hollywood studios, he thinks for a moment, then sighs: "[It's] like that joke about the man who's asked about the war: 'What would you say about your experience in World War II?' The man replies, 'I wouldn't give it away for a million dollars—but I wouldn't give you a damn dime to do it again.'" Even though Evan Foreman lost his case on appeal and was driven out of the film business, maybe he won in the end simply by having the ornery Fred C. Dobbs spirit to stand up to the major studios and spit in their eyes: "You have to understand, when these people throw the hand grenade in, in the past no one had ever stood up to them before with all this nonsense."

2.

An Expensive Hobby

The best-known film collector in the early 1970s to run afoul of the FBI is no longer around to share his story. At the time, the elfin, instantly recognizable British actor with the wonderfully musical birthname of Roderick Andrew Anthony Jude McDowall was experiencing a career resurgence. Since 1968, when he'd played the sympathetic chimpanzee Cornelius in Franklin J. Schaffner's epochal *Planet of the Apes*, Roddy McDowall had starred in three more films in the hugely successful series. The studio had left him out of the first sequel—the weird, dystopian *Beneath the Planet of the Apes*—but thankfully brought him back as Cornelius for the next, *Escape from the Planet of the Apes*. Even better, they reinvented his character as Cornelius's rabble-rousing, revolutionary son Caesar, leading his people—or chimps—to freedom in *Conquest of the Planet of the Apes* and *Battle for the Planet of the Apes*. In the former he gets to deliver one of the series' most memorable speeches: "We have passed through the night of the fires, and those who were our masters are now our servants. And we, who are not human, can afford to be humane. . . . So, cast out your vengeance. Tonight, we have seen the birth of the planet of the apes!" McDowall had become the actor most identified with the blockbuster series. In modern Hollywood parlance, he'd become "essential to the franchise."

And the *Apes* films weren't his only success: he'd also co-starred with Gene Hackman, Ernest Borgnine, and Shelley Winters in director Ronald Neame's gargantuan, melodramatic, and hugely entertaining *The Poseidon Adventure*, still by far the best of the early 1970s disaster movies. It was, all in all, a remarkable career turn for a man who'd started thirty years earlier as a slender child actor in *How Green Was My Valley, Lassie Come Home,* and *My Friend Flicka.* McDowall was, in a word, *cool.* He'd even been brought back as yet another chimpanzee, Galen, in the *Planet of the Apes* TV series, for which 20th Century Fox and CBS had high hopes. It was one thing to be a working actor—McDowall had always worked, since he was barely six years old, and he'd continue working up until his death in 1998. But to work and be successful, that was a rich reward for any performer, and especially one who loved the movies and Hollywood as he did.

It was in fact his deep passion for films—not just his own, but those of his friends and coworkers—that brought him to the attention of the FBI in late 1974. McDowall had been doing business with two film dealers that the FBI was keeping a close eye on: indirectly, Roy H. Wagner (later an Emmy-winning cinematographer on shows like *House* and *CSI,* and interviewed separately for this book), and directly, a notorious character named Ray Atherton. The Chicago-born Atherton would later appear briefly in director John McNaughton's savage 1986 cult hit *Henry: Portrait of a Serial Killer.* He played a pawn-shop owner who kills a man by breaking a television set over his head.[16] It was apparently typecasting for Atherton. He's been described by former employee Ted Newsom (who directed the delightful documentary *Ed Wood: Look Back in Angora*) as "perhaps the foulest-mouthed, most racist, anti-Semitic, misogynistic, hateful fucker I have ever met." Newsom, who has a way with words, goes on to say that Atherton would "go over to the liquor store across the street nearly on a daily basis . . . 9:30 AM or 10:00 or 10:30. More often than not, he'd be so totally hammered by 1:00 PM that he'd either go on a rant, at which point you couldn't work at all, or he'd segue into nappy time, and just pass out with his head on his desk. It was an impressive sight. He probably weighed 350 or 400 pounds, six foot two or six foot three, bald with a Friar Tuck fringe of hair. Horned-rim glasses."

Collector Mark Haggard, who knew Atherton well, says that he later did a brisk business selling documentaries on Church of Satan leader Anton LaVey, including *Speak of the Devil* (1995), which Atherton executive produced—and also, perhaps not coincidentally, had a church member working on his staff. "It's all bullshit," Atherton told Haggard one day about LaVey and Satanism. "But it interests people, and it sells a lot of videos."

Among his other offenses (and there were apparently many), Atherton ridiculed a group of Muslims that he regularly did business with. According to Newsom, "at least four times a day, they got out their prayer rugs, and bowed to Mecca, and did their business. Ray at one point stole one of their prayer rugs. He was drunk, I'm sure. Calling attention to it so everybody'd watch through the window, he went down to the parking lot and kept throwing it into the air, crying, 'Fly, motherfucker, fly!!'" All in all, a bizarre character for someone of McDowall's reputation to be doing business with. But Atherton had what McDowall and all other collectors desperately wanted, and that was access to prints.

According to an article in the *Los Angeles Times*, in November 1974, the FBI requested a sit-down interview with McDowall about his supposed dealings with Atherton.[17] Apparently, an unnamed informant had seen a list of films that McDowall was attempting to sell through Atherton and his associate Roy Wagner; a copy of the list was seized in a raid on September 4 at Wagner's home. During the initial FBI interview, McDowall admitted that he'd bought films from Atherton in the past, but when he was asked if he'd ever *sold* movies through Atherton (potentially a more serious crime), McDowall "declined to provide further information." Sensing they had a major target in their sights, the FBI and Assistant U.S. Attorney Chester "Chet" Brown moved in for the kill.

Of all the behind-the-scenes players in the early 1970s "film busts," the most active on the law-enforcement side—and the most opaque, personally—was Chet Brown. Looking back, he may not have been the main driving force behind the busts—certainly the MPAA, working on behalf of the studios, was pushing for the crackdown to protect their copyright interests—but Brown became the main figurehead, at least for a while, and much of film collectors' and dealers' ire was (and still is) directed at him. Roy H. Wagner, who was targeted in the Atherton–McDowall case, describes Brown as "an egomaniac" and adds, "He was so fascinated that he was doing something with the movie business. He was talking about the movie stars that were going to befriend him because he was going to save the movie business." Collector and electrician Peter Dyck, who was also targeted in the highly publicized film piracy arrests in 1975, still becomes enraged at the mention of Brown's name: "He *hated* film collectors.

It's like in *Patton,* when General Bradley says to General Patton, 'I do this job because I've been trained to do it. You do it because you *love* it.' Chet Brown was the same way." Even James Bouras, who was working for the MPAA at the time, says that Brown "obviously had ambitions of what he was going to do after he left the U.S. Attorney's office."

These judgments, many of them from collectors and dealers who felt personally singled out and harassed by the feds and the Justice Department, are obviously a bit biased. On the flip side, Brown's former boss at the time, U.S. Attorney Dominick Rubalcava, told me that Brown was "hardworking, enthusiastic, and focused. Chet was a hardworking guy. Again, in the U.S. Attorney's office, once you develop an expertise you get handed those cases. Some guys like doing bank robbery cases. Some like drug dealing. Some guys like fraud or IRS cases." Chet Brown obviously had a taste and talent for film piracy cases, and for several years his name appeared repeatedly in connection with film raids in the Los Angeles area. The most high-profile of these was directed at Roddy McDowall.

On December 18, 1974, the FBI, search warrant in hand, barged into McDowall's home in North Hollywood and seized some five hundred film prints and videotapes (the number was later revised to over a thousand videos and one hundred sixty 16mm prints.) The raid, which appeared in the *Los Angeles Times* a month later, on January 17, 1975, and was picked up nationally by news services, was a massive personal blow to McDowall's career, and by far the biggest "get" in the FBI's and Justice Department's war on film piracy. If they were trying to send a warning to other collectors and dealers, then the message was delivered loud and clear. Even now, forty years later, a number of collectors and dealers mention the McDowall raid as a watershed moment that kicked off a general wave of fear and paranoia that lingers in the collecting subculture to this day.

From the FBI's perspective, the raid was a great success. According to an internal U.S. government memorandum dated July 1975, the "recovery value of pirated motion picture films . . . and miscellaneous equipment which were seized from Roddy McDowall, prominent motion picture actor, during the execution of a search warrant at McDowall's residence" totaled $5,005,426. The memo goes on to state that "most of his collection was pirated." Among the films seized were prints of McDowall's own movies *Lassie Come Home, My Friend Flicka*, and several of the *Planet of the Apes* movies. How the feds arrived at the astronomical valuation for McDowall's collection is a good question. Even at the height of the underground film market, $5 million seems more like wishful thinking than reality. As a benchmark for comparison, dealers Ken Kramer and Jeff Joseph were selling prints around the same time to *Playboy* magazine publisher Hugh Hefner for the premium price of $500 for a black-and-white movie and $1,000 for a color movie. Even assuming all of McDowall's films were color and that he could sell them for the same high price, that's still only 160 16mm prints x $1,000 equals $160,000. The value of the videos is another matter, and in retrospect it may be those that the studios and the feds were most alarmed by, since it was apparent that McDowall was taping movies off TV and also transferring his prints to video. Ironically, in just a few years, your average American consumer would have just about the same number of videos taped off TV on their newfangled VCR or Betamax machines, maybe not quite as many as film buff McDowall—but nobody broke down their doors with a search warrant.

What happened next is not Roddy McDowall's finest moment. Faced with prosecution and a potentially crippling blow to his career, he rolled over and named names. Even using the term "named names" is politically charged, since it brings to mind Hollywood professionals informing on their coworkers to the House Un-American Activities Committee during the communist witch hunts of the 1950s. McDowall's situation was very different: he was the target of a legal investigation aimed at rooting out film pirates in Hollywood. To call McDowall a "pirate," though, as the government's internal memo implies, is a stretch—like many, possibly the majority, of film collectors Jeff and I interviewed, he'd turned to occasionally selling prints from his collection. Here he was, publicly linked with a guy like Ray Atherton, a Muslim-baiting, anti-Semitic loose cannon. Put yourself in McDowall's shoes, and what would you do?

What follows is an abbreviated transcript of McDowall's confession to the FBI, heavily redacted, with many names blacked out. It's a fairly remarkable document, often poignant in describing his childhood and career. It clearly shows his enormous, abiding love for the movies, and also the enormous stress that collectors were put under when they found themselves caught in the government's legal net:

February 14, 1975,
Los Angeles, California

I, Roderick Andrew McDowall, voluntarily appearing, hereby make the following free and voluntary statement. . . .

Personal History

I was born in London, England, on September 17, 1928. I became involved with modeling when I was six years old and when I was about nine or ten years of age, was hired for my first movie role. By the time I was twelve years old, I had performed in about eighteen films.

In 1940, my father sent my mother, sister and I to the United States because he felt we would be safer here with my mother's relatives and he was contemplating re-entering military service in England. Shortly after arriving in New York, through a strange set of circumstances, I was hired for a role in the movie *How Green Was My Valley.* This film subsequently won nine Academy Awards and made me a child movie star.

As long as I can remember, I have been totally involved with films and the movie industry. My mother used to take me to an old silent movie theater where I became familiar with the performances of many of the silent movie stars. As my acting career progressed, I met some of these silent stars in person and from these associations I became extremely interested in the history of film and stage.

I started my film collection during the mid-1960s as a result of my fascination for old movies and my interest in observing the progression of many actors and directors, starting with their first films up to their current work. I also had become interested in lost films and wanted to prevent films from becoming extinct, if possible. Also, studying these films helped improve my acting skills.

My film collection has always been a hobby for me. These films, mostly 16 millimeter with the exception of *The Ballad of Tam Lin* and some of the Errol Flynn estate collection of films which I purchased, have been an extraordinary delight for me and I feel that they contribute to film history.

At the height of my collecting, I believe I possessed about 337 films at one time. However, because as a collector I would sell, trade and purchase films, it is impossible to determine the total number of films I may have had in my possession. . . .

I decided to place a portion of my films on videotape cassettes because of the ease of storage, space saving advantages, and the longer life expectancy of videotape as compared to film.

I decided to sell my collection for the following reasons:

Many of them I had transferred onto videotape, some were films that I no longer had any interest in, and I knew that others would be playing frequently on television and could easily be videotaped. My films were sold for the same price for which I had purchased them; however, because I kept very few records of such purchases, this determination depended somewhat on memory. . . .

Prior to the current investigation, my understanding of the copyright law consisted of believing that as long as I did not show my films for profit, as long as I did not commercially attempt to earn money from showing them, it was not a violation of the copyright laws. . . .

I do not recall knowing of a studio ever selling their films to private individuals who are not in some way associated with the film industry. However, I was never in a position to be caused to dwell on how individuals outside the film industry obtained films. My life has been almost totally involved with films and the film industry both at work and at home, and meeting people who had films and film collections was an everyday occurrence for me.

Individuals From Whom I Have Purchased Films

Regarding the individuals whom I thought were collectors from whom I recall having purchased films, I can provide the following information concerning my association with them:

I became acquainted with [name redacted] in New York City (telephone [number redacted]) while I was living in New York City. I do not recall how we first came in contact with each other; however, I met him personally only once. At that meeting [name redacted] was desirous of selling a block of films, 26 in all, for a bulk sum. I was anxious to possess one of the films, so I purchased the block of films he was offering for sale. . . .

I do not recall how I first came into contact with [name redacted] from Tonawanda, New York. I believe I purchased and traded films with him, the last purchase according to my records being in 1971. This transaction consisted of my purchasing *The Magnificent Ambersons*, *Camille*, *Applause*, and *She Done Him Wrong*. I paid for these films with a check in the amount of $705.00. . . .

I do not recall how I first made contact with [name redacted], Chicago, Illinois, but it was some time during the 1960s. . . . I purchased *Planet of the Apes*, and according to my records, *Escape From the Planet of the Apes* from [name redacted] after he had moved to Los Angeles, and I would assume these films were delivered to my residence in person; however, again, I cannot be sure. . . .[18]

As I review the list of films which were seized during the execution of the search warrant on my home, I can provide the following information as to the persons from whom I obtained these films:

Giant—Given to me by Rock Hudson

Breakfast at Tiffany's—Given to me by Richard Shepard

. . . .

Persons With Whom I Traded Film

The following individuals are persons with whom I recall trading film:

[name redacted] of Thunderbird Films, do not recall which titles.

[name redacted] do not recall which films.

[name redacted], I also may have purchased films from this man; however I cannot remember for sure. I met him while making the *Planet of the Apes* feature movie at the studios. I did not care for him and soon discouraged his contacting me regarding my film collection.

Film Collectors

I am personally aware of the following individuals possessing film collections themselves:

Arthur Jacobs (deceased)

Rock Hudson

Dick Martin

[Name redacted]

Mel Tormé

[several names redacted]

. . . .

I have no partners in the business but the business does have a treasurer and a vice president. It is a corporation which was formed in California in 1972. I used corporation checks to purchase films in which I had appeared and to pay for videotaping of programs or films in which I had appeared such as segments of the *Hollywood Squares* episodes, *Planet of the Apes*, etc.

   Escape From the Planet of the Apes was produced in 1971. As I recall, when I learned it was to be shown on television, I made arrangements with [name redacted] to tape it from television. However, the television version of the movie had part of the final scene edited. This scene, a scene in which I get killed, required some very difficult and painful acting in that I was required to make a terrible animal noise which was extremely horrifying. The television version did not portray a portion of this scene and I was desirous to have the scene in my collection; therefore, I think that was the reason I purchased the complete film from [name redacted] in 1974. I desired a print which had the final scene intact.

Obviously, it's the final passages of the confession that are the most controversial, and the most difficult to read. It's one thing for McDowall to admit to his own collecting and videotaping, and even to name the dealers from which he purchased prints. It's another to willingly offer up the names of friends and colleagues like Rock Hudson, singer Mel Tormé, comedian Dick Martin (of *Rowan & Martin's Laugh-In* fame), and even the deceased Arthur P. Jacobs, producer of the five *Planet of the Apes* films that had made McDowall a major star again. (In 1973 Jacobs had suddenly died of a heart attack at age fifty-one.) Even though Jacobs was no longer alive to be concerned about the FBI knocking on *his* door, naming him (and what possible good could it do the FBI, since he was dead?) seems like an act of ingratitude at best on McDowall's part.

   As far as McDowall's legal troubles with the FBI and the Justice Department, the confession did the trick. On June 4, 1975, the *St. Petersburg Times* and other news outlets reported that McDowall had been cleared of all film-pirating charges in connection with the raid on his home. Further, "Assistant U.S. Attorney Chet Brown said the government concluded that McDowall committed no wrongdoing." Given the level of scandal we're now used to from celebrities, McDowall's troubles seem like barely a minor kerfuffle, but it was obviously a deeply scarring experience for McDowall, who dropped out of collecting altogether. To this day, internet users routinely refer to him as a "fink" for his confession—a sad judgment, perhaps, for an actor who gave so much to his profession.

Did it have any repercussions for him among his Hollywood friends, especially those he'd identified to the FBI? Apparently, there were no further arrests or film seizures made based on the names McDowall provided (although several names have been redacted). When I mentioned to *Hollywood Reporter* journalist and Turner Classic Movies host Robert Osborne that McDowall had named Rock Hudson to the FBI, he was genuinely surprised. Osborne, who knew both men well and even catalogued Hudson's private film collection, said that if Hudson had been aware of McDowall's confession, he never let on, and that this was "all well-known information about who was a collector and who wasn't." Osborne continued, "I don't think it was anything like the House Un-American Activities Committee. Also if you bought films from *The Big Reel* or something, they could have checks that you sent in to buy a copy of *Gilda*. I know that I was contacted at one time [by the FBI] and told it was against the law, but nobody ever asked to see my collection." Roy H. Wagner, who was (and still is) understandably reluctant to speak about his experiences, given his later career as a cinematographer in the industry, confided to me, "I talked to Roddy McDowall about this years later, and to Mel Tormé, and they both said, 'You were really set up [by Chet Brown].'" He paused, then added, "I did *Hart to Hart* with Roddy." It's a small industry indeed where two men caught up in an FBI film piracy dragnet wind up working together on *Hart to Hart*. Collector Tony Turano, who knew McDowall at the time of the film busts, said that "it broke [Roddy's] heart to lose his films. Of course it scared the shit out of everybody that had films. All of a sudden everybody went underground, and nobody wanted to talk about owning films." When I asked if McDowall stopped doing screenings at home after the busts, Tony replied, "Everything stopped. I never went to his house again. . . . Roddy had a beautiful film collection. He had beautiful prints. I guess he had the money to buy the best."

And what about Ray Atherton, the prayer-rug-waving dealer who touched off the firestorm? In a stunning blow to the government's much-touted war against film pirates, Atherton's separate convictions on five counts of copyright infringement and one count of interstate transportation of stolen property (for prints of *The Exorcist*, *Airport*, *The Way We Were*, *Forty Carats*, and *Young Winston*) were overturned in October 1977 by the Ninth Circuit Court of Appeals. As reported in *Variety*, "Driving a knife through the heart of the prosecution's theory, Judge Shirley M. Hufstedler said the copyright convictions were wrong because the government failed to negate the 'first sale' copyright doctrine which might shelter Atherton's trades. And in a second stab, the court said the government failed to show that the specific 16mm print of *The Exorcist* was worth the $5000 value that it would bring under federal interstate transportation laws . . ."[19] (The value placed on the *Exorcist* print brings to mind the astronomical price-tag of over $5 million the feds put on McDowall's collection.)

After that, Atherton continued in his dodgy trade in film and video unabated. According to his former employee Newsom, he married "a wife who he couldn't stand. . . . He was utterly dismissive and abusive to his family and in-laws when they weren't present. When they were around he came off more like Ozzie Nelson." Just to show that not everyone is all bad all the time, Atherton and his wife adopted a little girl whom he "adored," according to Newsom. "The earthquake in 1994 apparently terrified his little daughter, who was about two or three. Traumatized her. So he moved to Las Vegas, which he assumed was safer." When I asked what became of him in later years, Newsom chuckles: "Ray had huge tax problems. He didn't give a shit about the IRS. I remember once that this huge fat man was doing this exuberant dance, because he'd gotten a fifteen-thousand-dollar check—an advance for some project he'd proposed. I was happy because I knew I was gonna get paid that week. . . . But within two days of that, he was flat-assed broke." Six months after relocating to Vegas, he "simply dropped dead of a massive heart attack," Newsom recalls. "He was only about forty-eight, I think. But he was 150 pounds overweight. He would go through a bottle of goddamned rum in half a day."

In something of a final coda to the film-related hysteria that swept up Roddy McDowall, Ray Atherton, and many others, on December 14, 1986, the *Los Angeles Times*, in a tiny article barely four paragraphs long, reported that "a former federal prosecutor in Los Angeles has been charged with obstruction of justice and perjury in connection with an investigation of a fraud ring." The former prosecutor was none other than Chester

"Chet" Brown, Assistant U.S. Attorney during the early 1970s film raids. Brown was "charged with advising witnesses to deceive the grand jury . . . and later lying himself when asked about his role in the alleged cover-up attempt," related to a Pasadena-based fraud ring that provided false credit information about itself to get between $8 million and $15 million in merchandise. Although his later legal woes were completely unrelated to his role in the 1970s film busts, the news of Chester Brown's fall from grace was, not surprisingly, met with unrestrained glee by the former targets of his and the Justice Department's investigations; collector Peter Dyck, face nearly purple with rage, called it "poetic justice." The collectors' magazine *Classic Images* even reprinted the *Times* article about Brown's indictment in the fraud case in case anyone missed it. Brown was later disbarred, and although he appealed all the way to the U.S. Supreme Court, Justices Rehnquist, O'Connor, Scalia, Kennedy et al. confirmed the disbarment, ending his legal career.

3.

The Theodore Huff Memorial Film Society

"I had a heartbreaking moment last week: I threw four films away, actually put them in the garbage can. Beyond stinky—unsalvageable," Leonard Maltin sighs as Jeff and I settle into a snug back corner of his home office surrounded by densely packed bookshelves. In person he is just as you'd imagine him: medium height with graying hair and fuzzy beard, a relaxed, ingratiating manner—and a razor-sharp knowledge of cinema history. I ask what prints he had to toss out, and he winces, as if we were discussing abandoning his family pets by the side of the road. "A Ruth Etting RKO two-reeler called *Derby Decade* that I've always been fond of," he replies. "As soon as I opened the can, whoops! It was oozing white goo. I said, 'Let's see if we can get it through the projector one more time.' It was a singular experience in my life—the soundtrack played perfectly, unaffected. The image reversed polarity as we were watching. It turned to negative. We were watching the film vanish before our very eyes, and it left behind an ocean of white muck."

Trying to cheer him up, Jeff mentions that the negative still probably exists somewhere. "But it's lost *to me*," Leonard says. "The fact that there's some master copy somewhere in a vault does me no good." For good measure he lists the other "close family members" he had to part with: "One was another RKO short, my very favorite comedy with the team of Clark and McCullough, who had been Broadway stars and made a series of shorts for RKO in the thirties. My favorite was called *Odor in the Court*."

The third blow was a WWII propaganda short starring Robert Stack called *Keeping Fit*. "That was a nice old Kodak print, gone," he says wistfully. And the fourth? The Academy Award–winning *The House I Live In* with Frank Sinatra. Jeff mentions he has a pristine DVD copy of the Sinatra short he'll be happy to pass along. "Sure. Why not?" Leonard shrugs, but it's clear from his body language that he'd rather have his nice old Kodak prints back.

To call Leonard a "film lover" is something of an understatement. He is quite likely America's most famous and prolific film lover: as a critic for the *Entertainment Tonight* TV show for over thirty years, as a historian and author of a dozen highly regarded books, as host of the marvelous *Walt Disney Treasures* DVD series, and as creator and editor of the wonderfully bulky little tome *Leonard Maltin's Movie Guide*, which became as ubiquitous in American homes as a remote control.[20] (For good measure, he's also been spoofed on *South Park* and *Mystery Science Theater 3000*.) It's immediately apparent that for Leonard, "film love" is something highly personal—something that goes back to his earliest years as a collector and which has shaped his entire career and his home and even led to his marriage to his wife, Alice. As Jeff and I sit talking with him, we're surrounded by a veritable museum of posters, animation cels, painted portraits, books, magazines—pretty much anything film-related that you can imagine, and some you can't. (Alice even has an entire room in the house devoted to her personal hero, actor Ronald Colman of *A Tale of Two Cities* fame.)

"All I have ever collected were short subjects, live action shorts, cartoons, and some TV shows and trailers. No feature films," Leonard explains. When I ask why no features, he flashes a sardonic grin. Like most collectors, he can remember every print, good or bad, that's passed through his hands. "I bought for a very reasonable sum, maybe sixty dollars, a print of Alfred Hitchcock's *Foreign Correspondent*, which proved to be incomplete. That began and ended my feature-film collecting hobby when I realized there were pitfalls." Like many of the collectors Jeff and I spoke with, Leonard was part of the immediate post-WWII baby boom generation. Born in 1950 in Manhattan, the son of a singer and a lawyer/immigration judge, he was raised across the Hudson River in comfortably suburban Teaneck, New Jersey. "Our basement had a good throw," he remembers fondly about his childhood home. It's a reference only a collector or projectionist would get: "a good throw" means there was enough distance between the film projector and the screen for a proper image. "I grew up during that early stage of television programming when TV was a living museum of movies, and I became a TV junkie. So every day of my life, I watched Laurel and Hardy, the Little Rascals, and Warner Bros. cartoons, Van Beuren cartoons, Max Fleischer cartoons." How times have changed: in the early years of television, networks and local stations were desperate for cheap programming, so they licensed vintage features and shorts in vast bulk from the studios.[21] It is, paradoxically, how many collectors first fell in love with the movies, through a tiny black-and-white TV set screening afternoon reruns of *Abbott and Costello Meet Frankenstein*. It's also telling, because Leonard more than almost any other film historian or critic has used the medium of television to share and spread his love for cinema—even his beloved *Maltin's Movie Guide* was originally published as *TV Movies*.

When I ask about his earliest movie memories, though, they are of the classic kind: "My first cinematic memory is my mother taking me by the hand into the Guild Theater on Fiftieth Street, right behind Radio City Music Hall, to see *Snow White and the Seven Dwarfs* on a reissue," he recalls. "In those days there were continuous showings, so as soon as everybody was leaving one show, we went in, and I saw the last scene of the movie first. That was my first memory, seeing Snow White and the Prince going off into the sun in that golden finale." It's an ironic image, that Leonard Maltin's love affair with cinema should begin at The End. The Guild Theater is also where he experienced a turning point at the age of seven when he saw producer Robert Youngson's compilation film *The Golden Age of Comedy*. Although he's mostly forgotten now, Youngson and his compilation films in the late 1950s and 1960s featuring clips of Laurel and Hardy, Carole Lombard, Jean Harlow, Will Rogers, Harry Langdon, Mack Sennett, and others, introduced a young generation to the bygone geniuses of early film comedy. "Seeing this collection on the big screen was a transformative experience," Leonard recalls. "A couple of decades later I got to tell this to Robert Youngson, and that was a great delight."

Like many young collectors, Leonard began buying 8mm reductions of much longer films sold by companies like Castle Films and the cut-rate

Atlas Films and Ken Films for prices ranging from $1.95 to $5.95.[22] "I had the Headline Edition of W. C. Fields in *Never Give a Sucker an Even Break.* Their version was titled, wait for it . . . *Hurry Hurry.* The reason was that it was simply a chase scene from the movie," Leonard says with a smile. To this day he stays connected to his earliest years as a collector and proudly shows us time-worn but still charming 8mm film boxes he has in his office, including one for an Oswald Rabbit short from the long-gone Cine Art Films, which he holds as gently in his palm as if it were a newborn baby chick. "I am now nostalgic for the boxes, advertising, and even reels and cans, and I buy them sometimes as objets d'art," he observes about the fragile ephemera of movie love that fills his, Alice's, and their daughter Jessie's home. In high school in Teaneck, he started a movie club because he was part of the audiovisual (A.V.) staff that maintained the school's 16mm and slide projectors. "Another long-demolished institution in American life," he sighs nostalgically. His memory for detail is astonishing, and he never forgets a good joke or a bad pun: when he rented a print of Hitchcock's *The 39 Steps* to screen for the movie club for the sum of four dollars, he recalls, "one of our members said, 'That's like ten cents a step!'"

It's no surprise that one of his first jobs was film-related, working for a man named Milton Menell at Select Films Library in Manhattan, where Leonard put together 16mm rental programs such as History of Animation, Comedy, and more. When I ask if his efforts were successful at increasing film rentals, he smiles: "Some of them were modestly successful—and even that may be an optimistic statement." Leonard obviously has great affection for Menell, who was less a film buff than a film *hondler,* to use the Yiddish expression: "He'd buy anything in bulk because he could sell anything. . . . I have a print [from him] of my favorite two-reel Charley Chase called *The Pips from Pittsburgh,* co-starring the beautiful Thelma Todd. As Chase says to Todd in the film, 'Did you come clean from Pittsburgh?'"

Not everyone inspires fond memories, though. "The most infuriating man in the film rental business was a guy called Charlie Mogull of Mogull's Film Rental Library," Leonard says, still irritated after more than forty years. "When I was writing my book *Movie Comedy Teams,* somebody told me Charlie Mogull had a print of Clark and McCullough's four-reel Fox Movietone 1929 short called *Waltzing Around.* I'd been warned that Charlie

27

was incredibly difficult to deal with. So I called him up. 'Waalll, we'll need references,'" he drawls, imitating Mogull's voice, then follows with a laundry list of Mogull's inane, time-consuming demands. "He was in business *not* to do business. Infuriating," Leonard says, cheeks flushed with anger.

It was, in fact, while researching and writing his books *Movie Comedy Teams* and *The Great Movie Shorts* in the early 1970s that he got hooked on collecting. "I started collecting with an academic purpose, the most lethal kind of collecting, because I need an example of the *Strange as It Seems* series. It's not very good, but I need to have an example of it," he sighs, but it's clear that he didn't put up much of a struggle against the collecting bug. "Then I started a class on the history of animation in 1973 at the New School for Social Research in New York City. They gave me a rental budget, and I intended to rent Disney cartoons and silent animation from the Museum of Modern Art and various 16mm distributors. Nothing went right. Everything went wrong," he recalls. "So I started collecting cartoons purposefully, which was a dreadful path to go down. Because now I needed an example of an early Terrytoon, a middle period Terrytoon, a late period Terrytoon, etc. That's how my cartoons collection suddenly expanded." It's worth pointing out that the so-called dreadful path Leonard went down gave birth to his masterful, hugely entertaining book *Of Mice and Magic: A History of American Animated Cartoons* in 1980, still the definitive work on the genius of Chuck Jones, the Fleischer brothers, and other titans.

The New York film buff community in the 1970s was filled with fascinating, long-gone characters like collector Herb Graff and Leonard's self-described "hero and unwitting mentor," William K. Everson. The soft-spoken, genteel, and veddy-British Everson was a hugely important and influential figure as a film historian, professor, collector, and archivist. After a brief career in the early 1950s as a film publicist, Everson dedicated himself full-time to writing about and teaching cinema, and to preserving as many endangered films as he could get his hands on. (He also, coincidentally, worked with Robert Youngson on the silent-comedy compilations that so impressed the young Leonard.) I studied with Everson myself at NYU in the mid-1980s, where he screened forgotten gems like the superb *Bulldog Drummond Strikes Back* (1934) from his own private archives. I once delivered a term paper to Everson's apartment and got a quick peek at his legendary film collection, which was stacked in hallways and rooms everywhere I looked, the apartment floorboards sagging under the weight of prints.

Leonard's friendship with Everson literally changed his life. "Bill ran a film society called the Theodore Huff Memorial Film Society.[23] Theodore Huff wrote the first great book on Charlie Chaplin, which is on my shelf there," he says. "It was a secret film society: you simply had to know about it, it was not printed anywhere. Everson rented a hall on Union Square. The group later moved to the School of Visual Arts, where he used an amphitheater room. At the Huff Society he showed rare films every week." Besides Leonard, other regular attendees at the secret Huff screenings included noted writer and filmmaker Susan Sontag and *Castle of Frankenstein* magazine publisher Calvin Thomas Beck, a bizarre figure long rumored to be one of the inspirations for Norman Bates in Robert Bloch's novel *Psycho*.[24] "There was more collective knowledge in that room than in most institutions of higher learning. These were the ultimate film buffs— if not the most socially adjusted human beings in New York," Leonard observes with a chuckle. "One night we were watching a film that wasn't very good called *The Wrong Road*, a Republic picture starring Richard Cromwell and Rochelle Hudson, where Cromwell was being unjustly pursued for a crime he didn't commit by a dogged Lionel Atwill." As the film ended and the lights came up, Leonard echoed one of Atwill's lines of dialogue, whispering aloud, "'You kids can start laughing right now.' Then the guy behind me said, 'I started laughing when I sold Bill [Everson] that print.' That's how I met Herb Graff," Leonard remembers. "Herb was in the garment business and worked for a shirt company, but movies were his passion. Another great story is when sometime later I ran into him coming out of a screening and he had a new overcoat on. I complimented him on it. He replied, 'Do you like it? This cost me *Top Hat*.'"

"Many collectors I met like Herb didn't have good marriages," Leonard says, echoing an observation I've heard a number of times. "Because this was their pursuit and not their spouses'—and they didn't share the hobby with their spouse. Which is why it was considered near miraculous when I met Alice at the Theodore Huff Society." Graff had invited Alice to come as his guest to the Huff that night but conveniently took sick—and asked Leonard to keep an eye out for her. "So that was our first evening together, watching two rare silent films." I ask if he recalls what movies they watched that night: "Of course," he replies without hesitation. "*Open All Night* with Adolphe Menjou and Maurice Tourneur's *The Whip*. We were probably the only couple—the only heterosexual couple—to emerge from the Theodore Huff Film Society. When we were engaged we went to Bill Everson's apartment, where there was film stacked in every corner and nook and cranny," he says, in a repeat of my own recollections of Everson's place. "Alice looked at me in horror and said, 'Our apartment isn't going to be like that, is it?' And I assured her it wouldn't be. And it never was. They'd say, 'Does she like films?' And I said, 'How could I get married to someone who doesn't like films?' But that was the prevailing stereotype among film collectors. You hear about football widows, and there were film collector widows."

Like his friend and mentor Everson, Leonard has taught film history for over four decades, currently at the USC School of Cinematic Arts. "One of the reasons I still show 16mm to my class is simply to keep the projectors whirring and to put a film image on the screen," he says. "I also like to show my students what film looks like. I'll unspool part of a reel just to show them film and sprocket holes and show them there was a relationship from one frame to the next that you can see with the naked eye." Jeff points out the perhaps sad but inevitable fact that most movies will never be experienced on the big screen again in front of an audience.[25] Leonard pauses for a moment: This is obviously a topic that cuts close to the bone. "Something's been lost but something's been gained," he finally replies. "We could have never envisioned in our wildest dreams something like Turner Classic Movies. That there is a channel showing pristine, uncut copies of classic films twenty-four hours a day? Unheard of. On the other hand, you used to be able to watch films in New York, on seven channels around the dial, every morning, every afternoon, all night long. I know that some of the oddities I have in 16mm will likely never turn up again in any other form—because they have no commercial value and only marginal historic value." So for every print of *Derby Decade* that turns to white goo and has to be tossed out, something small but significant has disappeared from our collective film consciousness.

In addition to his students, Leonard has passed his love of film directly on to his daughter, Jessie, who now works with him at his production company. "At one time she could thread the projector," he says. "She regrets that she's forgotten, but we may need to have a refresher course soon." Does he still screen his 16mm prints at home? "Not a lot. We used to do it fairly often, and it was fun having an audience. Our calendar and lifestyle changed, and that's the only reason we haven't done it too much lately." When I ask for his thoughts on the death of 16mm and 35mm film in the digital age, he purses his lips: "I find it amusing, as all these things disappear from our midst, that the iconography remains. If you want to say film visually, you show a strip of film. If you want to indicate a theater and projector, you show reels with a beam of light." Before we can continue with this melancholy topic, he interrupts with another Herb Graff/ William K. Everson story. Apparently Herb had scored a prize contact at a film laboratory that had access, wonder of wonders, to the vast Warner Bros. library. "He said to Bill, who he loved, 'If you could have any Warner Bros. feature in your library, what would it be?' And Bill said, '*Mr. Cohen Takes a Walk.*' It was a 1930s British quota-quickie which Bill had seen as a boy and always remembered. Herb requested it and got the print—which incidentally turned out to be a charming film—but it blew the connection, because no one had ever requested this negative before. This created such a wave of suspicion that the whole operation was immediately shut down!" It's a story only a film collector would love: how you're given the keys to the kingdom and blow it by requesting a title that's *too* obscure.

As much as Jeff and I would love to stay, we realize it's time to go, but even as I pack up my things, there's always one more story, and another story, from Leonard about his early collecting days in New York City, when he fell so madly in love with the movies. He remembers a close friend, Harvey Chertok, who worked at Warner Bros.-Seven Arts and hired him to write text for a film catalogue. He found out that Leonard was writing his book *Movie Comedy Teams* on the side and was desperate to see some rare titles. "Harvey picked up the phone and called someone at Bonded Films on the West Side and said, 'I'm sending somebody over, and you can let him borrow anything he wants, two prints at a time.'" It's a small act of kindness that Leonard still obviously cherishes. But then there are the wounds that never heal: "There was a man at Paramount, much like Charlie Mogull. When I tried to rent Martin and Lewis movies from Films Inc. with my hard-earned money, he had to approve every rental. They said, 'You'll have to write a letter.' I said, 'Why? It's in your catalogue for thirty-five dollars.' He wouldn't let me rent them, for money!" Leonard recalls with the indignation of a collector denied. "And then I met Harvey and found out how easy it was. For Harvey it was picking up the phone and making a call and showing a kind gesture. As opposed to that putz who was in business not to do business: *'Do you know what we have to do to screen one film? We have to call the salt mines in Kansas City and pay somebody to inspect the print!'* He gave me this whole long song and dance," Leonard says, shaking his head at the bureaucratic nonsense. Then he adds, almost as an afterthought: "Not that I'm bitter."

4.

The Tuesday Night Film Club

One of the most truly remarkable temples of movie obsession sits behind a dull faux-Tudor facade next to a place that sells barbecue equipment on a busy Burbank street. There's no sign outside to mark collector and former dealer Ken Kramer's office/theater/film vault the Clip Joint: walking by, the only hint is a faint, bittersweet odor of old film prints, which a projectionist friend of mine once likened to oil-and-vinegar salad dressing. But step inside and you're greeted by a world like few others: rare one-sheet posters for *Singin' in the Rain, The Thief of Bagdad*, and the 1940s *Captain Marvel* serial cover the walls. Rows of twinkling Christmas lights give a kind of magical, childlike glow to the shop. Everywhere you look, your eye is caught by pieces of movie history: a multihued Technicolor sign on the wall, a miniature *Nautilus* from *20,000 Leagues Under the Sea*, a grinning *Gremlins* figure in drag with a feathery headdress. In the back near the entrance to Ken's theater is an old-fashioned popcorn machine next to a life-sized standee of James Dean. What Ken calls his office is to the left, and it's literally overflowing with totemlike stacks of 35mm film reels; in fact you're lucky if you don't trip over a print as you walk through the Clip Joint. Opposite his desk is a giant banner for Roger Vadim's 1956 erotic classic *And God Created Woman*, starring one of Ken's personal favorites, Brigitte Bardot. The actual film storage archive is in the back, and it's a marvelous labyrinth cluttered with hundreds of classic and rare titles, where you have to crane your neck sideways to try to read the film titles.

Part of the fun of the Clip Joint is simply wandering around and seeing what you'll find. I'm convinced if Charles Dickens had seen this place, he would've titled his novel *The Old Movie Curiosity Shop*.

For several decades Ken was one of the most active film dealers and collectors in the country—not just most active, but best known, most controversial and most colorful. "I never believed in God and still don't," he says. "But I believed there was a god of film." That god has been both kind and cruel to him. His private collection is one of the finest anywhere and includes such treasures as a 35mm four-track magnetic stereo[26] Technicolor print of Otto Preminger's 1959 musical *Porgy and Bess*, probably the best in existence;[27] a superb collection of original Technicolor Disney features from the 1940s, 1950s, and 1960s; plus one-of-a-kind items like home-movie footage of Marilyn Monroe and Joe DiMaggio shot during filming of *The River of No Return* and outtakes from George Pal's sci-fi classic *War of the Worlds*. His arguments with fellow collectors, some stretching over decades, are legendary in the tight-knit underground community. He's been assaulted by thieves dressed as cops over a fifty-thousand-dollar film deal, used psychic Peter Hurkos to try to find a rare Technicolor print of *Gone With the Wind* that was stolen from his vault, had his life threatened by the mob for selling dupe prints of *Deep Throat*, and, by his own admission, in broad daylight broke into the home of a fellow collector he thought had ripped him off. During the 1970s he bought and sold prints to some of the most high-profile collectors out there, including Dick Martin of *Rowan & Martin's Laugh-In*, Sammy Davis Jr., Frank Sinatra Jr., Roddy McDowall, and Hugh Hefner. "When I was really wheeling and dealing in film, getting $30,000 a month—it took me a long time to address what money really was," Ken observes now. "Because it wasn't real." He's also shared a long and sometimes contentious personal history with my writing partner Jeff: the two were briefly partners as film dealers in the early 1970s, until Ken's then-wife Lauren left him to marry Jeff, shortly after they were discovered having an affair at the 3rd Annual Witchcraft and Sorcery Convention. (Yes, the 1970s truly were another decade.) The long-ago rupture between the two men has since been healed—at least as healed as it can be—but remains one of the best-known personal sagas in the collector world.

Ken is now balding, with big glasses and increasingly frail—but in his 1970s heyday, when he briefly flirted with the porn industry, he would have fit right into the cast of *Boogie Nights,* with his dark beard, mustache, and paisley shirts. I wish I could adequately capture his sense of humor; he's rarely serious and is always looking to make a bad pun. Like a number of film collectors, his sense of comic timing comes from growing up watching Abbott and Costello, Jack Benny, and Bob Hope and Bing Crosby. (Ken describes a high school friend as having graduated "magna cum moron.") He's a bit like Johnny Carson, Ed McMahon, and the *Tonight Show* band rolled into one.

Ken swears he hasn't bought any prints in years—and then proceeds to talk about his latest find. He spotted an ad in *The Recycler* newspaper that advertised "*Deep Throat* poster, loose film reels—four hundred dollars." Ken wound up paying twice that but got a 35mm print of *Deep Throat* with 50 percent color left and an excellent Fuji color print of *The Devil in Miss Jones.* "But that's not even the good stuff," he grins. "The guy had an original 35mm black-and-white print of *A Hard Day's Night* and, even better, a complete British Technicolor print of *Let It Be.*" He claims someone's already offered him over three thousand dollars for the *Devil in Miss Jones* print alone—but he's not selling (for now). For guys like Ken, it's almost impossible to give up wheeling and dealing after an entire lifetime in the underground film trade. "I bought a couple Disneys I already had, and then said, 'Why am I doing this?'" he notes about another recent purchase of prints of *Alice in Wonderland* and *101 Dalmatians.* "It was just the impulse, a bargain," he says, shaking his head.

Like all obsessive collectors, he remembers the ones that got away: "Years ago I went through one of those phases where I swore to my then-wife that I wouldn't buy anything more. A guy called me up that month and said, 'I've got the Cowardly Lion costume from *The Wizard of Oz.* Do you want to buy it for eight hundred dollars?' I asked him if it included the mask." He pauses, waiting for me to react. "That's a joke—there was no mask for the Lion outfit. I turned him down." (There were reportedly several Cowardly Lion costumes created for the film; one sold at a Bonham's Turner Classic Movies auction in 2014 for over $3 million.) "I had one of the first movie poster stores anywhere," Ken remembers. "I hired a guy to paint the sign outside the store, and instead of cash I told him he could pick out any poster he wanted. He picked an original one-sheet for *Gone With the Wind,* the one with the flower border. The thing sold for fifty or seventy-five bucks back then." The list of lost treasures is endless: "I had the original Ming the Merciless costume from the *Flash Gordon* serial, the one with the big collar. Gave it to Debbie Reynolds when she was opening her costume museum in Vegas. Don't know where it is now. Poor Debbie. So many people stole from her over the years."

There's a photo in the corner of Ken's shop of one that didn't get away: "I spotted an ad in the paper and called the guy up. He said, 'I've got this big Frankenstein dummy. I think they used it outside a store or movie theater.' He wanted seventy-five bucks for it." Ken wound up with the dummy just ahead of a competing buyer but wasn't sure what he'd bought. "I'm looking at it later, and I can't quite figure out what it is. The face is really badly painted, so I send it to a friend of mine to repaint. He calls me up and says, 'Ken, do you know what you have? I stripped off the paint and underneath is a life mask of Karloff's face, beautifully painted in green.' I say, 'What?!' He does some more research and calls me back: 'Look at the final scenes of *The Bride of Frankenstein*. There's the Frankenstein figure surrounded by flames. But if you look closely, you'll see he's not moving— it's a model of him. They probably didn't want to risk hurting Karloff. Your dummy has the exact same clothes, they're torn in the same place. You've got an original prop from *The Bride of Frankenstein*." I ask him if he still has it, but he shakes his head sadly, saying he sold it years ago at a memorabilia auction. "My Frankenstein dummy sold for $37,000. Imagine what it'd go for now." To cheer him up I say, sure—but at the time that was a lot of money. And after all, a prop is just some plaster and paint that we assign an artificial value and meaning to. You sell this stuff and use the money for something more important, like buying a car or pursuing a pretty girl, real memories. Ken nods half-heartedly, but I can tell he doesn't believe me—he'd rather still have the Frankenstein dummy or the *Gone With the Wind* one-sheet. That's part of the illness of collecting.

On Tuesday nights Ken gets together with a bunch of buddies that I'd loosely call "The Cinecon Crowd" for dinner at the family Thai restaurant next to his office, followed by a screening.[28] This particular Tuesday there's about half a dozen film buffs—all men, of course. As we walk into the restaurant, Ken gestures to one overweight friend: "He's got diabetes like me, but he doesn't pay any attention to what he eats. He always falls asleep halfway through the movie. He'll gobble down half a bowl of candy and then pass out from the sugar." Of course, Ken's theater is always well stocked with Twizzlers, bite-sized Hershey's, and soda—very generous, but maybe he should hide them when his diabetic buddies are around. To say the Tuesday Night Film Club isn't the healthiest bunch around is an understatement: they're mostly mild mannered, but highly excitable when discussing film trivia, and look a bit like those odd albino cave creatures that grow genetically adapted to life in darkness. Ken's had a series of major and minor health crises over the past decade—heart attacks, diabetes, you name it—which have slowed him down considerably. In one of his rare moments of seriousness, he talks about his declining health: "I can't do many steps. It's the diabetes. I went to a meeting on Wilshire a while back, and coming down the steps I misjudged the last twelve steps and fell backwards. It took two guys to help me up," he says quietly. There's a long pause. "It's so hard. Your mind is still the same—but whose body is this? I always have to be careful when I walk in a room now. I have to look where I'm going to sit so that I can be sure to get back up again."

Compared with popping a DVD in the machine, it takes a lot of energy and bother to project a film print. There's a whole ritual involved, so it's good to know that Ken is still doing his screenings for the faithful. Tonight's crowd includes Mike Hawks, a slender man in a baseball cap who works at Larry Edmunds Bookshop on Hollywood Boulevard and recognizes me from my Cinematheque days. "The internet had already practically killed us, and now the recession," he says about the book business. "I don't know how we're hanging on, but we are." There's also Stan Taffel, who's one of the co-organizers of the annual Cinecon convention (with Robert S. Birchard). During dinner Stan mentions that he's recently bought a film package from the estate of a deceased collector in Palm Springs. I ask what was in it, and he rolls his eyes: "I never met the guy, but he was a gay Nazi. I'm not kidding: a *gay Nazi*. He had a bunch of movies all about WWII and the Nazis. One of his prints was the Julie Andrews film *Thoroughly Modern Millie*. With it was a little metal can marked 'Jew Outtakes.' Remember in the movie there's a scene where Julie dances at a Jewish wedding? He'd gone in and cut the whole scene out, and put it in this little can." The regulars at Ken's screenings come and go, depending on who's squabbling with who, but there's no denying the core audience is dwindling. "When we first started showing movies, people wouldn't even ask what you were showing—they'd just turn up," Ken recalls. "Now you say, 'I'm screening *Gone With the Wind*.' 'Oh, really?' 'Yeah, and Clark Gable's gonna be there in person.' 'Let me see if I can make it.'" He compares the death of film to—what else?—one of his favorite movies, director William A. Fraker's elegiac 1970 western *Monte Walsh*, starring Lee Marvin. "He's one of the last cowboys, and everything he loves is going away. Especially now, where everything *we* love is going away, I can really relate to it," Ken says.

He was born in 1943 in Plainfield, New Jersey. His father worked in the jewelry business early on but kept feeling the tug of show business: at one point he worked in vaudeville with famous western swing bandleader Spade Cooley, who later went to jail for the murder of his second wife, in 1961. "He was always 'on' like me, and they never saw the anger. He had a good sense of humor, he used it all the time," Ken recalls of his father. The family relocated to the West Coast when Ken was growing up; he re-members a stream of colorful visitors to their house, including midget star Harry Doll of Tod Browning's *Freaks*. Ken started buying 16mm prints in his mid-teens from a family friend named Leroy Scott, who had secret contacts at local film labs—Ken's earliest exposure to the black-market film underground. One of his first illegal film raids was breaking into the Gilboy film depot as a teenager with a high school friend to grab a print of *West Side Story* that happened to be sitting outside. "We were running away, and [my friend] kept yelling, 'We're going to get caught, Ken!'" he recalls with a chuckle. "And I said, 'We will if you keep shouting my name!'"

After high school he began working at Hollywood Film Enterprises lab in the mid-1960s, followed by MGM Studios Film Library and Technicolor. But he soon found himself in trouble again, this time for breaking into United World Films, Universal's 16mm division, to steal prints, for which he spent three days in jail. His partner in planning the break-in was his young wife, Lauren. A dark-haired beauty with a white streak in her hair, she was born in 1947 and as a child was a victim of the infamous Georgia Tann/Tennessee Children's Home Society black-market baby scandal.[29] As a result she struggled with abandonment and health issues for the rest of her life. She met Ken in her early teens and by age fifteen had already had a child with her first husband, Ira, whom she soon divorced. Together she and Ken had one son, Jay, in 1965, who recalls growing up in something of an unconventional environment: "We had a dining room table; always on top of it was a projector. We never ate at the table." Jay would occasionally accompany his father dropping off film to customers. "I remember several trips to the Playboy Mansion, growing up," he says. "As a kid I didn't know what the Playboy Mansion was. I remember driving up, and security came up, saying, 'Thanks, Ken,' and taking the film inside." I ask Jay if he was aware of his father's unusual line of work, and he stifles a laugh. "I thought that was a career. As a kid, I didn't know it was illegal," he replies. "I thought money grew out of his pocket, because he always had money. He'd always pull out big wads of money."

One of the deep ironies of the rivalry/friendship between Ken and Jeff is that Jeff has become something of a personal historian and Boswell to Ken, having inherited many memories and even personal effects through Lauren, who was married to both men. (She passed away in 2007.) Many times during our discussions, Jeff gently corrects Ken's occasionally bumpy recall or produces personal items like Ken's first union card to help prod him. "I'm sorry, I'm a little shocked," Ken says at one point in amazement, staring at long-lost photos from an amateur porn film he directed in the early 1970s, which Jeff hands to him. Another time Jeff produces an old ad Ken took out announcing, "*Repairs anyone! I repair 16mm sound projectors.*" Jeff confides, "Lauren was the one who actually did the work, but Ken had to be the front for it, since she was a girl. Nobody would hire her if they knew it was a girl repairing film projectors." Although Ken tends to deflect questions about his and Lauren's marriage with a joke, Jeff—who met the couple in May of 1971—recalls that theirs was not a peaceful marriage. "Have you ever been around a couple who are just screaming at each other all the time?" Jeff recalls. "And Lauren gave as good as she got when it came to arguing."

In 1971 Ken also began his brief flirtation with the adult film business, shooting amateur porn loops—often eight or nine a day—at a building on Las Palmas in Hollywood. "Guys got paid fifteen dollars a session, girls twenty-five dollars, and I'd hear their boyfriends telling them, 'This is a great way to break into the movie business.' I'd take the girls aside and tell them, 'Listen, if you ever want to work in the film business, don't shoot porn,'" he recalls. Ken soon branched out on his own and with backing from his film-collector friend Dick Martin directed a porn spoof of *The Man from U.N.C.L.E.* super-spy series called *The Man from S.N.A.T.C.H.—*

now, perhaps thankfully, a lost film. It wasn't his last brush with porn: when *Deep Throat* (1972) and *The Devil in Miss Jones* (1973) became huge hits, Ken got in on the action by making illegal dupe negatives of both for a theater in Las Vegas. "Half the theaters running those pictures were running bootleg prints," he says. "The bottom line is, they were being busted every day, so they'd come every two weeks and buy fourteen prints of each. They were making so much money, they could afford to buy them from me." It was a lucrative business until he got a call from a distributor asking if he had more prints of *Deep Throat* and *The Devil in Miss Jones* to sell, and he drove out to meet the man and his partners. "They ask me some general questions like, 'Are the prints in good condition?' And I say, 'Yeah, they're really good quality.' 'How much do you want for them?' 'Five hundred dollars apiece,' I say. The guys look at me and say, 'You realize these are our movies you're selling.' I try to crack a joke: 'Well, I'm willing to go down on the price then.'" He shakes his head, remembering his brush with the mob. "Eventually I wind up giving them the prints for free, and they tell me, 'If we ever find you selling our movies again, we're going to kill you.'"

If his experience in the porn business was brief, his career as a film dealer was just kicking into high gear. Jeff, who was eighteen years old when he met Ken and Lauren, was fairly astonished at the older man's access to prints: "At the time Ken had a great contact at C.F.I. [Consolidated Film Industries], and he was getting mint things straight out of the lab. Brand-new reels, brand-new prints. I'd come into his house, and right against the couch here are 2,000-foot reels of film: Here's a row of season one of *Star Trek*, here's season two of *Star Trek*, here's season two of *Mannix, Mission: Impossible, The Love Boat*," Jeff remembers. "Ken was selling this stuff all over the country. He was the *Star Trek* guy for months." It was in fact the famed sci-fi series that first brought them together, when Jeff purchased a 16mm *Star Trek* print from Ken—and promptly bounced the check. "I remember that, too," Ken says with raised eyebrows. "That's because you cashed the check too early. I told you to hold onto it for another day!" Jeff protests. Given all that's passed between these two men as friends, rivals, film dealers, and collectors, it's ironic that the bounced *Star Trek* check has now become a running gag with them. It even creeps into their most painful shared memories. At one point Ken recalls downing an entire bottle of vodka in desperation at his crumbling marriage. I ask what prompted this alcohol binge. "Well, Lauren and I got caught having an affair for the second time, and she and I split up the coast to Oxnard," Jeff responds. "You still owed me for the *Star Trek* episodes!" Ken adds in mock outrage; then he gives a long sigh. "But I knew things weren't working with her."

Although his personal life may have been messy, the 1970s were heady days for Ken professionally. He was getting a steady stream of prints from contacts at labs and film salvage companies, and turning them over for good profit. A regular client was Hugh Hefner: "One Christmas I wanted to get some extra money, so I called [Hefner] up and said, 'I know you love Disney, and I've got a couple of Disney prints.' Hefner said, 'Well, I'm interested, but I won't pay more than $1,000 each.' At the time the top price for them was like $200, $225." It turns out Hefner was willing to pay a flat rate of $500 per black-and-white feature and $1,000 per color film, so Ken and Jeff began rapidly scouring lists from other dealers, buying cheap prints for $25 to $50 and reselling them to Hefner at a huge markup. Their other big income stream came from an unusual source: South Africa. At the time there was a cultural embargo against the apartheid government, which prevented the major media companies from selling their film or TV series there. So an enormous black market developed, where South African buyers would purchase vast quantities of old prints here in the United States. Back in their country, hundreds of film rental shops sprang up, like precursors to video rental stores, where for a few dozen rand people could rent a 16mm projector and episodes of *Mannix* or *Mission: Impossible*. The trade was, of course, highly illegal, but a number of dealers I spoke with (including Jeff, who spent two months in jail for selling prints to South Africa) took the risk. I ask both Jeff and Ken if they had any qualms about selling to the apartheid-era pariah. "Only until I saw the check," Jeff responds bluntly. "I just rationalized it and justified it because it was so much money." Ken adds, "I was more scared than he was," and his caution may have saved him. "I took a couple of bucks less and had them meet me here in L.A. and take the stuff. I didn't want a record, and I was getting paid in cash. I was getting what, twenty-five bucks less than you?" Ken's refusal to ship prints directly to South Africa may be the reason why, of all the major dealers active in Los Angeles at the time, he was one of the few not caught up in the infamous film-piracy arrests of 1975. "We'd take the money and say, 'I want to go to New York'—and spend twenty thousand dollars on a trip. Because it was always coming in. It was like paper," Ken says now of the river of South African cash. "We weren't in the real world. Let's put it that way."

"I was a collector first. I just fell into it, really," Ken observes about his transition to dealing. To this day he is a collector first and a dealer second—and it's an important distinction. One of the discoveries he's most proud of is a cache of nine lost cartoon shorts in a box of trailers he paid fifty dollars for in the mid-1990s. The shorts were part of a series called "Animaland" made by an overlooked animation pioneer named David Hand. "He was the director of *Bambi* and *Snow White and the Seven Dwarfs*; next to Walt he was the big honcho at Disney. In the mid-1940s he brought the union in and Walt went ballistic and they fought. He went to England on his own, and that's where he did these nine cartoons on his own. They were never shown outside of England," Ken says about the shorts, with titles like *Ginger Nutt's Forest Dragon* and *It's a Lovely Day*. Working with Hand's son, Ken made film-to-tape transfers of his original IB Technicolor prints and rereleased the films in 1998, to wide acclaim. One of his other treasures, his 35mm four-track mag Technicolor print of *Porgy and Bess*, took several years and a good deal of luck to assemble. Ken purchased an incomplete print of six reels from Jeff, then managed to find a collector in Utah with four more reels. That still left one reel missing due to vinegar syndrome—which he thankfully found through the Widescreen Society in Long Beach. "I didn't know how rare it was until I showed it at the American Cinematheque, and then I started getting calls from all over the world to borrow the print," he says. Ken's love for IB Technicolor is well known: when the dye-transfer processing plant shut down in Hollywood in 1975, he and several other collectors took out an obituary ad in *Variety* mourning the death of IB Technicolor.[30] Of all the Technicolor prints in his archive, the crown jewel may be an original 35mm print of Hitchcock's *Vertigo*. Although it recently topped the *Sight & Sound* critics' poll of the 50 Greatest Films Ever Made, *Vertigo* wasn't particularly successful on its first release, meaning there were no restrikes in Technicolor, and fewer than a half dozen original 35mm prints in good condition survive today. "If you saw the restoration, it was very good, but if you saw them compared, there's so much lost on that film. The key thing is the first time he sees Kim Novak in a bar," Ken says. "It's almost three-dimensional." But even an admitted IB Technicolor freak like Ken is philosophical about it. "Dye transfer doesn't make a bad movie good," he says—then Jeff chimes in, "It just makes it pretty." Perhaps his sweetest moment with *Vertigo* came recently: "I got a call from someone at Universal. They're doing a new Blu-ray edition of *Vertigo*, and they're not happy with their colors, so they want to check it against my print," Ken says with barely disguised emotion. "I always dreamed about getting a call like that."

"That was my alternate life, was movies," he observes about his love affair with cinema. "My happiest times were going to movies." Almost inevitably, Ken is now actively trying to find a buyer for his film collection. "I can't really imagine the day when I won't have film prints to show," he says, looking around his shop. But he also knows if he waits much longer, the value of his collection will continue to drop. "I used to enjoy running a 35mm print: 'Oh, a changeover!' But now, it's an ordeal," he admits. For his film screenings he asks one of his younger friends to come in and operate the projectors. These days he is mostly retired from his longtime business licensing stock footage at the Clip Joint and usually comes to the office to watch films at night with his buddies. I ask which of his hundreds of prints it will hurt most to part with. "*Deep Throat,*" he answers immediately—then cracks a grin. His dad's sense of shtick is still with him. "Oh God. Well, the Disneys for one, because all the classics, all the DVDs don't look anything like the prints," he finally says.

Until then he'll continue to do his regular Tuesday Night Film Club, where much of the fun involves a heated debate over which film to watch, and then even more activity as Ken tries to actually *find* the print in his crowded film vault. This particular night, Ken and his regulars finally arrive in a very roundabout way to the business of watching a movie. They settle on showing a 16mm Technicolor CinemaScope print of an obscure Robert Ryan/Virginia Mayo/Jeffrey Hunter western called *The Proud Ones*, which plays like Howard Hawks's *Rio Bravo*, only with its balls cut off. Beforehand they screen two chapters of a forgotten 1926 silent serial called *Officer 444*, directed by John Ford's much-less-successful brother, Francis, and costarring his nephew Phil Ford. The good thing about silent serials is that you can ask questions while they're playing and no one gets upset. Ken's diabetic buddy in the rear explains during the film that Francis Ford had been a contract director at Universal a few years before: "But I think he had a drinking problem, because he wound up doing these cheapie states' rights movies that were sold off territory by territory." The crowd ventures to guess out loud that *Officer 444* was shot in and around Los Angeles—someone observes that the rolling hills in one car chase looked like Chatsworth, or maybe Glendale predevelopment—and in fact, the outdoor locations, the views of a still relatively unspoiled L.A., give it more interest than it probably deserves. The most excitement it generates is when a getaway car zooms past a remote roadside diner with a sign reading, "El Camino Inn," and Ken's buddies debate where the hell that was, but in the end nobody can say for sure.

5.

Rock Hudson's Hidden Film Vault

"I've lived in New York for twenty-five years, and I've never shown a movie here. But I still have my film prints," observes TV host, journalist, film historian, and collector Robert Osborne. "There's something very difficult about giving them up. That was such an important part of my life; it was so meaningful to me." With his silver-white hair and his always-dapper suit and tie, he is something like America's official ambassador for Hollywood history. A longtime journalist for *The Hollywood Reporter*, he's written a number of highly regarded books on the history of the Academy Awards. Since 1994 he has been an omnipresent fixture on Turner Classic Movies as the channel's primary host (and before that, as host on The Movie Channel for nearly a decade). He's been described by Susan King in the *Los Angeles Times* as "a delightful hybrid of Walt Disney and Walter Cronkite," which captures much of his charm and the familiarity he brings to the subject of film, having been close friends with many of the stars he discusses, including Bette Davis, Rock Hudson, and Olivia de Havilland—whom he still calls every Sunday to chat with on the phone, as he has for the past thirty-five years. "When I got my print of *Gilda*, I thought I'd never be able to see it again. Now I've introduced it, like, twenty-five times on TCM over the last eighteen years," he observes wryly about the changes in media since he began collecting in the late 1960s. His comments underscore a deep irony: it's much easier to be a film lover these days. But with this ready availability, something indefinable has been lost since the days when

Osborne and his friends would huddle together over a noisy 16mm projector. "We started collecting because we wanted access to films," he says simply. When you can find a movie with a few clicks of a mouse, is it as special?

When we speak, Osborne is in what he describes as a "chilly New York," although he's grateful that he can now tape his TCM material there instead of having to commute to and from Atlanta. In his early eighties, he still keeps up a remarkably busy schedule, and even more remarkable, he's kept his boyish enthusiasm and love for the movies intact. He was born in 1932 in Colfax, Washington, and grew up during the WWII era. "All the adults were really focused on the war effort, and I was ignored by them, so I spent a lot of time at the movies as a child," he says. Although he doesn't go into detail, there is more than a hint of loneliness in his memories of his small-town childhood. Without much cash to spend, he began collecting on a modest scale, acquiring 8mm Castle Films reductions of classic Laurel and Hardy comedies. After graduating from college with a degree in journalism, he traveled out to Los Angeles to pursue a career as an actor and was accepted as a contract player at Lucille Ball and Desi Arnaz's Desilu Studios in the late 1950s. He made appearances in several *Desilu Playhouse* episodes and was even seen, very briefly, in the pilot for *The Beverly Hillbillies* in 1962—although, perhaps wisely, he decided to take Lucille Ball's gentle advice when she suggested his future was in writing, not acting. He published his first book, *Academy Awards Illustrated*, in 1965.

Around this time he became friends with a dancer and film collector named Jeff Parker, who'd appeared in films like *Twist Around the Clock* and *Gypsy* and later danced in the Ginger Rogers Revue. Osborne gives Parker credit for introducing him in Hollywood film-collector circles—and also, just as important, to many of the golden-age stars who were still alive. "We didn't have any money, but enough money to buy cheap wine and spaghetti," he says fondly about those early collecting years. "We'd go over to his house, and, being a dancer, he got to know these people. Jeff would have Eleanor Parker over and show her numbers and talk about that." Other dance legends who appeared at these private screenings include, astoundingly, Vera-Ellen, Fayard Nicholas of the Nicholas Brothers, Cyd Charisse, and Ginger Rogers. "Jeff had been in her nightclub act and ran *The Barkleys of Broadway*. It seems strange now, but this was an era when people didn't care about Ginger Rogers." It's an indelible image, of Osborne, Parker, and their young, impoverished, and film-crazy friends sitting in the dark with these great stars, watching clips of classic MGM-musical dance scenes. It's also easy to understand why he finds it hard to part with his film prints, even if he doesn't screen them anymore. "What money we did make we'd usually spend on collecting," he recalls. "It was great, because those people [like Vera-Ellen, Charisse, and Rogers] were around, and they loved having young people interested in their work."

In the late 1960s he went to work as a publicist for a PR firm called Pat Fitzgerald & Company and through the owner became friends with another Hollywood legend and film collector: Rock Hudson. "He found out I was an avid film collector. He'd loan me copies of his films," he says about Hudson, whom he still regards with great affection. To illustrate what a dedicated collector Hudson was—at least of films he appeared in— Osborne recalls that the actor refused to do a film called *Pretty Maids All in a Row* with director Roger Vadim at MGM, unless the studio agreed to give him a print of that and another movie, *Something of Value*, that he'd made with Sidney Poitier. "As a favor to him I went through his whole collection and decorated the cans with the title on, so it was easy to read," Osborne says. To return the favor, Hudson surprised Osborne by buying him a brand-new 16mm sound projector—the first one he ever owned. I ask if Hudson had an interesting film collection, and Osborne suppresses a chuckle: "He didn't have much of a collection except his own movies. Rock was somebody who was a great guy, but he lost interest if you weren't talking about him," he replies with candor. "The way you could perk him up was ask him a question about *Giant*, and then he joined the party again."

For a film buff like Osborne, those must have been glorious days, hob-nobbing with the star of *Written on the Wind* and *Pillow Talk*. "Rock had this wonderful house up in the Hollywood Hills, kind of a big sprawling place. It looked like a ranch all on one level. He had a separate entertain-ment room with couches and a stage so that people could get up and do acts. He'd have Carol Burnett there, and he would sing at the piano," he remembers. "He didn't sing that well, but he was charming with his sing-ing, and he was so attractive and tall and likable. He used to have parties there and get roaring drunk. When he was at his own home, he was very relaxed, and he would show movies in that room." Hudson soon invited Osborne to come over and screen some of his 16mm compilation reels of classic musical numbers. Soon, though, there were dark rumblings in the collector underground that caused paranoia even for a Hollywood legend like Hudson. "The FBI was after film collectors then and put the terror into them. When Rock found out about Roddy [McDowall] and them taking his film collection, Rock had a side room built in his entertainment room. Right off the entertainment building, he built a film vault—but it was kind of in the back so you didn't notice it," Osborne recalls. "What he did was he got bricks and bricked it up so it looked like the fireplace, so nobody knew it was there. So when they [the FBI] did come to investigate, they couldn't find it, and they never bothered him."

One of Osborne's favorite stories of his collecting days shows how, as the adage goes, for the want of a nail the kingdom was lost—or in this case, for the want of a print. Through his good friend Jeff Parker, he made a contact at Columbia Pictures who'd surreptitiously loan Osborne private studio prints on Friday night to watch over the weekend. At the same time, through his job at Pat Fitzgerald's PR company, he came into contact with a client of the firm's, producer Ross Hunter, the man behind hits like *Imitation of Life, Pillow Talk,* and *Airport.* "Ross was looking for another film to do. He ran into Cary Grant one night at a dinner party, and they got to talking, and Cary said, 'Say, you should remake a movie I did called *Penny Serenade.*' It was Ross's kind of movie: he loved stories that were big and splashy and elegant and kind of melodramatic." Grant—who, like Rock Hudson, apparently liked to collect prints of his own movies—even offered to lend Hunter his personal copy of *Penny Serenade* to show to the executives at Columbia Pictures.

What happened next sounds something like a slapstick sequence out of a Blake Edwards film. Hunter decided to throw a lavish dinner party for the Columbia execs, capped by a surprise screening of the original *Penny Serenade* to convince them to finance a remake. "It's getting close to the night of the dinner party; it's maybe a Wednesday, and the party is on Saturday night. Hunter calls up Cary Grant to borrow that print. A house man answers and says, 'I'm sorry, but Mr. Grant isn't at home—he's away on a cruise.'" In a panic, Hunter calls Osborne, who says not to worry, he can get a print of the film from his inside contact at Columbia. "My friend at Columbia said, 'No problem, nobody ever checks it out. But I can't let you have it until Friday.' So Friday comes, I go over at five o'clock. The guy says, 'You're not going to believe this—somebody checked it out.'"

"Ross has a conniption fit. 'That ruins my plan. Is there something else I can borrow?!'" Osborne recalls with a rueful chuckle. "So I'm going down the list of films they have available for Ross: 'There's *Gilda* . . .' 'No, don't want that,' Ross said. '*Born Yesterday*?' 'No, don't want that.'

'There's *Lost Horizon* . . .' Hunter considers it for a moment. 'Hmm, that's interesting. Why don't you borrow that one?' I took a couple prints home for him—and on Saturday night he decides to show *Lost Horizon*."

Even by the standards of bad movies, Hunter's 1973 musical remake of *Lost Horizon* is in a category of its own. It is, in short, a colossal flop, and the last theatrical feature the producer ever got to make. "It ruined Burt Bacharach and Hal David, the two most successful composers in the business. For a time it ruined Peter Finch. It ruined Liv Ullmann's Hollywood career; she was coming off all those great Ingmar Bergman movies. Sally Kellerman had just done *M.A.S.H.* with Robert Altman, and her career never recovered." Osborne breathes in deeply, then heaves a long sigh. "It's this movie that destroyed all these careers, and it's all because we couldn't borrow this print of *Penny Serenade*!"

6.

Lockdown

The Windsor Palms Care facility in Artesia, California, is a sandy-colored, low-slung building with a peaked roof in front, almost like an old Googie-style restaurant. It sits, fairly anonymous, on a broad, well-kept street lined with palm trees as its name implies. I arrive twenty minutes late on a swelteringly hot Tuesday morning in July after struggling through traffic. I'm here to talk with one of Windsor Care's more colorful and notorious patients: Alfred "Al" Beardsley. His name may not be familiar to most people, but his place in the annals of modern American criminal history is.

"You know this is a lockdown facility?" my partner Jeff says as I meet him outside. "Apparently there are dangerous or violent patients inside—they can't just walk in and out." The point is underscored by a red sign at the door that bluntly warns: "Please Don't Give Out Cigarettes or Lighters Because We Don't Want Our Residents To Start Any Fires." As I sign for a guest badge at the door, the female clerk there jokes with us flirtatiously. When I ask if it's okay to bring in a case of Coke for the man we're visiting, she smiles, "Oh that's fine." A beat later Jeff adds, "I'm assuming it's that kind of Coke; maybe he wanted the other kind," which gets a laugh out of her. I'm guessing she doesn't get too many working the front desk here.

There are elderly patients wandering the halls in a semi-daze as we wind our way through the bland, antiseptic corridors. Jeff knocks at the door of Al's room and calls out his name; he's dozing in bed in a semiprivate room. "Oh hi," he says as Jeff introduces us. "Did you try to come by yesterday?" he asks, a bit confused. Of all the people we spoke to for this book, Al Beardsley—projectionist, convicted film pirate, and (much later) sports memorabilia dealer caught up in one of the most famous criminal cases of the past quarter century—evoked by far the strongest reaction. One man, first assistant cameraman Brian LeGrady, nearly exploded in an apoplectic fit at his name: "That guy almost single-handedly destroyed my love for film collecting and my marriage!" Projectionist and collector Mike Schleiger of the Egyptian Theatre rolled his eyes when I brought up Al: "If he walked into a booth, you did not want to take your eyes off of him. Because when he walked out you'd be missing something." Search his name online and you'll find articles referring to him as "a delusional menace" who "once heard voices telling him to overthrow the mayor of Burbank, California."[31] I'd even been warned not to give out my phone number or personal details to him.

In person, lying in a hospital gown, Al is a far cry from the image others had painted of him: he's tall and gaunt and speaks slowly; his right hand is paralyzed and hidden up to the middle forearm under a white bedsheet, and his chin and his face above his upper lip are moist and sweaty. His thick, bushy, red-gray eyebrows are one of his most distinctive features: they look like chalkboard erasers somebody has attached to his forehead. By his own account Al was born in 1961 in Albany, New York. He grew up firmly middle class. His father was a piano restorer; his mother a homemaker, in the parlance of the day. He credits his grandfather Alfred Antoinette with starting his obsession for the movies: "My grandfather was the head of the projectionists union in New York, used to let me go to work with him. I'd sit in the booth and watch him do his thing. I said, 'This is what I'm going to do—I don't care if there's no money, I want to do it.' My grandfather implored me not to do it. It's something I would have liked to have done the whole rest of my life, actually. It was just fun to run a movie. Do the curtain. Do the sound call. Take care of the equipment. Do the changeovers. Steal the print on your way home." He cracks a big smile at this last comment: Al is obviously aware of his notorious rep and even asks several times during our interviews how he'll be portrayed in the book. "As fairly as possible," I respond, which seems to satisfy him.

I can't help asking Al about the injuries that brought him to Windsor Palms. He replies that he was the victim of a hit-and-run in Santa Ana: a car jumped the curb and struck him, leaving him in the bushes like "a piece of trash or a transient." When I ask if the police found the driver, Al responds somewhat mysteriously that he knows who did it, but he's not pursuing the perpetrator. I push him further, and he finally mouths something that seems to be the name Bob. Jeff and I exchange looks. "Bob? Bob who?" Jeff asks. Al shakes his head: "No. *With the 'M.'*" We finally understand what he means—it's the mob.

After picking up the projection bug from his grandfather in his early teens, Al worked at a string of local Albany-area theaters, including the Turnpike Drive-In, the Latham Drive-In, and even the X-rated Cinema Art. After high school he moved to the West Coast with union card in hand and wound up at the Topanga in Woodland Hills, the Bruin and the Odeon in Westwood Village, and others. "I had an obsession with Clint Eastwood," he says. "I grew up with Eastwood and James Bond and Burt Reynolds. Was never a big Charles Bronson fan. I liked that era. I look at all these people now, and I could be standing right next to them and not know who they are. Back when movie stars were movie stars." It was his appreciation of celebrities that led to a chance encounter that would have lasting consequences. While projecting at the Fine Arts Theatre in Beverly Hills, he spotted football legend and actor O. J. Simpson and a date waiting in line for a screening of *The Gods Must Be Crazy*. "He was wearing this beautiful blue business suit, just knock your socks off," Al recalls today. "It was O. J. Simpson in his prime." Even now, in his frail voice, he sounds a bit smitten by Simpson's charisma. He waved Simpson and his date into the theater for free. After this kind gesture, the two men became friends. "Not best friends, but *friends*," Al points out, and they would occasionally see each other in Westwood Village, where Al would let Simpson in for free.[32]

In 1986 Al was hired by comedian Redd Foxx to run the screening room in a building Foxx owned. A year later he leased his own theater from musician Kenny Rogers, dubbing it the Sunset Screening Room, and began running it as a high-end private facility for directors and studio executives to watch dailies. Around the same time, Al made his first contacts in the shadowy world of film collectors through one of the best-known dealers at the time, Emil Varga. Varga, who was originally based in Detroit and later Arizona, seemed to have an almost magical network of suppliers across the country who kept him stocked with rare 35mm and 70mm prints; a number of former collectors Jeff and I spoke with referred to him with obvious affection and envy. Radio deejay Jim Zippo (who adopted his last name from a rubber "Zippo the Chimp" mask he used to wear screening *Planet of the Apes* in his teens at a theater in Lake Arrowhead) once drove out to visit Varga at his home in Sun City outside of Phoenix. He remembers the dealer as something of an "old-timer," with a comfortably middle-class house with elegant furniture. But the garage was literally stuffed to the ceiling with massive 70mm prints of *Circus World*, *The Alamo*, and *Chitty Chitty Bang Bang*, which he often ran at home: "He got these Japanese 70mm machines, and they sounded like machine guns," Zippo says. "It was just blowing my mind." Al shares the same fondness for Varga, whom he describes as an elderly, frail man in blue overalls, who "liked to make the sale. Lived the good life. Had a lot of friends. Loved film. I went to his funeral—they actually buried him with a reel of film."

Through Varga, Al met another key operator in the underground print market: Gunther Jung at Pix Fix film rejuvenation lab. Jung, whom we spoke with separately, was born in Germany in 1929 and immigrated to the United States in 1938, at the brink of WWII. His family settled in the Bronx, where his father worked as a steel engraver. After two years of college, Jung left to work for a company called Filmtreat that did chemical scratch removal on used prints. He moved to the West Coast in the 1960s and started his own operation; when I asked who came up with the name, Jung (who speaks in terse, one- or two-sentence answers) shot back: "I was sitting at a bar one day having my usual beer, and I thought, 'What's a good name for a company? We fix pics—so 'Pix Fix.'" When I spoke with him, Jung flatly denied any involvement with film dealers or collectors. But Al insists that Emil Varga sent him to Pix Fix to repair a print of *Rain Man* that Al had bought. "I walked into the [Pix Fix] office, sat my ass down on the couch like I was somebody, and I said, 'I'm here to exchange this reel, it isn't any good. I got it from Emil.' Gunther, like Don Corleone, told me, 'I don't give a fuck who Emil or you are. Tell Emil to stick that reel up his ass, and get outta my office.' My face was flush. I said, 'Holy shit, this guy is hot.' You know how Gunther was. Tough guy New Yorker." Al remembers that it took a few weeks to gain Jung's trust: "The first print I bought from him was a mint LPP print of *The Wall*. I remember walking away to put it in the trunk of the car, and he says, 'Hey! I've got ears all over town.' 'What's that supposed to mean, a threat?' 'No, but I've got ears all over town.'" According to Al, he began working with Jung, getting a steady supply of rare prints through him. (Several other collectors we spoke with confirmed that Pix Fix was a well-known print source.) These days there's apparently no contact between the two men. When I mention Al's name to Jung, he responds: "Who, Beardsley? I don't know too much about him. I just know he was bad news." When Jeff presses him for details, Jung evades the question: "I can't remember exactly, but I know he was a Bad News Bear." For his part, Al still seems to have a grudging affection for Jung. "He'd think nothing of threatening you or busting your windshield. But you couldn't help but like him," he adds, mimicking Jung's distinctive Bronx accent.

With his own screening room and access to high-end clients with brand-new movies, along with a network of contacts gained through Varga, Al began working as a dealer himself. As opposed to many of the former dealers we talked to who are understandably circumspect about their black-market activities, Al is open and unapologetic these days talking about his inventive scams. One particularly brazen operation involved selling prints back to the very studio that owned them: "The deal was, we were both broke at Christmastime. Gunther was behind on the mortgage. He was at eviction proceedings. I just came up with a brainstorm of an idea: We had probably a couple hundred prints of *Terminator 2*. A couple hundred prints of *Air America*, all these old Carolco prints. I said, 'Gunther, if I can sell these prints back to Carolco, then we'll turn around and demand the salvage rights and sell the rights to Jeff, and he'll take care of it.' Gunther said, 'It'll never happen. They'll never go for it . . .' I think we made $10,000, $12,000." An even more outrageous act of larceny involved a rare and expensive 70mm print of *Lawrence of Arabia*. According to Al, he tried to convince Jung, who was in charge of rejuvenating the print after a run at the Fairfax Theater, to let him have it, but in this case Jung refused, saying there was too much heat from the studio. Al was in a bind, though, having already sold the print to a collector. So he hired a moving van and sent it to the Fairfax, who turned the print over thinking it was the studio delivery service. He quickly overnighted the print to the collector before anyone knew it was gone. Say what you will, but it takes some serious *cojones* to pull off a con like that. Henry Gondorff in *The Sting* would be proud.

For a while in the late 1980s, business was good, possibly too good, because Al's growing reputation and brazenness brought him to the attention of a growing circle of collectors. One of them would ignite a literal sheriff's department sting operation and a highly public, decade-long feud between the two men.

According to Al, he met fellow collector Craig Call sometime around 1988 or 1989: "I was running a film for Charlie Sheen at my screening room, and Craig just showed up and introduced himself. He had the gift of gab and sounded believable." Call, who spoke with us separately, is a teacher in his mid-sixties now, with a neatly shaved head; he has the athletic build of a lifelong dancer and choreographer, and also a kind of manic energy that erupts in occasional bursts and physical leaps. When I go to interview him, he insists on meeting me outside his Hollywood apartment and leading me into the back courtyard. "You'd never find it on your own," he says, pointing to the unmarked door to his apartment that's hidden next to the laundry room. "It looks like this is the entry to a storage room. Nobody knows I'm here," he confides. It's the kind of paranoia I've come to recognize in many older film collectors, who still live with the anxiety that someone will come knocking on their door one day.

Call was born in the early 1950s into a family with a long Mormon lineage, and grew up in New Mexico and Maryland. According to Call, the founder of the Mormon Church, Joseph Smith, had a vision that his great-great-grandfather Anson Call would "go across the plains and build a home for the saints in the west. My ancestors were part of that whole thrust of Mormons into Utah and California and even Mexico: these were American Mormons who built colonies in Mexico that are still there today. My ancestors had run-ins with Pancho Villa." Craig fell in love with movies at an early age and started, like many of his peers, collecting two-hundred-foot Castle Films 8mm reductions of classic Universal horror titles like *Creature from the Black Lagoon*, *Abbott and Costello Meet Frankenstein*, and *Bride of Frankenstein*. For him, love of movies trumped everything else—he remembers his eagerness in high school to get his hands on a new 16mm print from a distributor in England: "I was on the gymnastic team; I was the captain of the team. I remember vaulting over the horse and thinking '*The 7th Voyage of Sinbad* came in today—I can't wait to get home. It's waiting for me, it's right there!'"

It was after college, while working as curator of the Brigham Young University film archives, where he worked on the Merian C. Cooper Collection, that his twin loves, movies and the Mormon Church, collided. Call was privately screening prints from his collection for friends and fellow students; one was *The Sound of Music*, which happened to be distributed by a division of the church, Deseret Books, under contract from Films Inc. A student reported him to Deseret, which demanded he surrender his print. Even today Call is obviously still deeply wounded by the incident: "I went to my bishop. I said, 'I'm not breaking the law.' At the same time I was this really righteous kid and wanted to do the right thing. 'This print cost me a lot of money, are you going to pay me back for it?' The bishop said, 'Oh no, we just want you to give it up, along with all your other prints.'" Call refused to surrender his collection, and the incident mushroomed. Soon Call was contacted by the FBI, which had apparently been notified by Deseret Books. Call still refused to hand over his films. Thinking everything had settled down, he went on tour as choreographer of a Mormon-themed musical, when he got a frantic phone call from his mother: "She's crying and terrified because the FBI called her and said upon my arrival back in Maryland, I was going to be handcuffed, arrested, and put in prison for twenty years for the felonies that I'd committed with regards to handling copyrighted motion picture film. My mother was beside herself. We're this really Mormon family that never did anything to break the law." With the help of an attorney in Kansas well versed in film copyright law, Call eventually managed to get the FBI to drop the case, but the incident ruptured his faith in his own church. It's easy to see why he still lives behind an unmarked door.

Shortly after meeting Al in the late 1980s, Call began getting a stream of just-released, and even not-yet-released titles, like *Home Alone* and *Rocky V*, from him. Today it's hard to imagine the John Avildsen–directed *Rocky V* being the cause of so much trouble, but this is the one that did it. According to Call, in 1990 Al agreed to sell him a 35mm print of *Rocky V*, which had yet to hit theaters, but loaned it first for a private screening at the home of a projectionist named Ned Fairbairn, letting it be known that the print belonged to Call. (When I asked Al separately for confirmation, he couldn't recall the incident but confirmed he'd sold a print of *Rocky V*.) At the private screening was a man who happened to work for the film's distributor, MGM/UA, and who was understandably upset that someone owned a print of their brand-new movie, even a turkey like *Rocky V*.

According to Call, he was incensed that Al had attached his name to the illegal print: "I was so angry at Al. I said 'Why would you do that?! Why would you tell people?! This is a *new film*, you can't do that!' Al just laughed and laughed." Within a week Call was contacted by a film rejuvenator named Tom Ogburn, saying that MGM/UA wanted to see Call's print. Ogburn, now deceased, was another fascinating character in the Hollywood collector and dealer underworld. I knew him briefly in the early 1990s when he did print inspection for the American Cinematheque, where I worked as a programmer, and remember him as a loud-voiced, gregarious man who was always in need of money. According to Al, Ogburn had a bad gambling habit: "Every day at my screening room he would call me up: 'How ya doing? Got anything hot over there for the weekend?'—meaning movies that hadn't come out yet. I trusted Tom—I think everybody did who encountered him—but he was in bad shape financially." Ogburn's claim to fame was a chemical process he'd invented called Tomacote, that protected prints from scratches and extended their life; many collectors we spoke with consider it something of a magic elixir for film. He was even hired by Universal Pictures to frantically Tomacote several hundred release prints of Steven Spielberg's *Schindler's List* after the black-and-white prints began burning under the glare of too-powerful modern projectors. My writing partner Jeff, who knew him well, laughingly recalls that Ogburn was less than safety conscious: "[He] would smoke when he was using Tomacote: it was an oil-based film cleaner, and he's basically pouring gasoline on film while he's smoking!"

Call reluctantly surrendered his illegal print of *Rocky V* (which in true collector fashion he'd already sold to someone else). The next day he received a call from Ogburn, who said the studio wanted to talk with him, but when Ogburn and the MGM/UA employee came to pick him up, they instead drove him to a Culver City restaurant to meet with a group of men headed by Tom Sheil of the MPAA. After wining and dining Call, Sheil proceeded to say, "We've been watching Al [Beardsley] for a long time. We have photos of him taking prints out of theaters that are never returned. We know he's stealing from theaters, but we know he has other sources at film labs, and we want to know what they are." When Call said he was uncomfortable with that, Sheil responded, "You're going to be in a lot of trouble if you don't cooperate." After extracting promises that he could keep his film collection and that he would not be forced to wear a wire or be contacted by the FBI (with whom he'd already had several painful encounters), Call reluctantly agreed to help set up Al Beardsley in a sting operation masterminded by the MPAA. Given his past history of harassment by the law and even a department of his own church, it's easy to understand Call's actions, even if it meant betraying a privileged source in the underground network of film collectors and dealers, who depended in many ways on mutual secrecy and anonymity.

"At the time I was working at a chiropractic therapist office in Toluca Lake," Call recounts. "What happened was, the next thing I knew I was called at work by the FBI. They said, 'We're calling for Tom Sheil, we want to wire you.' I said, 'Excuse me??'" After Call steadfastly refused to wear a wire, the FBI dropped out of the case, and the MPAA went to the L.A. County Sheriff's Department, which agreed to handle the operation. On the day of the sting, the sheriff's department gave Call $1,500 in marked bills to pay Al for 35mm prints of *Predator 2*, *Home Alone*, and *Rocky V*. (In retrospect, it's almost a public service that Beardsley and Call were taking beauties like these out of circulation.) Call describes the day of the arrest: "I met Al at his screening room on Sunset Boulevard where he had everything. I tried to talk him out of it one more time—I wanted him to go free. But he refused. He wanted his money and wanted it now. He was helping me carry the film out to my car on the street. The sheriffs surrounded us and handcuffed us and put us in separate cars. I was shaking and scared; I'd never done anything like that in my whole life. I remember Al saying, *'You fucker! You turned us in!'* I said, 'Al, I did not—it was your big mouth that got us in trouble!' It was that kind of exchange as we were being put into the cars."

According to Al, he was caught unaware by the highly publicized arrest on December 3, 1990, which was widely trumpeted as showing the MPAA getting tough on film pirates once again. The impact on his business running the Sunset Screening Room was almost immediate: "I got such a reputation from that film deal that I was involved in with Craig Call. All the management was scared that I'd steal their prints. Hurt my ability to work in the end." To this day, he still blames Call and Ogburn—fellow members of the underground fraternity of film collectors and dealers—and not the

MPAA, for setting him up. If anyone thought the arrest spelled the end of it, though, they apparently didn't know Al Beardsley.

Business cards soon started circulating in the collector world marked with the MPAA's logo and stamped "Craig Call: Special Agent, Sting Operation." When I ask Al if he had anything to do with printing the cards, he flatly denies it, although he does say, "MPAA was considering suing me for using their copyright-infringed business card logos," which sounds like a left-handed admission of guilt. Much more public was a fairly jaw-dropping letter that Al sent out to an undisclosed number of film collectors, dated December 17, 1990, two weeks after the sting, which reads in part:

> Dear Fellow Film Collectors,
> I am sending you this letter as a courtesy, I have recently been set up by a "Man" named Craig Call. Mr. Call won my confidence about 6 months ago when He mysteriously moved to Los Angeles from Utah.
> Mr. Call set me up in a "Sting Operation" with the M.P.A.A. in order to receive a $15,000 reward.
> If you have any pending film deals with Call I would strongly suggest you cancel them to protect yourself and your family from arrest and prosecution.
> To date I have lost a total of 63 prints and my legal expenses are in the thousands.
> Due to pending litigation I will not go into the particulars of My case until I have been cleared of all charges, but I am enclosing a copy of a Legal Document that Call recently filed against Me (for His own protection). I will also keep all collectors updated on this case. . . .
> Please feel free to pass this letter on to other Film Collector's you may know.
> Yours Truly,
> Alfred Beardsley
> Cc: The Big Reel

Somewhat astoundingly, Beardsley included with this missive a Xerox of an injunction filed with the California Superior Court preventing *him* from harassing *Call*. How this would inspire "fellow film collectors" to take

Beardsley's side against Call is anybody's guess. In the injunction prohibiting harassment, Call made the following claims:

> Since that time [of the arrest] Defendant has made harassing phone calls at my home and place of business. He and "a friend" have impersonated Sheriff's Deputies in an effort to enter my home for theft and vandalism purposes. . . . The Defendant and his "friend" have called my personal friends and threatened to have them arrested (again impersonating Sheriff Officials) . . . and recently made threats against my life and well being in front of witnesses to the extent that I had to be warned by the MPAA to not even return to my own Apt. for a few days.[33]

The rivalry between the two men didn't end there, though. On August 9, 1999, the trade paper *The Hollywood Reporter* ran an unusual article headlined "'Lion King' print return bares a saga of revenge." In a twist worthy of Shakespeare, Call was attempting to sell a print of the Disney animated film *The Lion King* for one thousand dollars in the collector magazine *The Big Reel*, when the MPAA was tipped off by none other than Al Beardsley, who spotted the ad and saw his chance for some payback. He wrote a suitably outraged letter to the MPAA demanding they seize the print and prosecute Call. According to the *Reporter*, Call had already been tipped off that he'd been ratted out to the MPAA and voluntarily offered to surrender the print to them, which he claimed was "a junked print from England that was very, very worn" and that, quite magnanimously, he was "trying to sell [. . .] for a friend who need[ed] the money to help pay for a heart transplant operation." Call couldn't help sniping that there were dozens of other Disney films being advertised for sale in the same issue of *The Big Reel* and that he felt "singled out."

Even the deals-and-dollars-obsessed *Reporter* couldn't help being fascinated by the decade-long feud between the two film dealers and collectors. Al was ultimately fined more than $300,000 in the 1990 case and ordered to pay $200,000 in attorney's fees and sentenced to four years' probation but went bankrupt before he could pay the massive fines and fees. "Craig, for his own selfish reasons, chose to destroy my life," Al vented to the *Reporter* in 1999. "Now, he has the audacity to try to publicly sell *The Lion*

King. If he thought I was going to stand by and allow him to do it without a protest to the MPAA, he's sadly mistaken."

Al continued to have his own skirmishes with the law: around the same time, the October 30, 1999, edition of the *Burbank Leader* reported that Al had announced plans to run for the local city council—just as he was being placed in custody by two Burbank police officers. He'd gotten into an argument with the officers outside a fast-food restaurant, because his car stereo was too loud, and while they were questioning him, they discovered an outstanding 1994 warrant related to a DUI and driving with a suspended license. During the arrest Al told the police that he was employed by O. J. Simpson; and in a subsequent interview with the *Leader*, he claimed that he was "a personal assistant to Simpson and managed his memorabilia," and that he suspected "his association with Simpson played a role in the way he says officers treated him." And how did the cops suspect Simpson was his boss? Easy: the star's Hall of Fame football was sitting in the front seat of Al's car. Ironically, while the officers were searching the vehicle, they also discovered a film canister containing one of Simpson's movies (although it's not clear which of O. J.'s movie masterpieces it was: *Capricorn One*? *The Cassandra Crossing*?), and a seriously miffed Al noted that they "tossed it all over the place, treating it with no respect, like it was nothing." When I press Al further about the Burbank incident, he says it was all taken out of context. I ask if he can remember which of O. J.'s films was in the car, and he insists they were still photos, not a 35mm print, which may in fact be the case, because it was still photographs that led in part to the ultimate, fateful encounter between the two men that had started years before at a screening of *The Gods Must Be Crazy*.

By the early 2000s Al had long given up the Sunset Screening Room and working as a film dealer in a market that was quickly vanishing; he now was buying and selling sports memorabilia, apparently trading in part on his association and friendship with O. J. Simpson. His troubles with the law multiplied: in 2000 he was committed to six months in a psychiatric facility after he violently rammed his car into a vehicle driven by journalist Will Rogers, who'd written articles on Al that he disagreed with, to put it mildly.[34] After his release Al was charged with stalking a Riverside woman and, in a separate incident, threatening to kill a police officer after getting a citation for urinating in public, for which he was placed on probation. According to Al, in 2007 he was contacted by another memorabilia dealer he'd known for over twenty years, Bruce Fromong, who offered him a list of items for sale. Al wasn't interested in buying them himself but offered to help Fromong sell them for a commission. Separately, Al had been contacted by a man in the Bay Area who legally purchased abandoned storage units. The Bay Area man had recently made a fairly remarkable find—he bought an anonymous storage unit that turned out to belong to O. J. Simpson's mother and contained, according to Al, "thousands of childhood and growing-up photos of O. J. Simpson as an infant, up until his football days and of all of his siblings and children, wives, father, aunts, uncles." Al agreed to help him sell these items as well, again for commission.

Al was soon contacted by a man named Thomas Riccio, who's been described as "an ex-con whose rap sheet includes at least four separate felony convictions, including arson, prison escape, and stolen property charges," according to the website *The Smoking Gun*.[35] According to Al, Riccio "took it on his own to call O. J. and tell him that I had his family photos, football awards, trophies, all of this list. O. J. asked him to ask me if I would give him some samples. I took pictures of the items and photos and faxed them to Riccio, who faxed them to Simpson." Simpson apparently promised to give Riccio two hundred signed copies of his autobiography to sell if he assisted in getting the memorabilia and family photos back from Al and Bruce Fromong.

On September 13, 2007, Al and Fromong were lured to the Palace Station Hotel in Las Vegas under false pretenses: "Riccio said his client was a wealthy client from the software business and works, I believe, out of Vegas. We'd do the deal in Vegas. I agreed. Bruce agreed. Little did we know that O. J. had to be in Vegas at that same time for a wedding and was planning on wrapping up two pieces of business at the same time." After bringing the memorabilia and photos to Riccio's hotel room, he and Al went to the bar. "I had a drink and, I believe, a hamburger that Riccio paid for. He feeds you before he screws you," Al says dryly. Returning to the room, they waited with Fromong for the fictitious millionaire buyer to arrive. Instead, his onetime friend, the celebrity he used to sneak into movies for free back in Westwood Village, O. J. Simpson arrived with several companions.

"They were let in by Riccio. They all charged through the door," Al recalls. "There was a lot of yelling and threats. I went into shock mode. This happened quick, and I wanted to figure out what was going on. I didn't know if they were cops or crooks. They were all well dressed." I ask if he knew something was amiss when he spotted Simpson, and Al nods. "He started yelling at me. Told me he trusted me and was surprised to see me there. Thought I was a straight shooter, how could I be involved in having his shit there?" According to Al, two of the men were armed with guns. They frisked him and Fromong, disabled the phone lines, and demanded their cell phones; Fromong surrendered his, but Al refused. The entire encounter was over in about seven minutes. Bizarrely, it later came to light that Riccio recorded the encounter on audiotape in an attempt to get evidence that Al and Fromong were illegally selling the memorabilia; on the tape Simpson shouts out, "Don't let nobody out of this room. Motherfucker, you think you can steal my shit and sell it?"

"It was quick," Al remembers of the infamous incident. "They packed up everything in pillow cases and boxes. And O. J. was standing there like the town crier with his litany of bullshit, until somebody came up and whispered in his ear, 'It's time to go.'" After Riccio chased Simpson and the men into the parking lot to recover some of his own items they'd mistakenly seized, he returned, and "he said O. J. told him to tell me that if I told the *National Enquirer* about it he's gonna sue me. I said, 'Fuck the *National Enquirer*. I'm calling the cops.'"

Ironically, Al insists that he had no desire to punish his former friend Simpson, the celebrity he once so admired: "I just called the police to get my stuff back. I didn't want to press charges. Because O. J. that night, he went home, I went home. We made up on the phone, but the damage had been done." Simpson was ultimately found guilty on ten counts, including first-degree kidnapping charges for Beardsley and Fromong, and robbery and assault with a deadly weapon. Simpson's currently serving a thirty-three-year sentence for the crimes at the Lovelock Correctional Facility in Nevada. In yet another surreal twist to the case, while Al was giving national TV interviews about the Simpson assault, he was spotted by his startled parole officer (from the 2003 incident involving a threat to a police officer). Since Al was giving interviews in Las Vegas, he was obviously breaking his California parole. He was quickly arrested and brought back in handcuffs.

The notoriety from the Simpson case continues to follow Al around, although it's hard to see how this man, semiparalyzed, shuttled from hospital to hospital, has benefited from it. "I know my partner that went with me [Fromong], he lost everything 'cause of that case. He wound up losing his house, he got caught shoplifting at Costco for fifty bucks," Al observes sadly. "I said, 'Look, Bruce, I know you want to make money off this case, and it's going to happen for good or bad. Don't go hard on him; it's a bullshit case. They want to nail him for '94, and they want to use us, and you could see that." When I ask if he still considers Simpson to be a friend, Al simply replies, "He's in jail for a long time. I got my own problems." That, if anything, seems to be the last word on the subject. The gods truly are crazy.

I ask if I can take pictures of Al lying in bed for the book, and he agrees, then asks how they look. I show the pictures to him. "God," he whispers, appalled. I ask if he'd ever done any acting in his younger days. "No. Only in front of the courthouse: '*Not guilty*,'" he says with a weak grin.

The interview finally wraps up. Al looks glad for the company, although he's obviously exhausted. Maybe we caught him on a good day, but the Al we interviewed (on two occasions) was far from the notorious film pirate and "delusional menace" that had other collectors like Craig Call and Brian LeGrady fuming at the mention of his name. Instead, the Al I met was surprisingly lucid and frank, talking openly about his criminal past and dodgy activities like lifting a 70mm print of *Lawrence of Arabia* from the very theater that was showing it. I can't say I exactly liked him, but I don't think he was *trying* to get me to like him. He was just talking about the brazen cons and film switches he used to pull, that are now a thing of the past. And maybe in the end that's worth a little respect.

We walk past the other patients of Windsor Care listlessly wandering the hallways and approach the exit. Jeff has to reach up and push a black button on the wall to summon the front desk clerk. A sign by the button reads: "Please Be Aware of Patients Trying to Leave Behind You."

7.

South of Sunset Boulevard

It's a warm and slightly hazy May morning as I drive over Laurel Canyon from the San Fernando Valley, down the long winding descent toward Sunset Boulevard and West Hollywood. If you live in L.A. and you love the movies, it's hard not to think about the two Sunset Boulevards: the actual street and the classic 1950 film directed and cowritten by Billy Wilder. There have been any number of great films made about the movie business, but none that captures the awful, perverse blurring of past and present, youth and age, celebrity and anonymity like *Sunset Boulevard*. At the end of the film, Gloria Swanson descends the stairs with the weird grace of an aging ballerina and a look of frozen madness on her face before delivering the famed closing line, "All right, Mr. DeMille, I'm ready for my closeup." Then as she glides toward the camera, half–Cobra Woman, half-Vampira, the image literally blurs and dissolves, as if Wilder were acknowledging that she was slipping into that terrible gray zone between the actual making of a movie called *Sunset Boulevard* and the myth that would become Norma Desmond.

While working for the American Cinematheque in Hollywood in the 1990s, I made any number of attempts to get Wilder to come out for a tribute. I was patient—usually if I waited long enough I could get a filmmaker to appear in person—but not Wilder. He just wasn't interested. He dodged one invitation on the phone, saying, "I'd like to tell you that I have to rush down to San Diego in an ambulance to see my sick sister, but the truth is I just want to stay home and watch football." Then he hung up. But, if you wait long enough, strange things happen in Hollywood. For many years the nonprofit Cinematheque had announced one permanent home after another, only to see the projects fall through, but in the mid-1990s it took over Sid Grauman's legendary 1922 Egyptian Theatre and launched what became a $15 million renovation. As part of the fundraising campaign, they updated its prospectus with quotes from well-known film-makers. Most, like Martin Scorsese, Steven Spielberg, and Spike Lee, offered earnest, boilerplate, "We think the Cinematheque is a really terrific idea" statements. On January 14, 1998, I was sitting at my desk at lunchtime when our startled office manager, Nancy, came to the door. "Dennis, Billy Wilder is here to see you," she said and stepped aside. I looked up dumbfounded as the ninety-one-year-old Wilder shuffled into my office accompanied by an ancient secretary who looked, if anything, more infirm than he did. Wilder launched into a mini-tirade about the impossibility of getting anyone on the phone at the Cinematheque, so he could give his fundraising testimonial, and then fixed me with a blunt glare: "Do you take dictation, young man?" I mumbled yes, and then he delivered the following in his thick Austrian accent:

Once upon a time, I knew a blind director. He was legally blind. He didn't want any guide, anybody with a white cane or a seeing-eye dog. He directed a few good pictures, really remarkable for a blind man. Then one day—wonder of wonders—he saw. The idea that he could now see what he directed before, instead of just shadows and walls. What's more, he could write. Boy, did he rewrite! Two pictures altogether—one is still on the shelf at the studio, the other went straight to the toilet. He died before he was seventy. Poor schnook!

Wilder insisted I print it out so he could proofread it; he added a punctuation mark at the end of "Poor schnook!" dated and signed it, and then disappeared as mysteriously as he came. To this day I have no idea what Wilder's bizarre parable means. Is he the blind director who gets the double-edged gift of sight? And I'd even doubt the whole incident occurred except that I was there, and the Cinematheque printed his testimonial in their fundraising brochure. It was, all in all, a moment straight out of

Sunset Boulevard. This weird, unexpected encounter often comes to mind as I'm on the boulevard, but today as I cross over and drive south of the Directors Guild building, I have no idea that I'm about to meet Norma Desmond in the flesh.

The apartment building I'm looking for is a classic two-level Hollywood job with a central pool in the courtyard, the kind that underemployed actors and actresses tend to congregate around. But the pool is empty now; only a few brightly colored beach balls float on the surface. Behind a metal-gated door on the second floor is the man Jeff and I have come to meet: Tony Turano, former Broadway chorus dancer (or "gypsy" as he says), talent agent, casting director, and film collector. I've already been warned that Tony tends to fabricate stories, and sifting fact from fiction can be tricky: he claimed for years that he was the baby Moses in the bulrushes in *The Ten Commandments*, until confronted with the fact that it was Charlton Heston's son, Fraser, as clearly listed in the film's credits. Another story he likes to tell is that when he was a boy, he was a passenger on the RMS *Lusitania* when it sank.

Tony greets us seated in a motorized wheelchair, wearing gray sweatpants and T-shirt with stains under his arms and thick, square glasses. His left leg is missing. His raspy voice still has a hint of an East Coast accent. "I was raised in Brooklyn right down the street from a synagogue. You're either Italian or Jewish in Brooklyn," he says. "I used to sit outside the synagogue and listen to the rabbis. You know how many times I've heard Kol Nidre in my life?" Inside, his apartment is unnaturally dark, with the sun blocked out by dust-covered curtains; the main source of light is a huge flat-screen TV which is playing John Ford's *The Searchers* as I enter. The place has the odor of sweat and a slight smell of urine like it hasn't been aired out in quite a while. The first impression is of an antique store or a mortician's office with a morbid Egyptian theme: to the right is a creepy black bust adorned with a gold headdress, which turns out to be Claudette Colbert's from the 1934 version of *Cleopatra*; to the left is a poster from *The Ten Commandments* next to a vase of peacock feathers and, appropriately, bulrushes. A 16mm projector sits on the kitchen table surrounded by dozens of pill bottles. It's a telling combination, movies and medicine, since the two seem to dominate Tony's life these days.

As he leads us around the apartment showing off his prized costumes and props, I ask if I can take photos. He recoils in horror: "No, no. I haven't had my picture taken in thirty-five years, and never without my wig," he says excitedly. After I reassure him that his face won't be seen, he allows me to snap a photo of his hand clutching the priest's wooden staff from *The Ten Commandments*. As I sit down and open my computer, he remarks enigmatically, "You're sitting on Ben Hur, you know." I look at him mystified until he gestures to the dark blue couch: "There are four reels under Jeff and two reels under you." I've seen film stored in some odd places, but this is possibly a first. "I now have ninety-seven prints," he tells us proudly. "They're all over the house. That's why you're sitting on *Ben Hur*."

A Meals-on-Wheels driver knocks at the door to deliver Tony's lunch, as he tells us about a movie that survives—at least part of it—only in his memory. When he was growing up he saw a preview screening in New York of Rodgers & Hammerstein's *The King and I*, courtesy of his cousin Al, who worked for 20th Century Fox. Several numbers were apparently shot, including "I Have Dreamed" and "Shall I Tell You What I Think About You?" but were cut from the film before its initial release and have since completely disappeared. Tony clearly remembers seeing them at the New York preview. "It doesn't even pay to talk about it anymore, because nobody believes," he sighs, then abruptly bursts into song in his sandpapery Brooklyn voice: "There is very much I like in you, but it's also very true— that you're spoiled!" It's a strange and remarkable performance, watching this unshaven, wheelchair-bound former Broadway gypsy imitating Deborah Kerr. Jeff comments that his late wife Lauren had confirmed Tony's account, having seen the same preview print in Hawaii as a child, but that the missing scenes exist now only in memory. I've often wondered if it would be possible to extract the memory of lost films the way that Dumbledore extracts memories in the *Harry Potter* novels and relives them in his magical Pensieve. I clearly remember a luncheon years ago at Musso and Frank Grill in Hollywood with my director friend Curtis Harrington, who recalled in detail seeing a nitrate print at Paramount Studios of the now-lost 1929 Josef von Sternberg silent film *The Case of Lena Smith*, while writing his monograph in the late 1940s on the great filmmaker. The movie had vanished, but it still existed, however faintly, in the reflection of Curtis's aged eyes, where I could almost see it flickering. Now that he's gone, it too is truly *lost*.

I try to ask Tony to talk about his childhood, but I quickly learn this is a difficult subject. He dodges the question, bursting into song: "I was born in a trunk, in the Princess Theater in Pocatello, Idaho," he trills, quoting Judy Garland's famous number from *A Star Is Born*. It's apparent that everything for Tony can be turned, or deflected, into a song from a Broadway show or movie musical. Instead he proceeds to tell us about possibly the rarest film materials that he helped rediscover, one that didn't get away. Tony was at the home of his friend Hermes Pan, the legendary choreographer of Fred Astaire's *Top Hat, Swing Time,* and others. Pan had just installed a large-screen TV and asked Tony for help with the cables; while rooting around back there, he discovered a reel of film in a false closet. "I took it out and said, 'Hermes, what is this?' He said, 'Oh, I don't know, I've had it for years. I don't know what the hell it is.'" It turned out to be footage from the fairly forgettable 1940 musical comedy *Second Chorus*, starring Astaire and Paulette Goddard—but not just any footage.

"I brought this reel back to my house, put it on the screen, and to my amazement, it was the missing Fred Astaire number that everybody's been looking for for fifty years," Tony recalls with barely controlled excitement. "It was 'Me and the Ghost Upstairs,' the missing number from *Second Chorus*. Now, in that, Fred dances with a female in a shroud. Well, it's not a female—it's supposed to be a female, even wearing high heels—but underneath that shroud is *Hermes Pan*." Pan preferred to work off camera. His film appearances were exceedingly rare to begin with, and he'd appeared only once on-screen with his famed partner Astaire, in a number that was subsequently cut from *Second Chorus*. Tony had the foresight to videotape the missing sequence while the print was playing (he now wishes he'd made a 16mm dupe of the footage, but such is life). He returned the footage to Pan, and it later disappeared, leaving Tony's grainy video the only surviving copy. Watching it now, the sequence begins in fairly routine fashion with Astaire singing in front of an orchestra, "It's an ectoplasmic tapping / That disturbs my nightly napping," like a hepcat 1940s version of the *Ghostbusters* theme. Then Pan appears, completely hidden in a long gray shroud, towering over Astaire, and what follows is a truly remarkable duet between the two men who essentially redefined the art of dance on film. They are an exquisite pair on-screen, long-limbed and fluid and perfectly matched. While the Ghost played by Pan is technically "female," it's now apparent that it's a man under the gray shroud, and not just any man, but a dancer as brilliant as Astaire: at one point the Ghost picks up *Astaire* and swings him from side to side, setting Astaire in its lap. It's over far too soon. The entire duet is barely two and a half minutes long, but it's the only two and a half minutes we will ever have of these two men dancing together. When Jeff shows Tony that several bootlegs of his video have turned up on YouTube.com, he literally squeals with outrage: "But that's mine! That's from my copy!" he protests, then finally simmers down. At least the number exists and hasn't been lost, like *The Case of Lena Smith* or the missing songs from *The King and I*.

It's obvious that dance has been and still is central to Tony's life, so his current situation, disabled, confined to a wheelchair, is literally too painful for him to contemplate. (His leg was lost to diabetes.) He finally begins to open up about his childhood. He was born in Brooklyn in 1946. He claims his mother, Antoinette DeStefano, was a Busby Berkeley chorus dancer at one point and appeared in *Gold Diggers of 1935* and in *The Wizard of Oz* as the blonde with the hedge trimmers in the "Clip clip here, clip clip there" sequence. Her name doesn't appear in the credits for either film, but that's not unusual for anonymous chorus line girls. As with much in Tony's life, it's hard to tell what's fact and what's embroidery. She encouraged him when he caught the dance bug, but his father, Salvador, was dead set against it. Salvador, who had connections with the Mafia, according to Tony, was by his account a monster: "My father used to beat me, he used to whip me," Tony says in his raspy voice. "If anybody did to me what my father did to me then, he'd be in jail. I don't really want to go back there, because my parents are dead. It's all water under the bridge; that person no longer exists. I'm a disabled cripple, that's my lot in life." His voice goes silent. I find myself staring at the heavy gold chain around his neck and then, almost unavoidably, at the space where his missing leg would be.

"I'll tell you what a stupid collector I am of *The Ten Commandments*," he says, brightening somewhat. "On its rerelease in 1960 I had a reel-to-reel tape recorder, and I went over to my local theater. I was thirteen years old, and I asked the manager of the theater if I could bring in my reel-to-reel recorder and record the sound of the film. And for years that's what *The Ten Commandments* was for me, because it was never going to be on television: I had the whole movie on four reel-to-reel audiotapes." It's a touching image, of Tony playing his homemade audio over and over, reliving the images in his mind. It's also apparent that for him, as for many collectors Jeff and I spoke with, the movies were a balm and an escape from a painful family life as children, a place where they could feel safe, if only for a few hours. It's no wonder they continue to return there as adults.

The blank space in Tony's life, the period he refuses to talk about on record, is his years as a dancer. He'll only confirm that from age fifteen to thirty-one he was a Broadway "gypsy." He then rattles off a dizzying list of shows and movies that he appeared in as a background dancer, from the 1960s through the mid-1970s. In a later interview he confirms that he moved out to L.A. permanently in 1975; he worked as a fill-in dancer on TV's *The Carol Burnett Show* around that time, and that was apparently his last professional work dancing. He became a subagent at the Norah Sanders Agency in 1980 and then began work as a casting director in 1984, casting commercials for McDonald's, Pepsi, Lay's potato chips, and Peter Pan peanut butter, along with extras casting for features, or "under-fives," as he calls it in professional lingo, meaning actors with under five lines of dialogue.

Although he won't discuss his dancing days, he's remarkably open about the fact that he's a gay man and a film collector. As he quips, "I don't know a film collector who *isn't* gay." It comes as a surprise to me in a follow-up interview that Tony confirms he was married—not once but three times—and fathered two girls and twin boys. (One of the boys was later killed in a motorcycle accident.) He came out as a gay man at age thirty-five and apparently never looked back on his former life. When Jeff asks if Tony is in touch with any of his three surviving children, he bluntly responds, "No." Jeff presses him why not. "Because I'm gay. New topic," he says. I ask if Tony has any thoughts on why so many film collectors are gay men. He closes his eyes for a moment: "It's a thing of fantasy. It's like watching Fred Astaire: you get wrapped up in the beauty of his movement, and it's total escapism," he responds. "You *are* Fred Astaire. You *are* Gene Kelly. You *are* Rita Hayworth. You *are* Leslie Caron. You *are* Ginger Rogers. And I guess this desire for beauty and elegance turns a person's personality if he's male to the effeminate. Not a sexual desire but a desire for beauty and elegance which you can't get in today's world.

"I came out because I was in love with a man from the time I was a teenager and didn't know it," he continues. "I saw him on Broadway with Carol Burnett in *Once Upon a Mattress*. I became a fan and wrote him fan letters every week. He gave me his phone number and told me if I ever came out to California to look him up. So I came out to do a movie, and we became friends. He even got me a job on *The Carol Burnett Show*. On set one day another dancer turned to me and said, 'You're quite an item, you and Don.' 'What are you talking about?' 'It's obvious you're in love with him.' I'd even bought him gifts, like a turquoise bracelet. That's when I knew I was in love with Don. But it was never consummated. He had a lover at the time, a big talent agent. He lives in Florida now. I stayed in touch with him until his lover died. I guess all my life I've been looking for another Don."

As Tony talks he's interrupted by the arrival of a home nurse, "Nurse Norah," as he calls her, but he waves her off. "She was going to do a leg wrap and give me an arm flush, but she can come back later," he says dismissively. "She's working for me, I'm not working for her." He wheels around the apartment in his motorized chair, confined now to his kingdom of movie memories, recounting a stream of celebrity encounters real or half imagined: of being on the set of *Giant* in 1955 as a nine-year-old and seeing James Dean unzip his pants and take a piss in front of startled onlookers; of narrowly missing a private party at Sharon Tate's house the night she and four others were murdered.[36] My writing partner Jeff later adds, "I used to have a hard time swallowing some of Tony's claims, like the fact that he knew Michael Jackson." But then Tony wound up acting as middleman when Jeff sold a rare IB Technicolor 16mm print of the Beatles' *Let It Be* documentary to Jackson for three thousand dollars in cash. So that story was true. Another involves famed director George Cukor, who, like Tony, was an avid film collector. "Every Monday night Cukor had people over; he loved to cook," Tony recalls with obvious glee. "He told me about one night where Vivien Leigh, Marilyn Monroe, and Hurd Hatfield were at the table eating, and the first course was matzo ball soup. And when Marilyn Monroe was served the matzo ball soup, she tasted it and said, 'Oh, George, this is so *delishy-ous*. What is it?' George said, 'That's matzo ball, Marilyn.' And she said, 'Is there any other part of the matzo that's edible?'"

Besides celebrity contacts, Tony's work as a talent agent and casting director gave him a dependable stream of income, much of which he sank into print collecting and often more than he could afford. "I'd rather collect film than eat," he admits. "You sacrifice a lot of things because you want this print, or do something like edit 35mm trailers for a week to pay off a print because you can't afford it, which I have done. I did that for about two weeks to pay off an IB Tech print of *Carousel*." Like many collectors of his generation, Tony acquired exclusively 16mm prints; the smaller format was much easier to screen at home and store. The crowning glory of his collection is, no surprise, a rare British IB Technicolor 16mm print of the 1956 *The Ten Commandments*, which he bought from Jeff. "I still have that print. It's the jewel of my collection, and I'm just selfish enough that I have it in my will that when I'm cremated, the print is cremated with me, so that no one else will ever own that print. I'm just that sick," Tony says adamantly, and I believe him. Jeff later confirms that he's offered a number of times to sell some of Tony's prints and costumes to pay for a prosthetic leg, but Tony refuses to part with them. He'd rather have the movies than an artificial limb.

As the interview starts to wrap up, he brings out his proudest possessions, the ones he saves for the end, starting with an arm cuff that Yul Brynner wore in *The Ten Commandments*, which Tony calls an amulet. "Look at that baby . . . look at the workmanship," he purrs as he slips the jewelry onto his fleshy arm. He repeats the word several times like a mantra, each time accenting the syllables: "*Ahm-you-let.*" He manages to navigate his bulky chair into a corridor, where he opens a narrow closet. Inside are stacked more 16mm prints, and sitting on top of them, a battered cardboard box. He reaches inside and lifts out several old plastic bags marked "Technicolor," and after rooting around pulls out a woman's top embroidered with gold sequins. "That belonged to Marilyn Monroe," he says dramatically. "She wore it personally." I'm momentarily taken aback: I never thought I'd see one of Marilyn's outfits, but here it is.

He digs around and produces other treasures: a green sequined top also owned by Monroe, a stunning gold and black robe designed by Travis Banton for Claudette Colbert to wear in *Cleopatra*. "I also own Aaron's robe from *The Ten Commandments*," he announces. "It's all goat hair, hand-done . . . DeMille wanted everything authentic." He hesitates for a moment, as if he's trying to decide whether he should show this next item, then finally asks, "Do you want to see Marilyn Monroe's watch?" He pulls out a velvet jeweler's box. Nestled inside is a piece of jewelry that looks more like a bracelet, encrusted with jewels. I ask if the diamonds are real, and Tony shakes his head: "The only diamond she ever wore was the one Joe DiMaggio gave her. Everything else was baguette or crystal. Which is kind of funny because she's famous for 'Diamonds Are a Girl's Best Friend.'" Finally he stuffs Marilyn's watch back into the crummy plastic bag with the other clothes and returns it to the cardboard box.

As I pack up my computer to leave, something Tony said earlier comes back to haunt me. "Since this happened to me, nobody comes to see me anymore," he confessed, referring to the loss of his leg and his virtual imprisonment in his apartment. "It's kind of lonely. When I think, when your best days are yester. I had a life where . . . oh, good God, I went to Scandia [Restaurant] with Broadway actress Nell Carter. She said, 'I'll take six ounces of beluga!'" His eyes light up as he imitates Carter's high-pitched voice calling for more caviar, and more. As Jeff and I leave his apartment and walk across the courtyard, we see a pretty brunette with big Ray-Bans hiding her eyes, sitting with a male friend near the pool. They both look like actors. She looks up and smiles broadly. "You want to use the pool?" she says invitingly. "Sorry, didn't bring our suits," I smile back. "You don't need suits. You've got pants. You don't even need pants. Just swim naked. We always do," she giggles, with a hint of a tease. As I cross Sunset Boulevard again and head back up Laurel Canyon, I spot a pair of glittery high-heeled silver pumps incongruously strung over the traffic light cables at an intersection, the way you usually see old Nike sneakers that someone's chucked over the lines. Something about the high heels hanging there reminds me of Tony, the one-legged, wheelchair-bound Broadway gypsy who can't bear to talk about his dancing days.

8.

A Dying Art?

Is film collecting truly dying? As of the writing of this book, the major Hollywood studios have almost completely phased out striking 35mm prints of new feature films for commercial distribution, and the major theater chains are likewise completing their conversion of cinemas to digital projection. So, in short order, there will be almost no new supply of 35mm prints to feed the collectors market—and very few places to show them even if there were, outside of cinematheques and museums. Further, the picture and sound quality of Blu-rays is far superior to 16mm prints and nearly equal to 35mm in terms of home projection, although there is a passionate argument to be made for the *artistic* quality of projecting film on film. Realistically, given the choice, most people would prefer the pristine image of a new Blu-ray disc to a scratchy, possibly faded print. You can buy a new DVD or Blu-ray of *Singin' in the Rain* for a fraction of what an original 16mm or 35mm print will still cost you. In fact, when the sixtieth-anniversary edition of *Singin' in the Rain* was released on Blu-ray in 2012, I heard grudging admissions from several collectors that it was the best they'd ever seen the film look, period. With the introduction of 4K television sets (and 8K looming on the horizon), home viewing of new and classic cinema will continue to improve until it's on par with commercial theaters, at least in terms of image quality (if not scale).

That should spell the end of film collecting, but of course it hasn't. Even among fellow collectors Joe Dante and Jon Davison, there is disagreement about whether this is the end of an era—or the beginning of a new golden age. Although most collectors acquired (some would say hoarded) their treasures in solitude, for many years Joe, director of wicked, giddy genre classics *The Howling* and *Gremlins 1* and *2*, and Jon, producer of megahits *Airplane!, RoboCop,* and *Starship Troopers*, have maintained a unique three-way collection with director Tim Hunter (*River's Edge*).

Together, the three filmmakers have given something remarkable back to their art form by assembling a superb collection of 35mm and 16mm prints, including many rare and overlooked horror, sci-fi, and fantasy movies, much of which is now on deposit at the Academy Film Archive in Hollywood. Although Joe and Jon were interviewed separately for this book, I think it's appropriate that their stories—and their differing viewpoints—are included here, since their friendship and shared passion for film collecting goes far back, before their days in Hollywood.

"You cut your hair," is the first thing Joe says to me when I walk into his Renfield Productions offices on a sleepy third-floor corner of the former Warner-Hollywood Studios, now euphemistically renamed The Lot. He's got his feet perched casually on his desk; he's still perennially boyish-looking, with a gray vest and slacks that match his graying hair. I've known Joe for more than twenty years now, from my days programming at the American Cinematheque, where he would often loan prints from his, Jon's, and Tim's collection. He was and still is unfailingly helpful when it comes to tracking down obscure prints. At my request he once bought a 16mm print of the low-rent AIP flick *Daddy-O* (1958), starring accordion king Dick Contino, for a James Ellroy–themed night at the Cinematheque. After watching it, he said, "I think you need to pay me back for this, because I'm never going to watch that turkey again."[37] He provided many of his own ultra-rare prints for several retrospectives the Cinematheque presented on Italian pulp maestro Mario Bava, a personal favorite of his and mine. One of the most moving screenings I ever experienced was due in large part to Joe's collecting, a showing of the apocalyptic sci-fi drama *The Day the Earth Caught Fire* (1961) with director Val Guest in attendance at the Egyptian Theatre. After watching the film—in Joe's stunning, original 35mm B&W CinemaScope print—the entire audience of three hundred people stood up and gave Val a standing ovation *simply because the film was so damned good*. Val was literally moved to tears by the response. That, in many ways, is film collecting at its finest: giving something amazing and irreplaceable to the filmmaker and to the audience.

In spite of Joe's many years on the West Coast, he's still kept up his rapid-fire, East Coast manner of speaking. In fact, the earliest seed for this book was planted years ago in this very office, when Joe mentioned, to my surprise, that he rarely screened his 16mm prints anymore because of the effort involved. It's a sentiment he echoes today: "I love the experience of the movie, but if I really want to see the film without splices, without cuts, with good sound and picture quality, I run the DVD now," he admits. "The 16mm projectors didn't have such great sound to begin with. I'd run them through amplifiers—there was a whole giant Rube Goldberg setup to try to get them to sound better. I still have friends, Tim Hunter and Jon Davison, that only run 16mm; they don't run DVDs. It's a lost battle. Frankly, if I could sell out my collection to them, I'd do it, because we all three own it. Not every picture, but enough of them to make it complicated." Amazingly, the three have had very few disagreements over the years, although Joe confesses that they're currently selling off some of their less-sought-after titles on eBay. This leads to one of those moments that only a film collector would love, with Joe nostalgically discussing not great movies, but prints *nobody could get rid of, at any price.* "*The Basketball Fix* was on every list," he recalls. "It was an Allied Artists picture, and nobody wanted it. The other was *Arson, Inc.*" For a brief moment I can almost picture a forgotten warehouse somewhere still stuffed to the rafters with unwanted prints of *The Basketball Fix* and *Arson Inc.* (and, quite likely, the beatnik bomb *Daddy-O*).

Suddenly Joe sits up and slaps his desk, hard, startling me: "The studios are stamping out 35mm. *They don't want anybody to have it.* It's a pogrom. Think of it from their point: their goal is to eliminate the cost of storing and shipping prints. I believe that the future of 35mm revival theaters is over. The problem is, they say, 'You can run it on digital.' You can run *Casablanca* on digital, but the studios won't supply their B-pictures on digital, like *The Return of Dr. X.*" His comments illustrate a dirty little secret: that it's the B-pictures, the grindhouse and exploitation films, the routine programmers and ephemera like live-action shorts and cartoons that are most in need of preservation—what Leonard Maltin calls the films of "no commercial value and only marginal historic value." In the years to come, we may be looking at a second great wave of film extinction to rival that of the silent era, as hard choices have to be made about what gets saved and what doesn't—or, more likely, as overlooked movies simply vanish from neglect.

"In 1994 I did a picture for Showtime called *Runaway Daughters*, a remake of an old AIP delinquent picture," he says to illustrate his point. "I went to Debra Hill, the producer, and said, 'Are you going to cut negative?' She said, 'Why would we do that?' 'If you don't cut negative, they won't be finished.' She said, 'What are you talking about? We've got twelve films on D-1 video ready for delivery.' I said, 'There's a reason it's called D-1—because there will be a D-2 and a D-3 and so on.'" He throws his hands up in a gesture of resignation. "I knew then those pictures wouldn't exist in ten years, and they don't. They came to me and wanted to release the movie on DVD, and I said, 'I have a three-quarter-inch tape and a D-1, that's it." Jeff asks if the 35mm negative still exists. "They threw it out," Joe replies bluntly.

He leans back in his chair and heaves a sigh. "When we began collecting, we started because there was no other place to see these movies. Unless you stayed up until one o'clock in the morning to catch it on TV, there was no other way to see them." Even watching an old film on TV was no guarantee you were actually seeing *the whole movie*, since TV stations were notorious for randomly hacking up prints to fit predetermined time slots. "On *Million Dollar Movie*, *King Kong* started when they got to the island!" Joe says with a grin. "It was a ninety-minute show, so they cut the movie to seventy-five minutes. That's how everybody on the East Coast first saw it." Joe is, by his own description, another classic baby boomer. He was born in 1946 in Morristown, New Jersey, and moved around following his golf-pro father—but it was his childhood experience with polio at the age of seven that left a lasting impression. "I was convinced I was never going to walk again, which is a real bummer as a kid," he recalls. "The doctors told my mother I was going to be a cripple forever, and she didn't buy it. I did parallel bars, whirlpool baths, physical therapy, mainly. I don't know where they got the money for it, but they did." I ask if his bout with polio inspired his love for movies, but he shakes his head: "No, it made me want to be a cartoonist. I spent all my time drawing." It's a telling comment for a filmmaker whose finest movies, from *Gremlins* 1 and 2 to *Matinee*, are filled with a delirious, almost comic-book sensibility.

It was while living in the Philadelphia area in 1967 that he bought his very first print, of the sci-fi flick *The Gamma People*, from a high school kid named Jon Davison. Although he was three years younger than Joe, Jon already had connections with a well-known older collector named David Grossman, who taught at the Philadelphia College of Art and organized film screenings. Around the same time Joe became aware of the macabre horror and sci-fi films of Italian director Mario Bava, whose work was still confined to inner-city grindhouses. "It was very hard to find them in Technicolor," he says of Bava's films. "*Blood and Black Lace* was, and that's one of the first ones I bought." The going price at the time for most 16mm prints was between $100 and $175, significant money in the late 1960s for someone like Joe, barely out of his teens. He remembers plunking down $175 for a brand-new Eastmancolor print of Hammer Films' *The Revenge of Frankenstein*, but only so he could swap it out (illegally, of course) for an original IB Technicolor print of the same film at a rental place in Philadelphia. He even went to the extreme of cutting up and resplicing his pristine new print to match the old print, so the owners wouldn't catch on to the switch—an ingenious strategy, if more than a little nuts. "We were wild and crazy. We always operated under the proviso that nobody cared but us." His laughter dies down and his face grows serious. "And it turns out we were right."

His and Jon's shared fascination with old drive-in monster movies soon gave birth to Joe's first credit as a director, which Jon produced, *The Movie Orgy* (1968), a legendary underground compilation of old trailers and gonzo film scenes, which ran seven hours in length. Because none of the clips were legally cleared, it's never been released on home video, although Joe has preserved a shorter, four-and-a-half-hour version on digital from the original 16mm film elements. Even in his early days, his film collecting habit threatened to get out of hand: "In Philadelphia, I had a fourth-floor walk-up apartment, and all my prints were in my closet," he remembers. "The neighbor below noticed the ceiling above was sagging—little pieces of stuff were coming down." Before the ceiling had a chance to collapse, he decided to move out to California in 1974 to work for Roger Corman. "I remember Jon and I rented a truck to bring the film out here to the vault on Seward that it's still in." While working as an editor cutting trailers for Corman, he had a rare opportunity to see the legendary dye-transfer Technicolor facility just before it shut down: "I did the last Technicolor release trailer for *Amarcord*. Roger used to do a lot of stuff in Technicolor, because he ordered in bulk," Joe remembers, then continues as if he could still see the fabulously intricate inner workings of the plant: "They had a conveyor belt where the film was being printed, the dyes on top of one another, and in order to do that the film would traverse the entire building. At one point they'd come down to a console, and a guy would adjust the color on the fly. It was fascinating and thrilling to be there."

As the plant shut down, the employees emptied the vaults of treasures that had been hidden away for decades: "All the Technicolor prints they had in storage were just sitting there, they were out to be junked," he says, shaking his head in disbelief. "I remember prints of *She Wore a Yellow Ribbon*. There were a lot of prints of *Satanic Rites of Dracula* and *Thief of Bagdad*—amazing, original Technicolor prints. Answer prints from the 1940s—they could have been nitrate, who knows? It was a film collector's dream." His eyes practically shine, marveling at the riches he saw. "As a film collector in good standing, I felt it was my duty to steal as much of this stuff as possible before it wound up in Santa Monica Bay. But it was impossible: they had too much security." He pauses for a moment and clenches his jaw. "It was a tragedy. I'd just come out here. It was my introduction to how Hollywood cares about itself."

In 1976 Joe made his first full feature, *Hollywood Boulevard* (codirected with Allan Arkush), produced by his friend and fellow collector Jon, and they followed up two years later with the gleefully deranged drive-in classic *Piranha*. Joe's burgeoning success as a director gave him the means to indulge in his film-collecting hobby, and indulge he did. "I would be such a rich man if I hadn't spent all my money on movies!" he moans now. Among the ultra-rare 35mm prints he snapped up were Val Guest's *The Abominable Snowman* (1957), written by British sci-fi/horror legend Nigel Kneale, and James Landis's *The Sadist* (1963), starring Arch Hall Jr. To this day Joe's prints are the only readily available copies in 35mm, and despite their rarity, he still routinely loans them for retrospectives. "One of the reasons I have these prints is, if people ask me to run them I say, 'Yes.' There's a certain risk factor; they could get scratched. The whole thing is, *these movies were made to be seen by people*. Thirty-five-millimeter is the one format you can run safely in a big theater and have it look great." Of all the overlooked horror films he collected, though, the one he was most proud of rescuing was Bava's delirious, S&M-flavored Gothic horror *The Whip and the Body* (1963), starring Christopher Lee and Daliah Lavi. "It's the only 35mm print of that film I've ever seen," he says. "But it went vinegar. It was a tragedy. It was used for the V.C.I. DVD release, then it went to goo. I had to throw it out. . . . It was so painful."

I ask if he's made any sacrifices to pursue collecting film, and he shrugs: "Well, yeah. Of course. The money that you pay for the prints is money you'd ordinarily be spending on something else. Like life. Bringing up a child. Which I didn't do. For a while I had a lot of money, so I could spend it on film." Although he's curtailed his collecting in recent years, he'll still pick up a print if it's particularly rare: he mentions recently buying a 35mm print of Terence Fisher's *Frankenstein Created Woman* (1967) from England, because it was printed in Technicolor only overseas. At one point he made sure he received his own 35mm copy of every film he directed, so that at least one print would be available for screenings. "*Piranha*'s kind of faded but still runnable. It's the print they show when they run it at the New Beverly. . . . *Hollywood Boulevard* is kinda faded. *The Howling* was printed on a new stock where the only thing that faded was the blacks; the rest of the colors are fine." He still seems fairly shocked by how quickly film has been replaced by digital. "It's happened so fast. I remember going to see the first picture I ever saw screened on digital: it was a *Pride and Prejudice*–type movie. It was so bright, it was like a supernova," he says, shaking his head. "You're looking into a cathode ray tube on one hand, and you're looking at shadows on a screen on the other. Which one is more romantic?"

"The really sad thing is we're watching the end of era," Jeff notes. Joe's eyes light up, and he leans in: "*And it didn't have to be this way.* They could have found a way for digital and film to coexist, together, side by side."

"I collect more now than ever," Jon Davison enthuses soon after he arrives at my Burbank house, a few months after I spoke with his longtime friend and collecting partner Joe. Jon has a graying beard and pink, cherubic cheeks, and a distinctive, high-pitched voice that would have been perfect for an old 1950s UPA cartoon character—he comes across like your favorite high school science teacher. "It's a great time to be collecting, because a lot of people with libraries are divesting themselves of their prints," he continues, in contrast to Joe's bleak opinion. "They're older, they're passing away, and many films are appearing with much less competition for them. Prices have basically been stable for thirty years—dropping, perhaps." When I ask how often he buys films these days, he surprises me by responding two to three prints a week, most recently a 16mm Cinema-Scope copy of an obscure 1963 German thriller *The Mad Executioners*, based on an Edgar Wallace *krimi* (mystery) novel. The print came from Sinister Cinema, a cult distributor that specialized in exploitation and pulp-horror films and is now selling off its vast library of 16mm and 35mm on eBay. It's not the only treasure that Sinister Cinema is getting rid of, as Jon confides: "This weekend there's a 35mm *The Whip and the Body*, which I intend to put a big snipe on, because our print went vinegar. That was the print that the Cinematheque used to run." When I press him for how much he's willing to spend for *The Whip and the Body*, he shoots me a stern look: "Well, the opening bid is $399, and I am currently the only bidder. It's up this Sunday. So don't bid against me, okay?" He finally relaxes when I assure him I won't compete with him for it.

He met Joe in the mid-1960s at the Philadelphia College of Art through local collector and teacher David Grossman (although Jon notes they were formally introduced via phone by *Castle of Frankenstein* editor Calvin Thomas Beck, to whom Joe was contributing articles). I ask if Joe was a collector when they first met, and Jon chuckles, "No, I think Grossman and I sort of lured him into that fate." Grossman, whom Jon refers to as his mentor and a father figure, ran the only art-house cinema in South Jersey, the Carlton Cinema in Moorestown. Jon's actual father, an electronics engineer for RCA, and his mother, a clothing-store owner, separated when he was in sixth grade, the same year he began collecting films. "I would be surprised if there was not some cause-and-effect there," he says dryly about the impact of his parents' divorce and his gravitating toward film collecting. Grossman sold Jon his very first print, of David Lean's terrific, still underrated *Hobson's Choice* (1954), starring Charles Laughton. "David Grossman was a big film collector," Jon recalls. "I remember going to his house and the phone would ring and it would be someone like Mel Tormé on the other line. He would have these lists of films that he would be reading to Mel Tormé with prices attached."[38] Still in middle school, Jon soon began working for Grossman, traveling to nursing homes and swim clubs in the South Jersey area and running prints from the man's collection for the residents. Grossman would pay him fifty dollars a screening—excellent money at the time, especially for a middle-schooler—but Jon would invariably reinvest it buying more prints . . . from Grossman. It was an arrangement that apparently worked out for both, and Jon was able to score treasures like a 35mm IB Technicolor print of producer George Pal's seminal sci-fi film *Destination Moon* (1950) for the ridiculously low price of fifteen dollars. I ask if he's kept that very first print of *Hobson's Choice* he bought so long ago, but he shakes his head, saying he's upgraded it to a better copy. "I think even then I had a strong feeling that I was conserving these pictures by buying them and cleaning them and taking care of them," he observes about his early years. "I always had a sense that there were a very finite number of these things and they should be preserved."

Not long after they met, he and Joe began collaborating on *The Movie Orgy*, which marked a turning point for them as filmmakers—and as collectors. "I would often find pieces of film that I thought were amusing and send them off to Joe," he recalls of their creative process. "He edited it together, and I basically went on the road with it as the projectionist. Officially, I guess, I was the 'producer' and he was the 'director.' I think that's what IMDb says," he says with a grin. *The Movie Orgy* premiered at Bill Graham's legendary rock club Fillmore East in New York and got picked up by Schlitz Beer, who paid for Jon to travel around to college campuses screening it. It was a different era, when most universities had film clubs that showed foreign, art-house, and cult movies and had a huge influence on the developing tastes of the students. "With some of the cash generated from *The Movie Orgy*, we started buying films together. So our collection became jointly owned, because the money was from a joint project," he says of the beginnings of his and Joe's collecting partnership.

In 1968, while still touring with *The Movie Orgy*, he started attending NYU Film School in New York City. Looking back now, it was an incredible era, when people like future director Martin Scorsese, writer Terry Southern, film critic Andrew Sarris, and film historian William K. Everson were teaching at NYU. Jon dove headlong into what could only be described as the hippie film-freak lifestyle and opened his own short-lived theater, the St. Mark's Cinematheque, while also working as in-house projectionist for Graham's Fillmore East. "I was with the Joshua Light Show," he says. "I would run the movies between the acts. There was a little tiny platform way up in the air with a Bell & Howell Mark 300 on it. You could crawl out there and risk your life and thread this projector." I ask if he ever had to project while stoned, and he looks at me, startled. "Did I ever thread a projector while *not* stoned?" he replies, laughing. "If the Grateful Dead were there, and you had touched or drunk anything inside the theater, you were tripping—the water cooler or the Coca-Cola or anything." He would pick obscure shorts or cartoons that somehow tied in with the rock group playing that night. "I ran the climax of *King Kong* before the Jefferson Airplane went on," he says nostalgically. The audio of that cinematic moment was, amazingly, included as the opening track of the Airplane's 1969 live album *Bless Its Pointed Little Head*—making Jon Davison the only projectionist I know of to "play" on a Top 20 rock album. On the minute-and-a-half audio piece titled "Clergy," you can hear the rowdy Fillmore audience roaring its approval as Jon projects the famed ending lines of *King Kong*: "Oh no, it wasn't the airplanes. It was beauty killed the beast." (Apparently, the band wanted the piece titled "King Cong" in reference to the ongoing Vietnam War, but their suggestion was shot down by label RCA.) According to Jon, though, his pièce de résistance was a bizarre 1935 cartoon called *The Sunshine Makers* that he'd play at the Grateful Dead's request whenever they performed. "It's a Borden Dairy film where the hippie-like friendly dwarfs force-feed sunshine to the evil dwarfs," he says fondly.

By his own admission he's forgotten many details of his sex, drugs, film, and rock 'n' roll days—"I do remember that I traded an ounce of hash for a 16mm print of *Not of This Earth*," he remarks, almost as an afterthought—but the good times couldn't last forever. In 1972 he relocated to Los Angeles and gave up the hippie lifestyle, realizing, "It was too hard to do the job and be high at the same time." He started work in the publicity department of Roger Corman's New World Pictures, where his friend Joe Dante would follow within two years. He remembers Corman, with whom he is still close friends and sees several times a year, as "very buoyant, very enthusiastic, very direct, and very cheap." In 1976 he started the transition to full-time producing with *Hollywood Boulevard*, codirected by Joe and Allan Arkush and released through Corman's company. Coincidentally, it's a title that's on his mind recently: "I was just at the Academy Film Archive yesterday, where I dropped off a brand-new 35mm print of *Hollywood Boulevard*," he notes. "I'm going to try to print a number of 35mm New

World pictures before they stop printing film and put them at the Academy. Roger Corman has given me access to the negatives." The next on his list? His and Joe's third film together, *Piranha*, and Corman's overlooked, antiracist drama *The Intruder* (1962), starring William Shatner. I ask how much each new 35mm print costs, and he replies roughly three thousand dollars, all coming out of his own pocket. "I'd prefer if somebody else did it, needless to say, but I don't see that happening," he replies with a shrug, acknowledging that this is something of a one-man mission to preserve these films. "I know there will probably be very few surviving 35mm low-fade prints of these titles. I assume this will be the only print of *Hollywood Boulevard* that will ever be made low-fade. I expect the life of that print to be between fifty and a hundred years. By then the negative will be long gone . . . this little moment in time when people were making exploitation movies for Roger Corman."

(A few weeks after our interview, I e-mail Jon to see if he was successful in scoring the 35mm print of Mario Bava's *The Whip and the Body* on eBay, to replace the copy of his and Joe's that turned to goo. "The winning bid was $610. And it was mine," he writes back triumphantly.)

9.

The House of Clocks

It's a mid-June afternoon as I park my car in the Inglewood/Lennox area of Los Angeles near the airport. Jets roar by overhead. Down the block is one of those self-storage places you see all over the city, beside the Lone Palm Trailer Lodge with a faded 1940s sign out of a Raymond Chandler novel. At the corner of Lennox and Prairie is a bench with a torn and distressed billboard trumpeting *"Save $ With Academy Insurance!"* next to a large, fenced-in *carniceria* with a doubtful sign in front that reads *"Northgate Market Coming Soon,"* although it's unclear if the market is about to come or has already vacated the premises. It's a run-down neighborhood, lined with single-story homes with small fenced-in yards: some well kept with fruit trees, but many with dead grass blowing in the front. A sunny, half-forgotten neighborhood, the kind with teenagers cruising along on wide-handled bikes, riding the wrong way against traffic, or two kids in tandem on one bike steering another beside them.

A half dozen wind chimes make a cacophony as I walk up to the house I'm looking for, the home of former electrician and film collector Peter Dyck. For a moment it's not certain that anyone still lives here. The front windows are obscured by thick curtains along with an old theater sign that says, "Preview Tonight 8:30." The front porch is cluttered with Wisk detergent boxes. I bang on the metal screen door, and Peter's odd singsong voice soon answers. As I step through the door, I'm not quite ready for what I'll find.

Inside is the House of Clocks.

The first thing you notice is that there are clocks everywhere: twenty-seven by the owner's count. There's one by the door with a gray rubber alien face looming over it, and rows of them on the wall overhead. There are clocks in every corner, in the hallway leading to the bathroom, in the bathroom itself next to an old 1950s-vintage pay phone mounted on the wall with a red placard that confidently says, "You Can Dial Any Number In The Los Angeles Area." There's even a clock in the front room whose face shows a crucified Jesus, overlooking dusty plastic figures of Darth Vader and C-3PO. The clocks all show different times. In fact, I'm not sure there's one that shows the correct time. They simply hang there, tick-ticking away out of sync, with no apparent rhyme or reason.

The master of all these timepieces, Peter Dyck, is in his early seventies, with gray hair, rosy, slightly cherubic features, and a pot belly. He'd make a good Bilbo Baggins if he were a few feet shorter. When he speaks, he has the strangely mesmerizing cadence of a TV evangelist, with an unusually dramatic emphasis on words and syllables, and when he talks about his mad movie love, he does it with a religious fervor, repeatedly gushing, "*What a ride it was!*" as if he were on a roller coaster that he never wanted to get off of. Although he's retired now from active collecting, Peter was for several decades one of the best-known figures in the secretive L.A. subculture of dealers and collectors, and particularly important as one of the first to specialize in buying 35mm prints in the 1970s at a time when 35mm was considered either a "rich man's hobby" or the province of the studios and commercial theaters. (By the 1990s the trend had reversed: the larger-gauge 35mm, with its superior image and sound quality, had shot up in price and rarity.) He's also, not coincidentally, one of the more controversial people on the L.A. scene. As if aware of his thorny reputation, before my visit Peter asks me on the phone, somewhat mysteriously: "Have you noticed that film collectors don't speak well of other people? They only talk about the evil other people do. . . . They never shade in the evil that *they* do," he says, emphasizing the weirdly appropriate verb *shade* in his evangelist's voice.

After I get over my initial surprise at seeing the House of Clocks, the next thing that hits me is the overwhelming clutter inside his place. At first glance it looks more like an abandoned storage unit than a living room. How could someone actually live here? The greater part of the room is an impassable mound of ratty sofas, old blankets, extension cords, metal film cans, and dust-covered equipment. There's a 35mm projector in the far corner, but it's not clear that Peter could even get to it without serious excavation. He notices my eyes wandering around the room trying to take it all in, and he smiles enigmatically. "Do you know who the star of *High Noon* is?" he asks coyly, already knowing the answer. "People think it's Gary Cooper or Grace Kelly. It's not—it's the *regulators*." I look at him, confused, until I see him pointing to a row of his regulator-style clocks. "The true star of *High Noon*," he beams. Maybe this is the point to all the clocks, as the punchline to an obscure movie reference.

Jeff arrives shortly after I do and greets Peter like an old friend. He doesn't seem to bat an eye at the chaos and clutter. Peter shifts some stacks of old newspapers, and Jeff and I manage to squeeze into one corner near a beautiful French poster for *Gone With the Wind* overlooking a huge, colorful Stardust Casino slot machine. As Peter plops down, he points to another old friend: "That's a JAN projector," he says fondly. "'Joint Army Navy.' It's a military projector." I look to where he's gesturing: on the floor, covered with a thick layer of dust like white cake flour, are the exposed innards of what must be a 16mm projector, although it looks more like equipment from the deranged scientist's lab in *The Brain That Wouldn't Die*. Peter served in the U.S. Navy in the early 1960s, and it's where he was first trained to care for film and do proper changeovers. It's also, paradoxically, where he first learned to appreciate film as an art form: "*The Music Man, Summer and Smoke*," he recalls, closing his eyes and rocking back and forth. "Ohhhh, I could never get tired of it: *Flower Drum Song*. . . . The ship got reissues of *Les Miserables, All About Eve*, but the crew just wasn't interested in these old movies," he says. "The movie locker was a room about six by four feet. I watched these films myself in the locker and got a movie education." I can immediately identify with his experience of sitting in a tiny room with a rattling projector and being amazed by flickering images. For me it happened in a room barely bigger than a broom closet at the Museum of Modern Art in New York in the late 1970s, watching 16mm prints of Jean Vigo's luminous *L'Atalante* and *Zéro de conduite* and what survives of Erich von Stroheim's masterpiece *Greed*. I know how Peter feels as he sighs and takes another look at his old friend, the JAN projector, the same kind that allowed him to fall in love with the movies. It looks like it hasn't actually screened film in several decades, but he still keeps it close at hand.

Peter was born in 1942 and raised in southwest Los Angeles in a large five-bedroom house. Like a number of collectors we spoke with, he suffered the loss of a parent early on: his father died when he was six. His mother worked as a secretary to support the family, and he helped out "mowing lawns, pulling weeds, throwing newspapers to pay the bills," along with his two brothers. After leaving the navy in 1964, he struggled to break in as an electrician in the union-dominated Hollywood shops, until he got a recommendation from neighbor Dan Borzage, brother of director Frank Borzage (*7th Heaven*), and a notable character in his own right, who used to play accordion on John Ford's sets to lighten the mood. "Next thing I knew I was working on *The Beverly Hillbillies*, then *The Man from U.N.C.L.E.* and *Daktari*," he recalls. His electrical work soon put him in the homes of celebrities he'd only seen on-screen as shadows in the navy locker, actors like Raymond Massey, Groucho Marx, and Norma Shearer, and director Alfred Hitchcock. "I fixed his dryer outlet; he was amazed," he says about Hitchcock, then shakes his head sadly. "When I went up in the attic, you know what I saw? His film collection! *Rear Window*, *Vertigo*. Sixteen-millimeter prints, cooking up there." It's a strange image indeed of Hitchcock's own prints moldering away like the desiccated corpse of Norman Bates's mother in *Psycho*.

In the early 1970s Peter became friends with one of the darkest and strangest figures in the Hollywood film underground, Tom Dunnahoo of Thunderbird Films. A self-styled "film pirate" who once posed for the *Los Angeles Times* wearing an eye-patch, and who routinely passed out on the floor of his film lab drunk on Drambuie, Dunnahoo was one of the first dealers nailed by the FBI in 1971 for illegally selling dupe prints of copyrighted films.[39] Peter, who still regards Dunnahoo with fondness, did electrical work for him and brought him rare 35mm prints of titles like the W. C. Fields shorts *The Dentist* (1932) and *The Fatal Glass of Beer* (1933), which Dunnahoo would duplicate in 16mm for the collectors market. Peter got paid in prints of other films that he wanted. "But it's hard to find good prints, without scratches and splices," Peter recalls of his days tracking down these elusive titles. "It's like a car: if it's all beat up, people don't want to drive it." Possibly the rarest title that Peter uncovered was an original two-color Technicolor print of *The Toll of the Sea* (1922), a silent adaptation of *Madame Butterfly*, starring Anna May Wong in her first lead role, and written by pioneering female screenwriter Frances Marion. More than for the cast or script, it's notable as only the second Technicolor feature ever made. Sadly, one of the reels started "becoming goo" on Peter, a pointed reminder that when film goes bad, it goes bad quickly and completely.

While we talk, Peter repeatedly interrupts by showing Jeff handwritten lists of features and trailers that he and a friend have for sale. It's an irresistible distraction: "*Lady and the Tramp*, four-track mag. That's rare, I've only seen one other of that . . ." "And *Oliver*, too. They haven't gone vinegar yet." "Mag *Oliver*, that's a rare title." "Man, what a movie! Sir Carol Reed directed. Excellent." Try as I might, it's hard to keep them on topic. It's an ironic picture: Jeff, who gave up film dealing several years ago after he sold his massive collection of 50,000+ trailers to the Packard Humanities Institute, and Peter, who by his own admission has stopped buying and selling prints, and yet neither can resist going over the lists and discussing prices. Once a collector, always a collector. Like many I spoke with, Peter seems to have backed into selling prints as a way of feeding his habit, and it was this activity that, almost inevitably, put him on the radar for the FBI and the Justice Department in the early 1970s. It's a wound that has never closed for him. When I broach the subject, he digs around in the stack of old newspapers that he shifted for us to sit and, in surprisingly short order, retrieves several yellowed copies of the *Los Angeles Times* from 1975. The headlines still fairly scream out, "L.A. Film Piracy: Thousands Copied, Distributed" and "U.S. Indicts 16 in Movie, TV Film Pirating Case."[40] I'm frankly amazed that Peter is able to locate these telltale articles so quickly in all this clutter, but maybe he likes to keep them, like the JAN projector, close at hand. Jeff takes one of the papers from him and scans it silently. "This is my bust, and yours," he finally says, then proceeds to list the other dealers and collectors who were charged along with the two of them in the notorious 1975 film busts. I ask if I can take pictures of them holding the papers up, and both agree. It's a strange moment, photographing these men linked by their shared love for a dying medium and by their legal troubles four decades ago.

"There was always a sense of, yes, the FBI was watching you, because we always carried movies in bags or boxes, so if there was any picture being taken, they didn't have anything," Peter recalls of those days. "Nothing was mentioned unnecessarily on the telephone except a meeting time or place." His own troubles stemmed from his association with Roy H. Wagner, later a celebrated cinematographer, who was interviewed separately for this book. Both men confirm that Wagner put out mail order lists of prints for sale by Peter and other collectors, although they differ on the issue of permission: Peter says it was done without his knowledge; Wagner insists that Peter was aware but later reneged on the deal. According to Wagner, Peter's house looked much the same four decades ago: "There was film stacked everywhere. Peter used to come to work and he'd have his trunk loaded with film," he says. Much of the clandestine trade in prints was done from hand to hand, with no paper trail; putting out a list meant the risk of exposing yourself. "I was at Larry Edmunds Bookshop one day," Wagner remembers. "And a guy I knew who was a film collector came up and said, 'I think the FBI's investigating you.'"

When the feds burst into Wagner's home in September 1974, Peter's name quickly came up. He was arrested and charged several months later, but unlike most of the other men indicted, he refused to cut a deal. His trial was a short one: "Roy Wagner decided to do me a favor and not show up at the trial," Peter says. Charges against him were dismissed, but he openly admits that he was illegally copying at least one film at the time: "I did dupe *Paper Moon*, and they took these dupes to an expert on the stand during my trial. And they were so perfect he could not determine if they were dupes or originals," he says with obvious, if possibly misplaced, pride.

Although the arrest was devastating for him—"Now I was like a leper, because my name was in print," he says—he continued unabated in buying and selling prints. The late 1970s and 1980s were, if anything, his glory years. He talks about the prints that passed through his hands as if they were old lovers: "I tell you, when I got *Thunderball* back in the 1980s, I had a party at my house, and everybody was just laughing and jumping for joy. I said, 'I don't want to break anybody's heart, but I'm not going to sell it.'" When I ask if collecting was primarily a social impulse for him, he nods enthusiastically: "You know what was wonderful? We could do film deals or poster deals and I didn't have to run all over town. All the people came to my house. I had a big pitcher of punch, and popcorn . . . people could go outside and have a cigarette. The only time it was really rough was when I ran *Gone With the Wind*. They didn't get home until three AM!" His eyes glow as he recounts the gatherings gone by, and I can almost see the friends streaming out of his house into the cool night air, drunk on Vivien Leigh and Clark Gable and Max Steiner's score. Probably the rarest prints he owned during this period were two British IB Technicolor prints of *Star Wars*. Technicolor stopped its dye-transfer operations in the United States in 1974 but continued in the United Kingdom for several more years, with *Star Wars* being one of the last films struck in dye-transfer, in 1977. Technicolor copies of it have since become legendary, and to own a pair is almost unheard of.[41] "I have two of 'em: my 'everyday' print and my 'Sunday-going-to-meeting' print," Peter says, still referring to them in the present tense, even though he's since sold both. "You just can't imagine the camaraderie of those IB *Star Wars*." It's an odd choice of words, *camaraderie*, to refer to his relationship with an inanimate object like a film print, but it's quite obvious that for Peter, film love is highly personal. "My IB of *Bambi*—you know in the forest fire scene they hadn't finished coloring in the animals when they huddle on the island?—my IB of *Bambi* you could see the dust on the glass," he says, using the possessive "my." My *Bambi*, my *Star Wars*. For collectors like Peter, owning a particularly rare or beautiful print makes them partners in the creative process of filmmaking, at least in their minds.

In the end, it's the loss not of the prints themselves, but of the other collectors and film lovers that Peter feels so keenly: "The hobby's kind of reached its final resting place," he says, echoing a sentiment I heard over and over. "All the keynote participants are deceased, and the hobby just isn't what it used to be anymore. You got a real satisfaction out of getting together with other like-minded people. More and more I looked to getting old films because they have a lastingness about them that new films don't." One of the fellow L.A.-area collectors he no longer speaks with is former truck driver and graphic designer Rik Lueras, one of the few Latino collectors in the field.[42] The break between the two men had nothing to do with collecting, though. "I had a falling out with Rik. He alleged that I molested his son, which wasn't true," Peter says flatly. No charges were filed in the incident, which both men discuss openly—although their opinions of it differ greatly. The topic almost immediately changes to Lueras's habit of putting lemon oil on prints to try to extend their life span, which Peter seems much more comfortable discussing. Whether true or not, the incident—and how quickly he changed the subject—hints at a darker and more troubling undercurrent in the lives of many collectors: their inability to deal with or confront real emotional trauma in their lives, and how they retreat into the illusory safety of cinema fantasy.

Toward the end of the interview, Peter suddenly remarks, "One thing about the movie industry—you see, the studio people feel film collectors are not collectors. They're pirates." He uses the term that he and Jeff were publicly branded with forty years earlier. "The studios want to use just about the nastiest word, but one thing we all have in common is we love movies." It's a hopeful thought, that the former combatants could lay their arms aside and agree on one thing, their shared passion for film—but I'm not sure I believe it. Peter quickly moves on from such magnanimous musings: "You remember I had a beet-red print of *Giant*? Well, Louie Federici[43] ran it and borrowed a beautiful IB print of *Giant*. Afterward he sent it back to Warners, and you know what they got? A beet-red print," he says, face lighting up. "You swapped it out?" Jeff asks. "I did. And later I traded it to you for *Singin' in the Rain*. How about that, huh?" he says, savoring his past triumph as if it were yesterday.

The shadows are starting to lengthen. I suddenly realize we've been sitting here talking for hours with the twenty-seven regulator clocks tick-ticking away all around us, and it's nearly sundown. I get a little shiver up my spine, picturing Peter here surrounded by his decaying empire like Miss Havisham in Dickens's *Great Expectations* with her petrified wedding cake. I stand quickly.

As we leave I ask for one final photo of Peter outside his house by the "Preview Tonight 8:30" sign in his window. He points to it. "Louie Federici gave me that. It's from the Encore Theater," he observes. Then I snap the picture. Sadly, the Encore, and almost all the other classic Los Angeles repertory cinemas, are just a memory. Everything about him and that place, from the clocks in every room to the chaos of film reels and movie posters and dirty blankets and pill bottles and stacks of bills, screams *obsession*. Like so many collectors we spoke with, Peter truly and deeply believes in the magic of movies. Movies were and still are his one great love and his religion. You can sense that, listening to his evangelist's voice falling and rising as he talks about keeping all his friends out until the early hours screening *Gone With the Wind*. He's invested so much time and devotion into the movies, and he became part of that magic in some strange way—

and now it's all slipped away, and the friends have all gone, and even the rivals have gone. He's left by himself in the House of Clocks on Lennox Boulevard, with the shades drawn and the "Preview Tonight 8:30" sign in the window announcing a screening that never comes.

10.

Child of Frankenstein

Rik Lueras greets Jeff and me warmly at the door of his house in West Covina, California, one of those slightly funky satellite cities east of downtown L.A. where people are allowed to keep horses in their front yards. Rik is renowned for having a large and impressive collection of 35mm and 16mm prints, over four hundred features, including a number of Technicolor rarities, like a superb dye-transfer print of *The War of the Worlds* (1953) that I screened at the Egyptian Theatre for a fiftieth-anniversary tribute to the film, with actors Gene Barry and Ann Robinson in the audience, and possibly the only existing 35mm Technicolor print of Errol Flynn's *The Adventures of Robin Hood* (1938) printed on safety stock (at least one nitrate Technicolor print survives). There's something immediately likable about him as he leads us inside: he resembles a Latino Kenny Rogers or Santa Claus, with his fuzzy white-gray beard and barrel-chested build. Jeff had mentioned before we visited that Rik is one of the few Latino film collectors he ever dealt with. From what I've seen, film collecting was and still is very homogeneous—predominantly white and male. Why film collecting would appeal to and be accessible to mostly white men is a good question. Probably economics has a lot to do with it. Many of the collectors we interviewed came from solidly middle-class white families in the 1950s and 1960s and had the means to pursue a costly hobby like collecting film prints. "It's a very, very expensive hobby," Rik confirms. Race and culture certainly had an impact: the vast majority of Hollywood classics well into the 1960s, from *The Adventures of Robin Hood* and *Singin' in the Rain* to *The Day the Earth Stood Still* and *My Fair Lady*, featured pre-

dominantly white casts (and crews) and were aimed at a mostly white audience who would feel comfortable seeing themselves reflected on-screen.
It doesn't mean these movies *necessarily* excluded Latinos, African Americans, Asian Americans, or other groups from enjoying them, as Rik proves,
but for many years mainstream Hollywood (with a few exceptions) didn't
go out of its way to make nonwhites feel at home. This attitude was most
likely reflected in the collecting subculture.

I ask Rik if he was ever aware of being one of the only Latinos involved
in film collecting. "Oh yeah, I was very conscious of it," he replies without
hesitation. "For one thing, I never ran into another one. All my life, even
going through school, I looked like a white guy, and everybody thought I
was, until I started speaking Spanish." He continues: "I did run into a guy
who does linen-backing for posters, and he's from Mexico. He said, 'You're
the only *mexicano* that I know in all collecting. How does a guy like you get
started?' I said, 'I don't know. I'm just a human being, and I happen to be
Mexican, and it doesn't mean because you're Mexican you can't like art
and films and American films.' I was born here, I'm an American. In fact,
I feel more like I'm an American than a Mexican." Rik is an exception to
the film collector stereotype in another way: he's quite obviously a family
man, and that's another rarity. Many of the collectors we interviewed are
lifelong bachelors. One Louisiana collector put it succinctly: "I've got a
hobby that doesn't go over too well with being married."

Rik has some difficulty walking from a recent hip surgery as he guides
us to the back of the house. "I just turned seventy," he says. "I retired from
driving a truck about six years ago. Driving a big truck and making a lot
of money." He leads us past a heavy western-style wooden door and into
his personal man-cave. It's one of the most remarkable rooms I've seen
during the writing of this book. Many collectors display their posters and
memorabilia as trophies, but this is more akin to an art gallery or museum
installation. By the entrance is a fabulous assemblage of glass tubes, cop-
per wires, and a giant reflecting disk that looks like something out of one
of the 1930s *Frankenstein* movies. It turns out it is: the equipment was an
unexpected gift from Kenneth Strickfaden, the legendary special effects
electrician who created the whirling/sparking devices for movies from
the original *Frankenstein* (1931) to *Young Frankenstein* (1974). Rik went to

see Strickfaden speak at a screening in the early 1970s and struck up a conversation afterward; on an impulse, the special effects artist invited Rik back to his home to see his garage, stuffed from floor to rafters with dust-covered equipment from classic Universal horror films. He invited Rik to pick out some equipment to take home—and it's still the first thing you see when entering Rik's trophy room. The walls all around are covered with beautifully lit posters, mostly for classic 1950s sci-fi films like *Them*, and examples of Rik's own artwork, some in elaborate handmade frames, including a painting of the wicked Queen from Disney's *Snow White*. A Mexican poster for one of the 1940s *Superman* movie serials, here titled *El Superhombre*, sits in one corner. Overhead, a sinister, copper-sheathed Martian "Technicolor eye" from *The War of the Worlds* hangs from the ceiling, staring sightlessly.

One piece of artwork immediately catches my eye—a stunning black-and-white poster for the 1922 silent horror classic *Nosferatu*. I ask if it's from the film's original release, and to my surprise Rik tells me that he drew it, because he was dissatisfied with all of the existing artwork he saw for the film. The image is truly haunting: it shows the gaunt, spectral vampire astride a medieval-looking European city, with a whirlwind of plague rats spinning beneath him. It almost resembles a nightmarish Chagall painting. To the right is the large telltale glass window of a projection booth, but when I look inside, I see it's cluttered with an aluminum walker, canes, and medical equipment. "My medical storage," Rik shrugs sadly, admitting that age and infirmity are catching up with him. I ask if he's still able to run film after his surgery, and he shakes his head. "I don't do any of it anymore. I ran a few 16mm's the other day, and it tore me up, just walking carrying them."

Looking around at this striking assemblage of rare prints, posters, and memorabilia, it's apparent that Rik is something more than a retired truck driver with a passion for old movies. He was born in Albuquerque, New Mexico, in 1941. His given name was Ricardo, but he shortened it several decades ago to just Rik. He grew up in Los Angeles with his mail-carrier father and housewife mother, in a family of three boys; one of his brothers later died of Lyme disease from a deer-borne tick. Rik is still haunted by his agonizing illness. "At that time it was very hard to diagnose. We watched him waste away—it got to where he couldn't swallow. He had to spit instead of swallow. His eyelids wouldn't close." He credits his mother with inspiring his love for film: "She went to the movies all the time, and she knew how to use the bus system in Los Angeles. We'd get on a bus or trolley car. They had the little yellow cars with the cowcatchers in front, you see them in Charley Chase movies." His talent for drawing developed early on, hand-in-hand with his love for cinema. "In 1952 they'd reissued *King Kong*," he remembers. "I saw this picture in the newspaper, and I was drawing it. And my uncle came in and said, 'My goodness, did you do that?' I thought he was just blowing smoke, but from then on I just kept going.

"I remember this Chicano group got ahold of me, the Brown Berets," he continues. "They wanted me to do political posters for the Chicano movement back in the 1960s. They took me to this home with all these pictures of Pancho Villa, and everyone's wearing sombreros. But I didn't wanna be political—I loved this country, and I didn't wanna subvert anything. I did a couple paintings for them, and they said, 'Oh yeah!' But I wanted to get paid. And they said, "Oh no, we want you to contribute everything you do."'

After graduating art school, Rik worked as a freelance graphic designer, but by his own admission, he bridled at being told what he *had* to draw, instead of what he *wanted* to. Then, in the early 1970s, he abruptly switched to driving a truck. He claims it was a purely financial decision to give up on his art career. "I couldn't raise my family on it, not as much as I wanted to," he says with pragmatic bluntness.

Although he's reluctant to discuss his days driving a truck—"That was just a means to an end," he says when I ask him about it—it obviously gave him the financial security to acquire films on a large scale. The first print he ever bought was a copy of James Whale's 1935 *The Bride of Frankenstein*, starring Boris Karloff. "I didn't even have a projector yet," he recalls. "It was a good dupe—a very good dupe—but it was still a dupe. It bugs you. I looked at that thing: I was fresh as a daisy, and I said, 'Something's wrong here—it's gotta look better than TV.'" He shakes his head, remembering the sleight of hand and backstabbing that involved collectors trying to dump their inferior dupes off on each other: "Oh, the skullduggery that went on! 'You sent me a dupe!' 'No, I didn't send you a dupe!'" Although he was active in the collecting world for several decades, Rik maintained a distance from other collectors. "I was a very enigmatic guy. Nobody knew who I was, what I did, or where I came from," he admits. "I could see they were curious to death of who I was. They knew my name and that I had a family. My family always came first . . . I never invited very many of them here, because my wife didn't like it. Only the ones I feel are decent people I'll invite here." One thing Rik did become known for in the tight-knit subculture was his unusual and fragrant habit of putting lemon oil on his prints: "Lemon oil does not hurt the film at all, and it eliminates black lines," he says, somewhat defensively. "If they're real deep and getting green, forget it. But if they're light lines, it'll get rid of them. Every line bothers a collector if he's a purist. If I had a print of *Murder, My Sweet* with a few lines, I'd put lemon oil on it, and they'd be gone."

One collector that he did become close friends with was electrician Peter Dyck. At first glance they'd appear to be an odd pair, the tall, excitable, and gregarious Dyck and the burly, truck-driving, family man Lueras, who liked to keep his distance. "When I got started, Pete was very clever," Rik recalls. "He'd put up these big previews of coming attractions, and it was usually something you were after. He'd get your blood churning, and the next time you called him, it was somehow available. His favorite phrase was, 'You gotta throw some wood in the fire before you get heat.'" The two men obviously shared a passion for movies and the thrill of the hunt. "I would go to conventions and film places, and people would come up to me: 'Oh, there's Peter's buddy.' It's like I was friends with Billy the Kid or something. I said, 'What's it to you, ass?' He'd never done anything to me." Even though they had their inevitable squabbles over print deals, they remained close. "Pete and I ran so many movies here," Rik says with obvious nostalgia. "At the time he loved to drink, and I could keep up with him. He loved to drink Jack Daniels sour mash—he'd fill the glass up, half booze and half soda water. I got one of those seltzer bottles so he could have his booze." He hesitates a moment, then says simply, "We were friends."

When it came, the rupture between the two men was abrupt, and permanent. Rik asserts that Dyck made sexual advances to one of his underage sons. It's a charge that Dyck acknowledges but flatly denies. "He said he wanted to teach both my sons to be electricians. They were about twelve, thirteen at the time," Rik remembers. "They were already big guys, that's the only reason I let 'em go. They stayed overnight. Pete said, 'I want to take 'em out the next day.'" At around nine PM, Rik received a frantic phone call from one of his sons, claiming Dyck had tried to touch him on the leg and kiss him. Rik rushed over in his truck: "I get there and Pete's in the corner half drunk. He looked so sheepish and sunk in his chair. I said, 'The only reason I'm not kicking your ass is you look like someone who's sick.' Almost like in *Psycho*. I said, 'I'm gonna do you a favor because of twelve years of friendship and not call the cops.'" Whichever version of the incident you believe—and again, no charges were ever filed with the police—it spelled the end of an important friendship for Rik. He brings up Dyck's name repeatedly during our conversation. When I mention that Jeff and I interviewed Dyck separately at his house in Inglewood, Rik's eyes almost light up: "So Pete looks like he's going to last a few more years? He must've stopped drinking. What did he say about me?

"There's a movie, *King Solomon's Mines*, and Stewart Granger describes life as going around in a circle and you wind up with nothing," Rik says. "I've known so many film collectors that wind up with nothing. After the big chase, going after the 'great whatsit.' Meeting strange people and allowing them into your home." Like many collectors and dealers I've met, Rik almost invariably compares and references everything to the movies. Movies are a rich and bottomless language, not just of images but of snatches of dialogue, directors' and actors' filmographies, and, possibly most important, a point of reference. A fixed moment in time, a personal anchor to say, *When I was ten years old, I first saw* King Solomon's Mines, *or* Them, *or* The Day the Earth Stood Still. It's how we gauge the passage of time, in movies seen and loved. Rik doesn't have to explain to me that "the great whatsit" is a reference to Robert Aldrich's 1955 film noir classic *Kiss Me Deadly*, I know what he means. Now that he's past seventy, Rik has begun to think about the ultimate question, the white elephant lurking in the corner of every collector's movie hoard, *What happens to all this stuff after I'm gone?* In Rik's case, he's planning to pass the ball to his wife: "I tell my wife, after the hymns are over, what are you going to do? She's one of those purists who doesn't believe it's ever going to happen. The good thing I tell her is, 'You're not in love with any of it, so sell it and have a ball.' She says, 'Well, I want to have a ball now!'" He pauses for a moment, then admits that divvying up his vast collection of prints and posters among his three adult children is more problematic. "They even confessed it once when we had a family conference. I asked them if they ever thought about it, and they said, 'Yes,' the three of them. I said, 'You know none of this belongs to you.' They said, 'We know but we just wonder what's going to happen to it.' And this is just a drop in the bucket to what I have. I have a lot more posters. I didn't get into posters until much later. You find yourself after years and years on the top of a mountain. And it's just happened."

Rik pauses, gazing at his beautifully lit and lovingly assembled museum of movie love. I can't help looking across the room at an oversized glass diorama case. Inside stands a freakish vampire creature with a large domed head, at the bottom of a castle staircase, surrounded by gray, overgrown vines. Rik bought it for twenty-five dollars in the late 1960s; the owner claimed it was a production art mock-up from Tod Browning's 1931 *Dracula*, and it might well be. But it's not the strange creature or diorama that fascinates me, it's the fact that in the dust on the outside of the case someone has cryptically scrawled a single word, "*Nosferatu*," linking it with Rik's haunting charcoal-and-pencil sketch a few feet away. Next to the case, several cans of dust-covered paintbrushes stand silently, witness to Rik's twin loves, art and film.

But of all the objects in Rik's minimuseum, perhaps the most fascinating sit along the far wall. Neatly arranged under several magnificent framed posters for 1940s movie serials are a row of metal Goldberg film cans. The 35mm prints they hold are extremely rare: titles like *The Day the Earth Stood Still*, *The War of the Worlds*, *Casablanca*, *Dracula*, and *Frankenstein* would still bring thousands of dollars, even in today's shrunken film market. But it's what Rik has *done* to the Goldberg film cans that's so fascinating: he's hand-decorated the normally utilitarian, generic cans with gorgeous reductions of the poster artwork for each of the films. He's turned them into gemlike objets d'art in their own right. These film cans and the prints they contain are museum pieces, in fact. They are among the most beautiful and most bittersweet objects I've seen while writing this book, because Rik is no longer able to project these prints. His projection booth is cluttered with medical equipment, and his dodgy hip won't allow him to carry the heavy cans across the room. But still, he can't bear to be parted from them. So they sit there, unscreened, but still magnifi-cent. "Nobody could predict why you're into it," Rik says to me later, trying to make sense of his lifelong love for the movies and collecting. "It's just something that sneaks up on you, and all of a sudden it becomes part of your life. And you discover all these memories that come racing back. And even you try to describe for yourself, 'Why does this affect me so much?'"

11.

Have Some Onions, They'll Make You Fat

Although he'd likely scoff at the description, British film historian, documentarian, preservationist, and collector Kevin Brownlow is something of a living legend among lovers of cinema history, and in particular, the history of the silent era. His documentaries on cinema have set a high standard few others have matched, including *Abel Gance: The Charm of Dynamite* (1968), the epic thirteen-part series *Hollywood* (1980), and *Buster Keaton: A Hard Act to Follow* (1987). His elegiac, masterful 1968 book *The Parade's Gone By* is arguably the definitive portrait of the silent era, featuring dozens of interviews conducted by Kevin with Louise Brooks, Dorothy and Lillian Gish, Mary Pickford, Gloria Swanson, Buster Keaton, and others. It's one of the few truly great books about film that should be read by everyone, whether you're a movie buff or not. As a preservationist Kevin has been directly involved with rescuing and preserving dozens of endangered films, including most famously Abel Gance's long-neglected 1927 masterpiece *Napoleon*. Kevin's first feature film as a director, the disturbing and highly controversial *It Happened Here* (1966), codirected with Andrew Mollo, imagined what might have happened if the Germans had successfully invaded England during WWII. For me personally, Kevin's crowning glory is his brilliant second feature *Winstanley* (1976), a haunting black-and-white portrait of the ill-fated seventeenth-century Digger movement, which was brutally repressed by the British ruling class. In 2010 Kevin received a Lifetime Achievement Award from the Academy of Motion Picture Arts and

Sciences. It was the first time that a film preservationist has received an honorary Oscar, and entirely fitting it should go to Kevin.

When he and his Photoplay Productions partner Patrick Stanbury arrive at my Burbank house to talk with Jeff and me, Kevin's first words have nothing at all to do with film. His eyes light up when he sees a toy Paddington bear I have sitting in a frame by the door: "My aunt illustrated the first eleven Paddington bear books!" he says with delight and then asks politely if I'll take a photo of him with it to send to her. He's tall and slender, with thinning gray hair and glasses, and he's dressed quite properly in a suit jacket and tie, which he later asks permission to remove due to the stifling Los Angeles heat. His producing partner Patrick is fifteen years his junior, with shaggy brown hair and a scruffy, graying beard. When they talk there's a very funny give-and-take between the two men, constantly correcting each other in the way that only two incredibly knowledgeable film buffs would do, but it's always taken in good spirit. I give Kevin a quick tour of my house, casually pointing out a rusted 1930s-era film light, or what I think is a film light, in the corner of the den. He whips out a tiny flashlight that he apparently carries with him for just such occasions and examines it with keen interest. "It may be a prop," he says, pursing his lips in deep concentration. "It should have a plaque on it saying Mole-Richardson somewhere." I start to move on, but Kevin the historian isn't done with the mystery just yet: "Whatever it is, it wasn't a carbon arc light, I'm sure of that. You know if they'd just kept the glass on them, they wouldn't have caused klieg eyes." I ask what "klieg eye" is, and he instantly bugs his eyes out in exaggerated fashion. "Oh, that's what happened to actors in the silent film era. Cameramen removed the glass from the lamps to get more light, and the ultraviolet rays caused this terrible inflammation. It could take several days to recover. They'd have to put potatoes on their eyes to reduce the swelling. We now know that if they'd kept the glass in place, this wouldn't have happened."

"I never thought I'd live to be the age of people I was interviewing [for *The Parade's Gone By . . .*]," Kevin observes as I pour cups of mint tea for him and Patrick. "When they were talking about fifty years ago, it was *The Birth of a Nation.*" He pauses for a moment, then continues: "I remember showing my 9.5 *Napoleon* and saying, 'It's twenty-seven years old!'" I look at him confused, then ask if he's referring to a 1995 restoration of the film. He and Patrick both roll their eyes and reply in unison, "*9.5mm*," as if they're talking to a remedial school student who's just asked which end of the pencil he should use. I know a bit about film history, but I'm obviously way out of my depth with these two.

They first met in February 1975 when Patrick, who was programming a local film society in England, invited Kevin to come down to show several rare silent movies. "Do you remember what I showed that night?" Kevin asks teasingly, as if he's testing his old friend's little gray cells. Patrick thinks for a second, then responds, "The films you showed were *The Beast at Bay* and the *Silents Please* Paul Killiam version of *Variety*." Paul Killiam was a noted silent film collector who produced a pioneering TV series in 1960 called *Silents Please,* hosted for a time by comedian Ernie Kovacs, which featured reduced versions of silent classics. Although the notion of condensing films might seem like a sacrilege to most purists, apparently it didn't bother the young Kevin: "In fact they turned D. W. Griffith's boring *America* into a masterpiece at twenty-eight minutes by skillful abridgment," he says with a twinkle in his eye.

As with most collectors Jeff and I spoke with, Kevin's love for film goes back to his earliest years. He was born in 1938 in the mid-sized town of Crowborough in East Sussex. "My mother had gone out with my father the first time in 1926, and they went to see *The Four Horsemen of the Apocalypse* on reissue for Valentino's death. They were so broke that they couldn't get married for ten years," he says. Both his parents were commercial artists. "My father was Irish and was a really brilliant artist, but he couldn't get any work," he recalls. "So he became a commercial artist doing film posters. You think the lettering on all those posters was typeset, but they were all hand-drawn by some poor artist like my father. *Oliver Twist* by David Lean was one [poster he worked on]."[44] His parents were determined that Kevin wouldn't follow in their artistic footsteps, so they packed him off to boarding school at the age of three. It's where Kevin was first introduced to cinema: "An orphanage called Dr. Barnardo's would show a film as treats for us children. I'd never seen a film before, and yet I knew instinctively it was badly shot. It was filmed on our home movie gauge of 9.5mm. When I finally saw a proper film, it was a newsreel. This was 35mm, so you can imagine the impact of the brightness, sharpness, and clarity. I remember that first shot to this day: there were four naval officers walking towards the camera. To show you how prescient I was—the technical knowledge I had even then about cinema—I knew those four naval officers were going to fall into the theater. I was so disappointed when they melted off-screen." He pauses, then adds: "Then we saw *Snow White*, and I ran out screaming from the theater."

He recovered enough from the trauma of seeing *Snow White and the Seven Dwarfs* to develop a keen fascination with film, thanks to the silent films shown at his next boarding school. "The stuff we saw at the cinema in the holidays was what Alfred Hitchcock called 'photographs of people talking,'" he notes, doing a quite-passable imitation of Hitchcock. "The silents seemed fresher and occasionally a lot more daring." He begged his parents for a home movie projector, and the following Christmas they gave him a 9.5mm Pathéscope Ace that came with two shorts, a Mickey Mouse cartoon and a newsreel called *The Naval Review at Spithead 1935*. It was the beginning of Kevin's career as a film collector. "I quickly wore those out and went out into the streets looking for more," he remembers. "I came across a photographic shop which had a pile of 9.5mm films. They were one-and-six a reel, and I had ten shillings pocket money, which was an enormous amount in those days. And I bought the lot."

He shared his tiny cinematic treasures with his mother, and it was this that led to his first encounter with a forgotten masterpiece he would eventually spend over forty-five years of his life restoring to its former glory. "My mother was a Francophile; she nearly married a Frenchman. She thought French culture was 'it.' Anything French was much better than English," Kevin says. After locating a silent adaption of writer Pierre Loti's novel *Pêcheur d'Islande* called *Fishers of the Isle*, which Kevin's mother thought was "beautiful," he was desperate to find anything else French. After ordering an inferior 1924 movie, *Le Lion des Mogols*, from a film library, he tried to exchange it for another title. "They said, 'We've got *Napoleon Bonaparte and the French Revolution* in two reels.' I didn't want that, because I was sure it was a boring educational film with static engravings of battles and such," Kevin remembers with a shrug. "They said, 'That's all we've got left.' So I settled for it. I was home from school with flu, from which I managed a miraculous recovery when the film arrived. It was the finest piece of cinema that I'd seen."

It's taken for granted now that director Abel Gance's *Napoleon* (1927) is one of the greatest masterpieces of the silent era and a pioneering achievement in its use of rapid cutting and brilliantly innovative camerawork. Originally running over six hours, the film climaxed with a stunningly ambitious triptych effect using three cameras and meant to be projected on three screens. This innovative use of widescreen anticipated Cinema-Scope (and later, Cinerama) by nearly twenty-five years. Even in its day, the massive length and technical challenges of *Napoleon* proved too much for most distributors and audiences: in the United States it was released in 1929 by MGM, brutally shortened to a mere seventy-five minutes.

By the time Kevin saw his even-further-reduced version of *Napoleon* in the early 1950s as a teenager, Gance's masterpiece had been butchered and discarded for decades, passed over by even die-hard film historians. Although he had no notion at the time of "preserving" or "restoring" the film, Kevin recognized that what he saw was incomplete and a pale shadow of a much greater work. "I became obsessed with finding the rest of the movie," he says. "I advertised in the *Exchange & Mart*, that was a magazine just full of ads: 'Wanted: 9.5mm Films Especially 'Napoleon: Youth,' 'Napoleon: The Battle of Toulon,' etc." He was able to find enough 9.5mm reels to assemble a nearly ninety-minute version that he began screening privately for other silent-film buffs. At the same time he became, in his words, "an Abel Gance bore." He wrote to the great filmmaker care of the Cinémathèque Française and amazingly received a brief, polite reply. The story of Kevin's pursuit of *Napoleon* is filled with years of dogged research and persistence, and also moments of pure blind luck. One such twist of fate came after he'd shown a photo of Gance to Liam O'Leary at the British Film Institute. A few days later O'Leary happened to look through his glass door and saw a man passing by who looked exactly like the photograph. "He walked out his office and said, 'Hello, Mr. Gance!'" Kevin says with obvious delight. "Gance was astounded to be recognized, because he hadn't worked in twelve years." The director happened to be in London and had literally wandered into the BFI offices. Remembering Kevin's obsession with the French director, O'Leary called Kevin's mother, who telephoned him at his school. This was such a rare event that they assumed there had been a death in the family and let Kevin go, so he could rush over to the National Film Theatre to meet his idol. "He was the most charismatic character, even though he didn't speak English," Kevin recalls of his first meeting with Gance. Then he adds simply, "That was the beginning."

Although he never fully forgot about Gance or *Napoleon*, life pressed on; Kevin dropped out of school to begin working in the film industry. While still in his late teens, he and his friend Andrew Mollo started work on the project that became *It Happened Here* (1966), about Nazis successfully invading England. The heated controversy surrounding the finished film, which featured actual British fascists playing themselves and angered many Jewish organizations, launched his career. During the shooting of *It Happened Here*, he was invited to a private screening at the home of a well-known British film collector named Dr. Ken Elliott, who lived in Norfolk. "He had bought a 17.5mm projector accompanied by a print of *Napoleon*. It was tinted. It was seventeen reels long." Like the 9.5mm films Kevin bought for his own collection, 17.5mm was meant primarily for home use, not commercial distribution. Kevin, as he now says dryly, was "gobsmacked" when he saw Elliott's original 1920s print of *Napoleon*, which was far longer than any version he'd seen so far, including the one he'd assembled.

Despite his own amateur attempts to restore the film, and even after seeing Elliott's longer (but still woefully incomplete) version, Kevin still hadn't decided to work on a restoration of *Napoleon*. In the late 1960s the Canadian-born animator George Dunning, best known for directing the Beatles' *Yellow Submarine*, organized a festival of multiscreen films in London, for which he brought over some of the groundbreaking triptych sequences Gance had shot for the climax of *Napoleon*. It was the first time Gance's astonishing use of widescreen had been seen in England in over forty years. "I went over to Dunning's office hoping to get hold of it, and he said, 'I'm very sorry, I've sent the triptychs back,'" Kevin remembers. "Then Dunning said, 'But I've copied it before it went, and I think you should look after the print.' This was really the beginning of the restoration. I was forced into it, you see, by accident."

The following year, while working on his own acclaimed documentary on the director, *Abel Gance: The Charm of Dynamite*, Kevin was asked by the National Film Theatre to repair an original print of *Napoleon* brought over from the Cinémathèque Française. "It was in a terrible state. It was covered with oil, and some of the sprockets were ripped, and even some of the film," Kevin says, nearly wincing. "It was an original safety print of the film." When Jeff tries to correct him, saying it must have been nitrate if it was an original 1920s print, Kevin shakes his head firmly: "No, it was safety. They printed it that way originally. Because they had a rule in France after many members of the aristocracy had been killed by a fire at a charity bazaar in 1897. Whenever they had an important show and when children were involved, they paid the few extra cents per foot and showed safety film." Before the print was returned, he and a friend "borrowed it" (as Kevin mildly puts it) and had a dupe negative made: an illegal action, perhaps, but one that shows his increasing passion for preserving the film.

A major turning point came from a seemingly offhand remark Abel Gance made while Kevin was interviewing him for the BBC documentary: "He told me that they'd shot footage of *Napoleon* being made. I thought he was an old man having me on. I'd never seen footage that showed a silent film while it was in production." On the off chance that Gance was telling the truth, Kevin went to Paris to visit the archives of the Cinémathèque Française. In another strange twist of fate, the woman in charge of the archives happened to be Mary Epstein, the sister of Jean Epstein, director of *Le Lion des Mogols*, the silent film that Kevin had exchanged all those years earlier at the film library for *Napoleon Bonaparte*. She disappeared into the back of the archive shelves and returned with one big reel and several smaller reels. To Kevin's astonishment, the smaller reels turned out to be, yes, surviving behind-the-scenes footage of Gance during production. But an even bigger surprise was in store. "We look at the big roll, and it has all sorts of flash cuts of a snowball fight, and I remember from a book I'd read that the original *Napoleon* had a snowball fight that was a masterpiece of rapid cutting. I was obsessed with rapid cutting at that time, so this excited me enormously," Kevin recalls of that moment when he rediscovered the long-missing footage. "When she came back, Mary Epstein was very upset that I'd rootled through the can, but she ran it for us on the flatbed, and that was one of the most amazing moments of my life. It was the equivalent for me of that researcher who found a Leonardo da Vinci sketchbook in a Spanish museum."

Returning to England, Kevin put the rediscovered snowball-fight footage into his BBC documentary and showed it to director Gance, who was equally thrilled to find it still existed. (Ironically, when Gance himself tried to access the lost footage for a never-completed project he had in mind combining the earlier *Napoleon* with newly shot material, Epstein refused to let him have it—until Kevin went to see her and explained that he'd let Gance use the 16mm print she had made for Kevin. "At one point Gance said, 'You need two revolvers: one for Henri Langlois [founder of the Cinémathèque], one for Mary Epstein,'" Kevin recalls of the great director's exasperation.)[45] Hearing of Kevin's growing interest in restoring *Napoleon*, in 1970 David Meeker of the BFI reached out to a colleague across the channel, Jacques Ledoux, then secretary general of the International Federation of Film Archives (FIAF). Ledoux issued an appeal to film archives around the world to scour their holdings and send anything related to Gance's *Napoleon* to Kevin Brownlow c/o the British Film Institute. "So in it rolls, print after print," Kevin says of the riches that arrived from all over the globe.

Utilizing the newly arrived footage along with material from a 35mm blow-up of the Elliott 17.5mm tinted print Kevin had seen nearly a decade earlier, he labored on and off to produce a restored version while also working on his own documentaries. In 1979 he screened his nearly five-hour version of *Napoleon* to an astonished audience of film lovers at the Telluride Film Festival. The response was overwhelming and began to turn the tide of opinion on a film that is now justly regarded as one of the greatest masterpieces of its day. Ironically, when the topic of the Telluride screening comes up, Kevin's response is less than stellar. When Jeff asks him to explain, Kevin sighs: "The Telluride experience is what made Mr. Coppola say, 'Wouldn't it be wonderful if my father wrote the score for that?'" Following the rapturous Telluride screening, Francis Ford Coppola joined forces with restoration expert Robert Harris, who had bought rights for North America through his company Images Film Archive to present the film at Radio City Music Hall. But Coppola and Harris soon learned that the unions at Radio City would charge thousands of dollars more if the show ran over four hours. Ironically, the same problem had been faced by Gance at the Paris Opera in 1927, and he had cut it to three and a half hours for that engagement. Gance then showed his full version a week later. Kevin listed the sequences that could be cut to match the Opera version. Coppola and Harris agreed to do the same: present Gance's abridged Paris Opera version at Radio City, followed by the longer edition at other venues, but then decided to stick with their abridged cut. It was another thirty years before the full version with the Carl Davis score reached the United States.

The film was released by American Zoetrope to great acclaim, but because Coppola's name was attached to it, he received the lion's share of the credit, at least in the U.S. press. When I ask Kevin to talk about his experience with Coppola, Patrick steps in: "We won't talk about that for legal reasons," he says simply. End of discussion, but not of Kevin's work on *Napoleon*. In 1983 he produced an improved version, replacing all of the blown-up 17.5mm footage from Elliott's tinted print with material from original 35mm elements. Then again in 2000 Kevin premiered a further-restored version incorporating thirty-five minutes of additional footage discovered by the Cinémathèque Française, at close to five and a half hours running time. *Napoleon* developed into a collaborative project with the BFI, and the most-recent restoration is a collaboration between the BFI and Photoplay Productions, who jointly own it. This is by far the most definitive version of Gance's masterwork to date, although just under an hour is still missing from the full version that premiered in 1927. When I ask Kevin earlier in the interview to talk about *Napoleon*, he quips, "Have you got a fortnight?" and then adds, "Do you really want all this? Because it's not really about film collecting, it's film restoration." "Kevin, you start off doing this as a *film collector*—you're not doing it because you work for an archive," Patrick quickly corrects him, and he nods.

Like his partner-in-crime, Patrick developed his love for film and collecting at an early age. Their experience as British collectors mirrors that of many American collectors we spoke to, with some differences. Patrick was born in 1954: "Within days of the date Kevin saw *Napoleon*. I wish it was the same day as the first screening of *Napoleon*, because that would fit very nicely," Patrick says with a smile. His parents both worked for the telephone system, which was then part of the post office. On St. Patrick's Day in 1962, they took him to see William Wyler's *Ben-Hur*, starring Charlton Heston, which was still in its original release. "We came out and my mother said, 'That was good, but the silent version was better.' Silent version—what silent version? I'd only seen Chaplin films on TV," Patrick recalls. Like Kevin, he badgered his parents into buying him a home movie projector and soon began renting 8mm abridged prints of titles like

The Hunchback of Notre Dame, eventually moving up to collect 16mm and 35mm.

Jeff asks if collecting in 35mm was difficult in England, and Patrick nods: "There was an organization called the Kinematograph Renters Society, the KRS—in other words, the Gestapo—and they would go around threatening you if they found you were showing films you weren't supposed to be."[46] Smaller film gauges like 8mm, Super 8mm, 9.5mm, and 16mm were considered fine for home exhibition. "But nobody was supposed to have 35mm outside of commercial movie theaters," Kevin explains. "If you had 35mm sound films, the KRS would be after you." The organization's heavy-handed tactics sound suspiciously like those of the MPAA in the United States in the early 1970s. The best-known court case surrounding film collecting in the United Kingdom involved Bob Monkhouse, a popular TV game show host and film collector who'd produced a successful British TV series in the mid-1960s, *Mad Movies*, which featured clips from old silent films, many from his private archives. In 1979 he was charged with defrauding distributors of their rightful royalties. Monkhouse was eventually cleared of all charges, but much of his collection was seized and, sadly, destroyed. (When he walked out of the Old Bailey after his acquittal, the quick-witted Monkhouse still managed to quip, "It's terrible being a film pirate: you can't watch films with a patch over one eye and a parrot on the other shoulder."[47]) The KRS may have been vigilant, but they weren't necessarily the brightest bulbs when it came to examining the prints that passed through their hands. "My favorite story about the KRS was when [film preservationist] David Shepard went to see them," Kevin recalls. "The man who ran it was an ex-Army intelligence officer and David was told that there were lists of what all the collectors had. He said, 'Do you have anything on Kevin Brownlow?' 'Yes, we do have something on Kevin Brownlow.' And they showed him the list of films I supposedly had," Kevin says with a smile, then pauses for effect. He leans in closer: "At the top was a very strange title called *Have Some Onions, They'll Make You Fat*. Not a classic of the screen." Jeff and I exchange puzzled looks. I'm about to ask him if this was some food-related educational film in his collection, when Kevin continues: "What had happened was, the person who was sending it to me had wit enough to send the print with the tails heads out. If they'd been heads up, it would have said, 'Greta Garbo and Antonio

Moreno in *The Temptress*.' But at the end of reel one, there's a scene where Garbo's serving dinner and she says, 'Have some onions, they'll make you fat.' So that's how they listed the print."

"I got the impression that film dealers in the U.S. would try to take advantage of us European collectors because we were overseas," Patrick observes. "For example, in *The Big Reel* I found somebody offering a Scope edition of the first version of *Close Encounters of the Third Kind*. I was really into CinemaScope, and I happen to love the film." He paid his money for the print, but when it arrived he found, to his dismay, that the print was pan-and-scan flat, not Scope. "I phoned the dealer up and said, 'What happened to it? This was supposed to be a Scope print!' He said, 'It was a Scope print when it left me. Something must have happened to it on the way.'" Like almost all collectors, they remember the ones that got away or, in one case, never were. Patrick brings up the name of a dealer in Austin, Texas, and Kevin groans painfully, as if someone had punched him in the stomach. The dealer had taken out an ad in *The Big Reel* listing impossibly rare and/or lost films, including a five-hour "rough cut" of Leni Riefenstahl's *Triumph of the Will* and F. W. Murnau's long-vanished *Der Janus-Kopf* (a 1920 silent version of Robert Louis Stevenson's *The Strange Case of Dr. Jekyll and Mr. Hyde*, starring Conrad Veidt and Bela Lugosi in one of his first screen appearances). Even though they should have known better, Kevin and Patrick took the bait. "Not being sensible about this, and being collectors, we sent money," Patrick says. When I ask how much they sent the dealer for these tempting but nonexistent rarities, he shudders: "More than we would care to remember. I can't remember now. I don't want to; it was a painful experience."

For all the missed opportunities, there are also the small triumphs to go with the large ones like *Napoleon*. "I was contacted by a collector in St. John's Wood who said, 'I think I have a film that would interest you,'" Kevin says. "I shoot over. He goes to his air raid shelter, roots around, and brings out a can of film which turned out to be *Le Droit à la vie*, Gance's *The Right to Life* (1917). It opens very unusually, with a portrait of Abel Gance at the beginning of the film. I said, 'How much do you want for this?' He said, 'I don't want to sell it. I just want to know that *you* want it.'" Kevin bursts out laughing and then adds the ironic punchline: "In order to remind him who wanted it, he put my name in the can. And when he died, his widow thought he'd left it to me!" So she sent Kevin the print, free of charge.

To this day Kevin and Patrick continue to screen prints from their collections at home for their private pleasure, although not as often as before. When I ask which films they showed most recently, Kevin responds a 9.5mm print of the 1924 version of *Captain Blood*, starring J. Warren Kerrigan (later remade much more famously with Errol Flynn); for Patrick it was a 35mm print of Rex Ingram's 1926 WWI drama *Mare Nostrum*, starring Antonio Moreno, one of the first Latino film stars in Hollywood. And yes, there are still treasures in their archives waiting to see the light of a projector: Patrick mentions the 35mm negative of a rare British silent called *The School for Scandal* (1923), starring a young Basil Rathbone in one of his earliest roles, which he's hoping to raise money to preserve. "We don't know if it's any good. Being British it may not be!" he says with a self-deprecating grin.

Toward the end of the conversation, the topic of the transition from film to digital inevitably comes up. It's a pressing but somewhat troubling issue for these two men who have spent so much of their careers preserving *film on film*, including some of cinema's earliest treasures. In fact, the two are currently in L.A. for screenings of their acclaimed Photoplay Productions restorations of *The Phantom of the Opera* (1925) at the Academy of Motion Picture Arts and Sciences, on 35mm, and *The Cat and the Canary* (1927) at the Disney Concert Hall, on DigiBeta (or "Digi-*Beeta*" as Patrick says with his British accent), although the restoration was produced on 35mm. Kevin expresses guarded optimism about the future of digital preservation but fears "an enormous amount of stuff will be junked." Patrick has similar optimism, with reservations: "Digital is a big bogeyman to some people. It's certainly a big problem for silent film, because it's difficult to show silent film at the right speed with digital. It's a cost issue, because for the manufacturers of the projectors, the studios are the big customers and the cinema exhibitors—and there's no money in it for them."

12.

Restoring the Audience

"The collector scene is vanishing everywhere," replies Serge Bromberg when I ask him about the state of film collecting in France. "We are less and less. A few dozens. We used to be very young, we are not as young as we were," he admits in his clear but heavily accented English. "The film collectors are moving to digital or dying, and their widows are trying to get rid of the film." Although most of this book is focused on film collectors in the United States, there were—and continue to be—collectors in every part of the globe. In fact, the greatest film collector in history was quite likely a Frenchman, Henri Langlois, who, together with the marvelous, still-underrated director Georges Franju (*Eyes Without a Face*, *Judex*) and critic Jean Mitry, started the Cinémathèque Française in the 1930s. Langlois's private collection morphed into the great-granddaddy of film archives, and his overwhelming passion for cinema has made him something of a patron saint for film lovers.[48] By the time of his death in 1977, he'd acquired, scavenged, and rescued by some estimates over sixty thousand films for the Cinémathèque.

In the tradition of Langlois, Serge Bromberg has turned his passion for film collecting into a career as a world-renowned film preservationist, director, distributor, promoter, and tireless champion for cinema. Dark-haired, with a bit of a John Garfield quality, he speaks about cinema with an almost irresistible enthusiasm and a showman's sense of how to sell a good story. Through his company Lobster Films in Paris, he's been involved in the restoration of all surviving Charlie Chaplin films made between 1914 and 1917 and dozens of previously lost Georges Méliès films, including the recent painstaking restoration of *A Trip to the Moon* (1902)

115

from the only known hand-tinted color print of the film, discovered in Spain. In France he's a household name as host of the much-loved TV programs on film history *Cartoon Factory* (1993), *Cellulo* (1995–2001), and *Ça tourne Bromby* (1997–1999), and from 1999 through 2012 he was artistic director of the Annecy International Animated Film Festival. In 2010 he won a French César award for his superb documentary *L'Enfer d'Henri-Georges Clouzot* (codirected with Ruxandra Medrea), a thrilling cinema detective story reconstructing a never-finished project by Clouzot, famed director of *The Wages of Fear* and *Les Diaboliques*. "If I had remained a simple collector, I'd be totally nuts today," Serge confesses. "But turning the passion of film into the profession of saving and showing films kind of saved my life, because my job is my passion."

Perhaps the most remarkable aspect of his collecting is how he's managed to *popularize* long-forgotten films of the silent era, making them seem fresh and important. Nowhere is this more visible than in his live presentations called "Retour de Flamme," literally "Back from the Flames," which always include Serge igniting a piece of old nitrate film in front of a startled audience. Retour de Flamme began in 1992 when he was asked by a small theater in Paris, Théâtre du Nord-Ouest, to put together a show: "It was an old theater, but they'd removed the seats, and they'd put out the little tables and a bar—and you could watch the film and drink at the same time. I must admit it was bizarre, but nevertheless, they had a piano in house," he recalls today. "We said, 'We have some films, but they're nitrate and we can't run them.' They found a small institution that funded the restoration of an hour of nitrate." Among the films was a 1925 Stan Laurel two-reeler, *Pie-Eyed* (under the delightful French title *Picotin noctambule*), *Philips Broadcast of 1938* by George Pal, and what he describes as "two primitive French comedies of 1910." The night of the first show, he arrived at the venue at rue du Faubourg Montmartre—and realized he'd forgotten to hire a pianist. "I'd studied piano for fifteen years and still remembered my A, B, and C's. So I had to play. Of course the music was terrible," he confesses with a smile. "While the leaders were going through the projectors, I'd stand up and apologize for the quality of the music and explain where we found the prints, and why these films are so miraculous, all kinds of stories. And it worked. It's like a cocktail that worked instantly exactly, maybe because of my storytelling. Not because of my piano." For over twenty years now, he's performed Retour de Flamme around the world, most recently at the Telluride Film Festival and the Academy of Motion Picture Arts and Sciences. "It's fun to find films, to restore them, but it's much, much more fun to restore the audience," he observes.

Serge was born in 1961 in Saint-Maur-des-Fossés, a suburb of Paris surrounded by a loop in the Marne River. When he was nine years old, his father purchased a film projector and showed Serge a print of Chaplin's *A Night in the Show* (1915). It would have a lasting impact on him. After graduating from ESCP Europe Business School in 1983, he started his own audio restoration company, Lobster Films, in 1985. Throughout his career he's shown a canny knack for turning an admittedly obscure obsession with old films into a paying job. He is, as he describes himself, a "crazy film collector who is also a wise businessman." In 1988 he was asked to work on a sound restoration of Jean Renoir's 1935 film *The Crime of Monsieur Lange*. Lobster quickly became one of the first companies to specialize in digital audio work on vintage films, including Marcel Carné's *Children of Paradise* for Pathé. Serge is especially proud of his efforts on the films of Jean Vigo, the tragically short-lived genius of early 1930s French cinema, including the director's final film, the sublime *L'Atalante* (1934). "The film was cut down very, very early," he says of the movie, which later became a key influence on the French New Wave, most notably François Truffaut. "The only surviving long version was in London, that's where we got it. We took that sound because all the other prints had rerecorded sound. They'd used all kinds of noise reduction from the 1940s and 1950s that were totally destructive."

He met his longtime collaborator and partner at Lobster, Eric Lange, at a flea market in 1989. "He tried to sell me stuff. It didn't work out well," he says with a smile about Lange, who was attempting to sell him a 17.5mm projector. The two quickly hit it off and began working together, with Serge the visible frontman and Lange the behind-the-scenes technician. "He does not speak so much," Serge says of his friend and partner, with whom he recently directed the acclaimed documentary *Le Voyage extraordinaire*, about the making of Méliès's *A Trip to the Moon* and their restoration of the single, precious hand-tinted copy. "I don't know if he's shy or doesn't enjoy speaking. Basically he's the brain and I'm the voice." There's a pause as he considers this picture, then he amends it: "Okay, let's say he's the arms and I'm the voice, and we share all the brain." When the two men met, they had by Serge's estimation about fifty prints each. Now their combined collection amounts to a staggering 120,000 cans of film, spread out between two private vaults in Paris, the CNC Archives, the Cinémathèque Française, and the Academy Film Archive in L.A.

Their most famous find together—and one of the most astonishing discoveries of lost films, ever—occurred almost by accident in the late 1990s. Serge explains, "A man called an archive and said, 'I have a film by Méliès called *Paris—New York*. Does it exist and are you interested?' The man at the archive checked the catalogue of Méliès films, and there was no title of this kind listed. He thought the man had made a mistake, which was not the case. What happened was on the leader of the Méliès film, it said 'Paris—New York,' because he had an office in Paris and New York. He thought it was the title. The man at the archive turned it down." The owner subsequently contacted Eclair Laboratories in Paris, who recommended him to Lobster. Serge happened to be filming that day, so Lange agreed to drive down to the south of France to meet with the collector. It turns out the man had twenty films in his possession, and a fellow collector had another eighty films, which they'd purchased from a local antique store for one hundred euros. "Eric grabbed the things. He negotiated and got all the films—and he got back to the hotel, because it was too late to drive back to Paris, and spent two hours watching those films." There's a pause as Serge recalls the excitement and anticipation waiting to hear from his partner. "Eric called me that night. He said, 'These are pre-1906 nitrate, and if we announce a new lost Méliès film every year, you and I will be grandfathers before we announce the last one." The discovery, which they famously dubbed "Treasures from a Chest," was the cinema equivalent of discovering Tutankhamun's tomb: they had found over two hundred pounds of film, ninety-eight movies total from before 1906, including a staggering *seventeen previously lost Méliès films*.[49] I ask, almost as an afterthought, what the actual chest looked like that held these wondrous treasures. "They mention it as a chest, but we never got the chest," he finally admits. "That's what we imagined, that's the legend—how do you say, 'When the legend becomes fact, print the legend?'" He's quoting, of course, from another famous film, John Ford's 1962 classic *The Man Who*

Shot Liberty Valance, and it's a fitting coda to this tale of treasures from a chest that wasn't actually a chest.

As with any collector, there are of course ones that got away, even for a fanatical Méliès scholar and preservationist like Serge. In 2003 during a blistering heat wave in Paris, he was contacted by a woman who said she had an old film to sell. "She came to Lobster, and she took out of a plastic bag a roll of film that was all white, totally decomposed—except the middle was still there. We opened it and looked at the middle section that survived. It was *A Trip to the Moon* in black-and-white, but the last tableau was complete. That's all that survived of the print, but that's the part that did not survive in any other print. We asked her, 'Why is it that decomposed?' She said, 'It's because it was nice in July, but the film was a bit sticky so I put it on my window, and I was hoping the heat would dry it.'" Still hoping to salvage the precious middle section, Serge offered her 500 euros. "She said, 'I want 100,000 Euros.' I said, 'It's a bit too much.'" The woman left. After attempting unsuccessfully to sell it elsewhere, she returned a month later. There's a strain in Serge's voice as he continues: "But the film had melted from the first to the last image, and it was too late."

"Our best find is our next one. The one we'll do tomorrow," he responds when I ask if he has any favorites among his collection. He admits he has had to make sacrifices with his family to keep up his tireless role as film champion/promoter/preservationist. "Mostly because of my traveling—it takes a lot of time to do the shows. So I'm not often at home, and I'm sorry for this," he confesses. He grows contemplative when I ask him for his thoughts on the transition from film to digital. "I would put it this way: papyrus—the Egyptian way of leaves and bamboo—was the only way to write stories. But those stories have been translated and printed, and now we know those stories in translation," he says. "What's interesting is not the papyrus but the story." He acknowledges that for most audience members, even the ones that thrill to his Retour de Flamme shows, it's the images that count, not how they're presented. For him, as with other film collectors, the technology they cherish has made them men out of time in the modern world. "For us, being in a small room with a 16mm projector, it's part of the poetry, but it's our poetry. So many people now think it's a Stone Age technology—which it is."

While Lobster continues to preserve films in 35mm, at least for the present, Serge admits that they rarely make 35mm prints for screenings, preferring DCPs instead for digital presentation.[50] I ask which films they're currently restoring, and ironically one turns out to be *A Night in the Show*, the 1915 Charlie Chaplin short Serge's father screened for him when he was nine, which he's restoring digitally in 2K in partnership with the Cineteca di Bologna using material from the Museum of Modern Art and the Cinémathèque Française. I inquire if he feels like he's come full circle, restoring the film he watched with his father so long ago. There's a quiet pause. "How could I answer this?" he finally responds.

13.

A Woman in Film

Pennsylvania-based collector Hillary Hess is one of the few women active in a field that was, and continues to be, almost entirely dominated by men. It's not the only thing that makes her stand out: by her own admission she's drawn to films that are bizarre, strange, and forgotten by most people, even diehard buffs. "I would never buy a print of *A Christmas Story* or *Gone With the Wind* or *The Wizard of Oz*. Everybody has seen those movies," she shrugs. Instead, her taste runs to films like the indescribably weird *A Visit to Santa* (1963), which is something like Christmas as envisioned by David Lynch circa *Twin Peaks*. "It's only ten minutes long and produced by Clem Williams Films in Pittsburgh, Pennsylvania," she gushes. "I've never seen a film that violated every rule of filmmaking so quickly in such a short period of time. It's gloriously bad . . . I was really excited to get two prints of it." When I ask if she's ever felt out of place as a female collector in an almost all-male subculture, she laughs: "I've always been odd, so this is just one facet of the gem that is me." A moment later she grows serious. "In some ways I'm a fish out of water," she admits. "But I've never felt out of place in the community. Everybody's always been very welcoming."

Together with her radio-buff husband, John, Hillary continues to run vintage 35mm and 16mm films in their basement screening room. It's a unique American tradition that is sadly disappearing with the films themselves. Their home theater is no movie palace, but it's wonderfully warm and inviting, with a black-and-white checkerboard linoleum floor, old-school wood paneling, comfy lounge chairs, and a ten-foot-wide screen. Best of all, the booth is equipped with two beautiful 35mm Simplex E7 projectors that were purchased at a benefit auction from the Fulton Opera House in nearby Lancaster, Pennsylvania. At the time she bought them, though, Hillary didn't have adequate space, and they were temporarily put in storage. So she and John started shopping for a house that was big enough to fit them in. When I ask if she and John really bought their house to accommodate the projectors, she nods: "That was a very big part of it." Now *that's* a true film collector. Together, she and John put together themed programs, most recently a screening of Buster Keaton's *One Week* (1920) and *The General* (1926), with old intermission slides from the nickelodeon era and Hillary accompanying the films on piano. "We were trying to get people to forget they ever knew what a sound movie is," she says, then adds proudly, "One of my friends said, 'The best time I ever had was seeing *The General*. I'd never seen a silent movie before, but that was the best experience.' People don't know what they like until we shove it down their throats!"

Her motivation for collecting is also quite unique and has more to do with a keen awareness of history and the prints as a physical bridge to a lost era. "Movies are like a time machine," as she puts it. "You're seeing the preservation of a time and people who no longer exist, or no longer exist in that way. That's something that's always drawn me to movies, that kind of preservation." Most collectors buy prints because they love a specific movie, or the visual quality of IB Technicolor, but for Hillary, the print itself is a window into the distant past; she's like an archaeologist standing in front of a Mayan glyph and trying to imagine the people who carved it long ago. "It's important to have the closest thing to the real artifact. For me it's not so much the story you're watching, it's about the format, the experience. It has to be as close to the original as possible. Even if it's several generations away, you're seeing the same shadows that were there on the set that day. A DVD's great, but I know I'm watching reconstituted imagery, and it takes me a little further away, no matter how clear it is."

Hillary was born in 1964 in Lebanon, Pennsylvania, part of the Pennsylvania Dutch Country, an area rich in antique stores, auctions, and estate sales. "There were a lot of antiques around the house," she recalls of her childhood. "I was infused with this sense that the world didn't begin when I was born." Her first film purchase was by serendipity: "One time we were at an antique market in Adamstown, Pennsylvania. There was a small, small reel for a toy projector. It was 35mm, and it was for the little Keystone hand-cranked projector." The tiny reel contained clips from a Krazy Kat cartoon, a Charlie Chaplin comedy, and footage of Charles Lindbergh, but unfortunately it had a bad splice. So she turned for help to a much older and somewhat eccentric local figure, the man who would spark her lifelong interest in collecting.

"In our neighborhood, about a block and a half away, there was a little movie theater," she remembers. "Everybody in the neighborhood knew about this theater. They assumed it was built out of a garage, but I later found out the man built it purposely as a movie theater." He was a local collector and exhibitor named John Stegmoyer. In surviving photos he looks something like my own steelworker grandfather: he's wearing a thick red-and-black plaid shirt so typical of the Pennsylvania woods and has a deeply lined face and somewhat guarded eyes. At his makeshift neighborhood cinema, Stegmoyer would run Elvis Presley movies or the latest James Bond film with a Three Stooges short and a cartoon, all for half a buck. One screening stays with her to this day: "He showed *I Shot Jesse James*. I think it was Samuel Fuller's first movie. Stegmoyer said, 'The song you hear in it, "The Ballad of Jesse James," it wasn't made for the movie. It was actually quite old.' That's when 'Steggie' played his own vintage Edison cylinder recording of the song on the antique phonograph he had in the theater by the screen. That made such an impression on me. And again, he did it for ten-year-old and twelve-year-old kids. I don't know how many remember that, but I can remember it as clear as day. The connection, it put everything in context. I thought, 'Wow, he's doing this for a bunch of kids just because he cares that much.' You had to appreciate that."

Barely in her teens, Hillary brought her 35mm reel with the bad splice to Stegmoyer. "He said later, 'I couldn't believe this little girl was bringing up a film for me to fix,'" she remembers. It was the beginning of an important friendship. "As time went on we talked. When I was in high school, he said, 'You know, I have a bunch of friends.'" Through Stegmoyer, Hillary was introduced to an all-male circle of collectors in the area, men who were at least as old as her father, and many of whom had served in WWII and Korea. "A couple of them were projectionists during the war, in their unit, on their ship. That's probably how they got interested in it.

Those are the ones who hosted the movie parties, the gang accumulated the other members from co-workers and word-of-mouth," she observes. From her descriptions of the gatherings, they sound like pretty masculine affairs. "There was a lot of drinking beer and smoking while watching the movies," she admits with a laugh. When I ask if she was the only woman at these gatherings, she replies, "Sometimes the wives would come to watch something." I try to picture a teenaged Hillary among these older WWII-generation film buffs with their Pabst beers and their unfiltered Lucky Strikes—and it's a strange picture indeed. But she insists she always felt at home: "During the holidays, for instance, one person would show *White Christmas*, and the whole family would come in. It was always a family thing. There was never any competition or condescension among these people. They were really glad to have more people to watch their movies." It's obviously that very welcoming spirit of inclusion that she and her husband have continued with their own basement cinema.

She studied film history and production at Penn State but after college decided that a career in the movie business wasn't for her. "I found that I actually enjoyed the exhibition of movies more than the making of them," she readily admits now. Through her mentor Stegmoyer (who has since passed away), she was introduced to magazines like *Movie Collector's World* and began modestly, buying 35mm trailers of films starring her idol Marilyn Monroe, like *The Misfits* and *Gentlemen Prefer Blondes*. "I figured the movie itself was about the best collectible you could get of a movie star." Once she met her future husband, John, and they found a home for their Simplex E7s, she began acquiring more and more film. I ask if she has any favorites among her collection of oddities. "John would vehemently disagree with me, but one of my favorite films is *A*P*E* in 3-D," she responds without a moment's hesitation. "It's a Korean film that came out in 1976 to capitalize on the remake of *King Kong* by Dino De Laurentiis. In some places, *A*P*E* was called *Nuevo King Kong*; it's *Super King Kong* in Asia. See the poster online, because it shows the ape holding a shark, and it says, 'See Ape fight Deadly Jaws!' It's a rip-off of *Jaws* on top of everything else. The poster is part of the enjoyment of the movie. I tell people, 'Look at this poster, and tell me if the movie delivers everything the poster promises.' It's in 3-D, that's what got me. It's the famous movie where the gorilla gives the helicopters the finger. It's so horrible but it's so funny."

"Maybe I'm just like a contrarian," she says about her fondness for ou-tré and bizarre cinema. "When people think of old movies, they think of films like *Casablanca*. When I seek out stuff, I seek out the really oddball. Sometimes the worse, the better for me." She pauses for a moment, then continues. "That came from my friend John Stegmoyer. He said, 'Every movie is worth watching.' To some point I can understand what he meant. I would give every movie at least one chance. Somebody worked hard on it somewhere." She and her husband have slowed down their collecting somewhat, although she continues to buy 16mm prints off eBay, most recently *Mr. Dynamite*, a forgotten 1941 programmer starring Lloyd Nolan as a ballplayer who tangles with Nazi saboteurs, and ironically, the Dick Contino–starring juvenile delinquent picture *Daddy-O* that fellow collec-tor Joe Dante succinctly calls "a turkey." "May you unhinge your jaw laugh-ing at that!" she says admiringly of *Daddy-O*. As the conversation wraps up, I ask again if she has any thoughts on being one of the few women in the collecting subculture. "I only know of one woman who's my age who's as obsessed with old movies," she confirms, then adds: "I can't give you an actual reason why the content itself should have such a gender bias. Maybe it's the same reason why guys like old cars, because they want to revisit their youth. They go for the cars they couldn't get when they were kids!"

14.

Captain Ahab and the Triffids

In Herman Melville's magnificent *Moby-Dick*, still arguably the greatest and most profound novel in the English language, and one instantly familiar to generations of befuddled high school students (like me) who grappled with its ornate language and cosmic themes, the book's ferocious antihero finds himself possessed by a singular, literally monstrous obsession. It's an obsession that propels him and the crew of the *Pequod* on to their eventual fate. As Ahab says in one of the book's most memorable passages, "Swerve me? The path to my fixed purpose is laid with iron rails, whereon my soul is grooved to run. Over unsounded gorges, through the rifled hearts of mountains, under torrents' beds, unerringly I rush!" The mad purity of Ahab's purpose is breathtaking. At the very end, as the white whale is destroying his ship, he fights on, crying, "To the last I grapple with thee; from hell's heart I stab at thee; for hate's sake I spit my last breath at thee." If this passage is familiar, it's probably not from *Moby-Dick*, though. More people know it today from the sci-fi movie *Star Trek II: The Wrath of Khan* (1982), quoted by Ricardo Montalban's dying, defiant Khan as he attempts to kill Captain Kirk.

Many collectors are associated with a certain type or genre of film, but mention restoration expert Mike Hyatt's name, and you will almost invariably hear this: "*The Day of the Triffids*." It's his torment and his pleasure, a more-than-thirty-year odyssey that occupies roughly the same place in his life that the whale occupied in Ahab's. This comparison may sound far-fetched, but it's not. For over three decades Mike—who has worked for a number of now-vanished film labs in L.A. and assisted on the restorations of *Spartacus* and *My Fair Lady*—has waged a lonely one-man battle to preserve and restore this particular movie, at all costs. For those who aren't familiar with it, *The Day of the Triffids* is a thoughtful and still-engrossing 1963 science-fiction film directed by Steve Sekely, based on the postapocalyptic novel by British author John Wyndham. Its plot (which was borrowed from heavily by Danny Boyle's 2002 zombie film *28 Days Later*) revolves around a merchant sailor, played against type by American musical star Howard Keel, who's recovering in a London hospital from eye surgery. He removes his bandages to find that most of the earth's population has been blinded by a freak meteor shower that has also scattered seedlings for voracious, man-eating plants called triffids, which grow to terrifying height. Intercut with Keel's struggle to escape the alien onslaught are scenes of an alcoholic scientist (Kieron Moore) and his long-suffering wife (Janette Scott) trapped in a lighthouse by the triffids; these scenes were directed by an uncredited Freddie Francis and added to the film at the last minute to give it a stronger ending. The triffids themselves may be a little crude by today's visual effects standards, but there's something weirdly beautiful and convincing about their strange, herky-jerky, shuffling movements. The film, like many of the great sci-fi and horror movies of the 1950s and 1960s, has the eerie, somnambulant quality of a waking nightmare. When I ask Mike what about it fascinates him so much, he pauses for a moment: "It has this profound effect on an audience, because it feels like everything is doomed. Everything they've gone through to find a solution has failed. The lovers, who you care about, are in their last moment alive, almost at the brink of suicide. And then there's this unexpected and tremendously moving ending of hope. I've seen people crying in the audience. A lot of people love it, including Tim Burton. There's talk of doing a remake right now."[51]

That said, it may be a little hard to understand someone spending three decades on one movie. When I mention Mike's odyssey to fellow collector Mark Haggard, he responds, "That takes my breath away. I can see doing that for a John Ford film or a Howard Hawks or a William Wyler. But

Day of the Triffids with Howard Keel? If *She Wore a Yellow Ribbon* were in that state, I could see getting caught up for a decade or so. But *Day of the Triffids*? It's just a movie!" Mark's "it's just a movie" may be pretty funny—but there's no reason that *The Day of the Triffids* should be any less important or preservation-worthy than *She Wore a Yellow Ribbon* just because it's a sci-fi film about man-eating plants from outer space. In fact *Triffids* might deserve preservation *more*, because it was made by an independent producer and doesn't have the resources of a major studio to protect it. Would I spend thirty years of my life to save the film? Probably not—but then, I'm not Mike Hyatt.

Mike is medium height with a trim salt-and-pepper beard and red hair just starting to gray at the fringes. If I were casting a movie of *Moby-Dick*, he would not look out of place as a nineteenth-century Nantucket seaman. I've known Mike for a number of years through my former job programming for the American Cinematheque, where he frequently loaned rare sci-fi and horror prints for retrospectives. Like many collectors, he can be very friendly and eloquent, but also remarkably intense. Former film dealer Allan Scott, who hired Mike to work for him at a film rejuvenation facility, bluntly remembers that Mike "got on [his] nerves, he kept chanting all the time," a reference to Mike's passion for Nichiren Buddhism, which he's practiced since the 1970s. Based on the teachings of a thirteenth-century Japanese monk, Nichiren Buddhists believe that, essentially, the Buddha is in all of us, and thus we can all achieve enlightenment in our lifetimes. Mike's interest in Buddhism was inspired, in fact, by cinema. In 1975, to the despair of many film lovers at the time and since, Technicolor shut down its operation making dye-transfer prints. Mike visited the plant the week it shut down with his friend, famed science-fiction author Ray Bradbury. "Dye transfer to me was like being in heaven, the color was so pure," Mike recalls of that bittersweet final visit. "Everybody felt so terrible. At that time, dye-transfer prints were the only prints where the color lasted, because Eastman prints faded. It was a wonderful day, but it was so sad. I was so depressed over it, and that's partially why I started to practice Buddhism. All I could think about anywhere I went is, 'Why are they letting this wonderful thing go away?'"

Mike was born and raised in Los Angeles and grew up just downhill from the famed Ennis House designed by Frank Lloyd Wright and known for its use in Vincent Price's *The House on Haunted Hill* (1959). His mother was a housewife, and his father a cocktail-lounge pianist, who can be seen performing briefly in the 1950 film noir *Between Midnight and Dawn*, with Edmond O'Brien. His first fateful encounter with the film that would change his life was in 1963 when he saw *Triffids* at a matinee at the long-gone Paradise Theater. When his father was late picking him up, he stayed with his brother, eager for a second showing. "That's when I was really impressed. It was as good or better the second time around," Mike remembers clearly. Had his father been on time, who knows if fate would have inseparably linked him and the triffids?

His own interest in film collecting began in the early 1970s when he was running a college film series and couldn't get a print of George Pal's *The Time Machine* to screen. "At that time I decided if I could somehow buy a print from a collector, I'd hang on to it to make it available," Mike says. "That's the thing about collecting, it's really for people who love the movies. It's a custodial thing. You try to keep the print as close to its original condition as possible." He thinks for a moment, then continues, "It became a spiritual thing after a while, because I realized that the movies I loved were not the same as other people loved. For example, your writing partner Jeff loved the musicals. Some friends I knew loved the animated films. That was their responsibility. I loved science fiction and fantasy. That became part of my raison d'être." At the time, he couldn't have imagined that his raison d'être would one day become *The Day of the Triffids*.

"I didn't get involved with *Triffids* initially as preservation," he says now, looking back on a quest that's absorbed much of his life. Around 1975 he simply wanted to find a print of the film to screen at Louis Federici's Encore Theatre revival house but discovered there were none available. He tracked down the film's executive producer, Philip Yordan, to whom the film's rights had reverted. At the same time he also befriended the director, Steve Sekely. It was, he observes, "a spiritual synchronicity of being in the right place at the right time." Sekely loved the film but openly wished some shots were better. "Most of the effects were terrific, but money and time kept others from being finished correctly," Mike says. He began thinking more and more about the movie. "I thought the film was still powerful and solid, but contemporary viewers would have a hard time forgiving those shots. I thought, 'There must be a way to make this movie fly with a modern audience.' And then, 'What if those shots were improved and made to look as if they had been there all along?' The rationale came from reading Truffaut's book on Hitchcock, as the master discussed the context and collective value of each image."

It was this relatively benign idea to improve some of the visual-effects shots that led him down a slippery slope. By 1982 Yordan confirmed that he'd sold his interest in the film to its original writer, Bernard Gordon, and his then-partner, Richard Rosenfeld. Gordon was a prolific scenarist who'd been blacklisted in the 1950s and forced to write under the pseudonym "Raymond T. Marcus" on films including *Earth vs. the Flying Saucers* and *Zombies of Mora Tau*. He spent years in the shadow of Yordan, working for him on films such as *Circus World*, while Yordan took on-screen credit. (After Gordon's death in 2007, he was posthumously granted sole writing credit on *The Day of the Triffids*, which had previously been credited to Yordan.) Mike made a presentation with storyboards and drawings of his ideas, and Gordon and Rosenfeld sparked to the notion of improving the visual effects and overhauling the film for a contemporary rerelease. But in the middle of discussions, Gordon decided he and his partner wanted to make their money more quickly: "Bernie was bitter at the blacklist and having been denied his *Triffids* credit. He also felt he'd been cheated and brushed aside by the film community. So he was now trying his hand as an entrepreneur." Gordon decided to release the film on home video, but because a single sale couldn't generate enough money, he devised a plan to sell a number of legitimate but time-limited, nonexclusive licenses to a group of paying (but substandard) VHS labels. Mike was dumbstruck: "I told Bernie, 'You're muddying the public's perception of the film and ruining its chances for a rerelease.'" Some of the budget video labels carried public domain titles, and although *The Day of the Triffids* was copyrighted and properly renewed, this caused some people to mistakenly think the film was in the public domain, too—and cheap. "Hyatt, you're interfering!" Gordon shot back when Mike warned him his plan would devalue the film. "Keep in mind that Bernie was the person who wrote the film— probably his best work. And now he was forced to show a financial return on an investment. The years of suffering only made him more cynical. At that point the film's reputation meant less than the money it could immediately generate. So we had a fight and a huge falling-out," Mike recalls sadly. It should have spelled the end of his interest in the film on a professional level, but it didn't. Twelve years later he reapproached Gordon, who'd softened since their falling-out. Mike's career had advanced in the field of film restoration, and he'd just completed work on *My Fair Lady* with preservationist Robert Harris. To Mike's surprise, Gordon gave him access to the original 35mm negative of *Triffids*, but what he discovered was sad: "It was falling apart. It also had thousands of specks of embedded dirt throughout from a treatment performed in a release to laserdisc home video. The dirt translates as minus-density spots. These are pure white specks that appear like little stars. It creates a wall, a psychological block between the audience and the film, because you become aware of these spots." Mike was brought on to work on a restoration. He was made a partner in lieu of payment, for one dollar.

Seeing the sorry condition of the original camera negative seems to have set the hook deep in Mike's psyche. The film's distributors had run over 150 release prints directly off the negative. "It's a miracle it survived without losing footage," he observes. In the middle of repairing the film, he got a call from Gordon, who'd sold his rights to his partner Rosenfeld. But Rosenfeld was in turn short on cash and was now offering him some rights on *Triffids*. "I basically took all the money I had out of the bank and bought these rights, which were for North American theatrical and home video, from Richard," he recalls about that fateful decision. "Now I was involved in a restoration not just because I loved the movie, but because I owned it, too. The rights enabled me to restore and release it however I saw fit."

What he didn't know at the time was that he hadn't clearly bought the film. Unknown to Mike, Rosenfeld had previously sold an option agreement on a package of films, including *Triffids*, to a well-known Dutch distributor named Jan Willem Bosman Jansen. Bosman Jansen showed up unexpectedly one day at the lab where Mike was working, demanding his *Triffids* negative. Words passed between them, and Mike hired an attorney. After a three-year legal battle, he and Bosman Jansen settled out of court, with Mike retaining the rights he originally purchased. "The legal battle was never acrimonious. The great thing about Jan Willem was his ability to see past the troubles. Once we settled, we became friends. He then made me restoration supervisor on all the films in his library," he says.

The legal battle to hold on to *Triffids* was small potatoes compared to the actual restoration of the film negative. More than anything, it's this dogged, single-handed mission that has inextricably linked Mike and the film in the minds of other collectors worldwide. "I returned to working heavily on the film in 2004," he says about the unbelievably arduous and painstaking process of manually removing the stuck-on dirt. Nowadays it's work that would be done completely digitally, with a restoration expert sitting at a computer workstation, but not in Mike's case. His description of the process is lengthy but well worth reading: "I'd had training working on *A Hard Day's Night*, *Tom Jones*, *Sweet Smell of Success*, and *The Great Escape*, removing dirt by hand. I developed this technique using a jeweler's loupe and a needle, and using a recent print of the film as a guide to where the specks were. I'd line up the original camera negative with a frame counter on a bench, and then using the recent print on a Moviola, I'd wind down to the frame and very gingerly, holding my breath, pick the dirt out of the negative, which is the only way it would come out. There were so many specks on each frame that I had to break down the image on the Moviola into an imaginary sixteen areas: four down and four across to find each speck on each shot, and I would run from the beginning of the shot to the end of the shot focused on that one area, and then go back to the beginning of the shot focused on the next area. Each time I ran across a speck, I'd return to the negative, gently wind it down to the correct frame, locate it with the loupe, and gingerly pick it out. So each shot in the film was reviewed sixteen times on that Moviola. There are maybe a thousand shots in the film, I've never counted the number. I estimate I must've removed over twenty thousand specks from the one negative of *Triffids*. Maybe as many as thirty thousand specks."

Imagine for a moment sitting by your lonesome at an editing bench, gently handling the fragile, already deteriorated negative of *The Day of the Triffids*. You're examining each teeny-tiny frame through a jeweler's magnifying loupe, and plucking out infinitesimally small specks of dirt with a needle.

Then imagine doing this *for years and years*. It's work that seems to belong to another age, like a medieval monk copying an illustrated manuscript by candlelight.

"It produced an absolutely perfect image. Flawless," Mike says. When Jeff asks how much he's spent total on his quest to preserve and restore *Triffids*, he thinks for a moment, then sighs, "Over one hundred thousand dollars." It's an investment that he will likely never see back, but it should be obvious by now that he didn't do it for the money. His restored version of *The Day of the Triffids* screened to great acclaim at the Turner Classic Movies Film Festival in 2009 in Hollywood and at the Museum of Modern Art in 2010 in New York City. "People were amazed at the power of the film and that the color is so beautiful. It looks like IB Tech," he says with pride.

Jeff asks if after all this time and effort Mike is finally finished with *Triffids*. He shakes his head. It goes without saying that he will most likely never be done with the movie, nor the movie with him. In April of 2014, after this interview, Mike bought the rest of the North American rights to the film. Later, in October, he purchased all the worldwide rights to *Triffids*, with the exception of five countries owned by the BBC. Because of advancements in digital technology, he plans to travel to Poland to scan the film at 4K resolution and complete the restoration, replacing missing frames and reregistering cut-in dissolves more accurately than ever. Unfortunately, this will also mean losing the expensive color timing, and in many ways, it means going back and beginning again.

Was it all worth it? "Absolutely," says Mike. "Now anyone will have a chance to own their own copy of this film looking and sounding exactly as created, and it will be even better than that. Both versions will be available: the original, perfected, and the alternate, improved. It will be the kind of movie that families can share together at holidays. Everyone should have a love they can complete. Mine is the luckiest I can think of: something that moved me as a kid will one day enable me to leave behind a special message of faith and hope. In my own way it makes this world a better place. When it comes down to it, what's better than that?" It's a grand and optimistic thought, that a single film could make the world a better place—and it's also clear that his obsession with the movie continues, undimmed. It's hard not to think that they are bound together now, like Ahab and the whale. Mike Hyatt and the triffids. Melville's words come back to haunt me, out of the mouth of the great captain himself: "They think me mad—Starbuck does; but I'm demoniac, I am madness maddened! That wild madness that's only calm to comprehend itself!"

Evan H. Foreman, owner of 16mm Filmland, shooting home movies in the early 1960s in Mobile, Alabama. (Photo credit: Howell Foreman.)

A boy's treasures: Leonard Maltin cradles the fragile cardboard covers to *Oswald the Rabbit* and *Dick & Larry* cartoon shorts, part of the disappearing ephemera of film collecting. (Photo credit: Dennis Bartok.)

FBI Seizes Films From Actor

BY ROBERT RAWITCH
Times Staff Writer

FBI agents have seized from actor Roddy McDowall more than 500 copies of motion pictures and television shows as a part of a federal crackdown on the multi-million-dollar film piracy industry, The Times has learned.

The films and television shows were seized Dec. 18, after the FBI was granted a search warrant of Mc-Dowall's North Hollywood home, court records revealed Thursday.

In an affidavit filed with a U.S. magistrate to justify the warrant, FBI agent Theodore J. Bowler stated that the actor admitted in an interview that he had bought an unspecified number of films from Ray Atherton.

The FBI has identified Atherton as a "large scale dealer in the purchase and sale of illegally produced or stolen major motion pictures."

Bowler also stated that McDowall, 46, is suspected of attempting to sell a portion of his film collection through Atherton and Ray Henry Wagner of Northridge. Wagner is described by the FBI as an associate of

Roddy McDowall

Atherton and a dealer in stolen or illegally produced motion pictures.

Efforts to reach McDowall for comment on the seizure of his film collection failed. Neither he nor his attorney returned The Times' calls.

Federal authorities first learned of

McDowall's extensive film and video cassette collection from an informant who said he had seen a list of films McDowall was attempting to sell through Atherton.

A copy of the reported list was seized in a raid on Wagner's home Sept. 6.

A second FBI source in December bought a motion picture from Atherton and the check the source used to pay for it was endorsed by "R. A. Mc-Dowall," the affidavit stated.

In an interview with the FBI Nov. 29, McDowall said he had purchased films from Atherton. But when asked if he had ever sold films through Atherton, the affidavit states, "Mc-Dowall advised that this investigation obviously had very serious ramifications and he declined to provide any further information."

Simple possession of material that infringes federal copyright laws is a civil violation, but willful infringement for profit is a misdemeanor punishable by up to one year in jail on each count.

Asst. U.S. Atty. Chester Brown, who

Please Turn to Page 6, Col. 4

FBI SEIZES 500 FILMS FROM RODDY M'DOWALL

Continued from First Page

is heading the federal grand jury investigation into film piracy, said he could not comment on the McDowall matter. But it is known that McDowall has not appeared before the grand jury.

Among the films and cassettes seized from the actor's garage were his own first pictures—"Lassie Come Home" and "My Friend Flicka"—and his most recent efforts, the "Planet of the Ape" series.

Also seized, however, were more modern films like "Dirty Mary and Crazy Larry," and a host of comedy and dramatic television shows from

"Maude" to "Henry Fonda as Clarence Darrow."

Los Angeles
Times
CC   PART II
FRIDAY, JANUARY 17, 1975

January 17, 1975: *Planet of the Apes* star Roddy McDowall's FBI arrest makes the *Los Angeles Times*, setting off a wave of paranoia in the collecting and dealing subculture that lingers to this day.

Ken Kramer, in the mid-1960s.
(Photo credit: Lauren Jones-Joseph.)

Jeff Joseph (left) and Ken Kramer
stand outside the nondescript
entrance to Kramer's magical office/
theater/museum, the Clip Joint.
(Photo credit: Dennis Bartok.)

Caught in a candid moment, Jeff
Joseph (right) looks at the stack of
prints recently acquired by his one-
time partner, friend, and rival, Ken
Kramer (left). (Photo credit: Dennis
Bartok.)

Ken Kramer operating the 16mm projector at the Clip Joint for the Tuesday Night Film Club. (Photo credit: Dennis Bartok.)

The view from Ken Kramer's desk. (Photo credit: Dennis Bartok.)

Ken Kramer's private film archive, one of the finest in the United States. (Photo credit: Dennis Bartok.)

Turner Classic Movies host, journalist, historian and collector Robert Osborne. (Photo credit: Turner Classic Movies, courtesy of Robert Osborne.)

Former film and sports memorabilia dealer Al Beardsley, photographed at the Windsor Palms Care facility in Artesia, California. (Photo credit: Dennis Bartok.)

Choreographer and collector Craig Call. (Photo credit: Dennis Bartok.)

A rare image from 2007 of former Broadway "gypsy" Tony Turano, who disliked having his photo taken. (Photo credit: Hebe Tabachnik.)

Film and medicine bottles: the reality of Tony Turano's life at the time he was interviewed for this book. (Photo credit: Dennis Bartok.)

Gremlins and *The Howling* director Joe Dante discussing his lifelong passion for film collecting at his Hollywood office. (Photo credit: Dennis Bartok.)

RoboCop producer Jon Davison, who enthusiastically believes this is a golden age for film
collecting. (Photo credit: Dennis Bartok.)

Peter Dyck at his home in Inglewood, California. (Photo
credit: Dennis Bartok.)

Peter Dyck clutches a yellowed copy of the
Los Angeles Times from May 1975, with the
infamous "U.S. Indicts 16 in Movie, TV Film Pirating Case" headline. He and author Jeff Joseph
were among those charged in the case. (Photo
credit: Dennis Bartok.)

Woody Wise and Ray Atherton (right),
who were among the 16 dealers
indicted on film piracy charges in
1975 by the U.S. Justice Department.
(Photo credit: Woody Wise.)

The House of Clocks. (Photo credit: Dennis Bartok.)

Rusted film cans, from Peter Dyck's collection. (Photo credit: Dennis Bartok.)

Rik Lueras, one of the only Latino collectors in the homogeneous underground community. (Photo credit: Dennis Bartok.)

Film historian and restoration expert Patrick Stanbury. (Photo credit: Dennis Bartok.)

Beautifully decorated film cans: objets d'art in their own right. Part of Rik Lueras's superb collection of 35mm prints. (Photo credit: Dennis Bartok.)

With his ever-present flashlight Kevin Brownlow tries to identify the maker of a vintage film light belonging to author Dennis Bartok. (Photo credit: Dennis Bartok.)

French preservationist Serge Bromberg of Lobster Films. (Photo credit: Serge Bromberg.)

Hillary Hess with one of her 35mm projectors in the background. (Photo credit: Mike Zortman)

Mike Hyatt, the man who's devoted more than three decades to saving a single film, the 1963 sci-fi classic *The Day of the Triffids*. (Photo credit: Dennis Bartok.)

Something Weird Video founder Mike Vraney (center) with arms around two of his exploitation heroes, producer David F. Friedman (left) and distributor Dan Sonney. (Photo courtesy of Mike Vraney.)

Paul Rayton, head projectionist at the Egyptian Theatre. (Photo credit: Dennis Bartok.)

Mike Schleiger demonstrates the quickly vanishing skill of film handling and preparation. (Photo credit: Dennis Bartok.)

Matt Spero in his home film vault. (Photo credit: Dennis Bartok.)

The interior of Matt Spero's home theater. Many of the decorations were salvaged from former movie palaces that were being demolished. (Photo credit: Matt Spero.)

Former projectionist and die-hard union officer Lee Sanders. (Photo credit: Dennis Bartok.)

Mike Schleiger holds two carbon rods in each hand to illustrate how movie projectors at one point used them to create a brilliant carbon arc light. The rods burned down quickly and had to be replaced often, though. When carbon arc projectors became obsolete, the role of the projectionist was greatly reduced. (Photo credit: Dennis Bartok.)

Jeff Joseph stands inside the cavernous interior of the former Gilboy depot, where he once took part in the ultimate film collector "score": a warehouse of prints abandoned by its owner. (Photo credit: Dennis Bartok.)

Brian LeGrady, who also took part in the Gilboy "score." (Photo credit: Dennis Bartok.)

Phil Blankenship stands next to a wall of VHS tapes in his Hollywood apartment. Part of the younger generation keeping collecting alive, he's assembled over seven hundred horror, sci-fi, and grindhouse prints, including rare treasures like 35mm copies of Dario Argento's 1982 giallo *Tenebrae* and George Romero's 1978 zombie classic *Dawn of the Dead*. (Photo credit: Dennis Bartok.)

Every film collector's holy grail: a frame from Tod Browning's long-lost 1927 horror film *London After Midnight*. But is it real? Ask collector Jack Theakston. (Photo credit: Jack Theakston.)

Jack Theakston in a typical pose: inspecting film. (Photo credit: Jack Theakston.)

Mike Williamson, who continues to keep the tradition of 16mm backyard screenings alive at his Burbank, California, home. (Photo credit: Dennis Bartok.)

Jeff Joseph holding the January 11, 1975, *Los Angeles Times*. (Photo credit: Dennis Bartok.)

Longtime friends and rivals Ken Kramer (left) and Jeff Joseph in 1972, when they were briefly partners in the film trade. (Photo credit: Lauren Jones-Joseph, courtesy of Jeff Joseph.)

Jeff Joseph in 1974, aged twenty, shortly before he was charged with illegally selling film prints. He's holding his margay, Sabu, who would later inspire the name of his film company, SabuCat. (Photo courtesy of Jeff Joseph.)

Future collector and radio deejay Jim Zippo in 1962, aged nine, proudly clutching home movie editions of *Rodan* and *Abbott and Costello Meet Frankenstein*. (Photo credit: Franklin M. Pollitt, courtesy James G. Pollitt.)

Author Dennis Bartok. (Photo credit: Marja Adriance, courtesy of Dennis Bartok.)

A dumpster filled with junked 16mm projectors. (Photo credit: Steve Newton.)

15.

Something Weird

"I know I have the largest sexploitation archive on earth. Not just the commercial value of it, but in the collector sense," says home video distributor and film collector Mike Vraney. For nearly twenty-five years, Vraney's company Something Weird Video has plumbed the incredibly strange and sleazy netherworld of mostly forgotten sexploitation films, including such subterranean subgenres as nudie cuties, nudie roughies, nudist colony films, and white-coaters. A visit to Something Weird's website brings up choice titles like *Nude on the Moon*, *Olga's House of Shame*, *Shanty Tramp*, and *The Curse of Her Flesh*. The sheer volume of obscure films that Vraney has rereleased—over 2,500—coupled with his support of neglected grindhouse auteurs like gore-meister Herschell Gordon Lewis (*Blood Feast*, *Two Thousand Maniacs!*), subversive softcore queen Doris Wishman (*Double Agent 73*, *Deadly Weapons*), and producers David F. Friedman (*The Defilers*) and Harry H. Novak (*The Agony of Love*), is fairly amazing. These are orphan films in the truest sense of the word: bastard cinema that was made to pry money out of people's pockets and then to be discarded, lost and forgotten, if not for someone like Vraney. If you're a cinephile, it's easy to get excited about the rediscovery of the lost 1912 silent *Richard III* or the missing footage from Fritz Lang's *Metropolis*, but how about Friedman's *She Freak* or Lewis's *Scum of the Earth*? These are exploitation movies that still *feel* like exploitation: crude and rude, with the stench of the peepshow clinging to them.

I ask Vraney what it is about sexploitation films that so appeals to him, given that he's devoted much of his adult life to these movies. "Number one, they were plot driven. They're not like pornography of the 1970s, which have like zero plot," he answers without hesitation. "These men thought they had to actually *make a movie*. The other interesting thing is they were shot in four, five, six days, tops. So whatever fad was going that week, say, the Hula Hoop, would show up in that movie."

Vraney is tall, gregarious, and good-looking, with shaggy sandy-colored hair just starting to go gray at the edges, and an unabashed love for all things involving punk rock, comic books, movies, and naked women. "The girls were wonderful, lots of beehive hairdos, sexy underwear, sexy lingeries," he says enthusiastically. "The one thing that my collectors love more than anything is a big hairy bush, and that whole giant underwear and nylons and hose and garters. Because for the last twenty years, everybody is hairless—they look like aliens." He's well aware that even in the underground world of film collecting, he's in something of a class by himself. When I mention that he's one of the last collectors we're interviewing, he gives an appreciative laugh: "It makes me feel like I'm at the bottom of the barrel—or below the barrel. It's okay, because what I specialize in is under the barrel as well, which I'm very proud of. I wasn't out there trying to collect the classics, or preserve or find *Gone With the Wind*'s missing footage." He's proud to be, as he describes it, a "film scavenger."

A longtime resident of Seattle, Washington, Vraney was born there in 1957. His father was an engineer for NASA and Boeing who worked on both the Saturn V, the rocket that carried man to the moon, and the classic Boeing 747 airliner. "I grew up during the 1960s when *Laugh-In*, all these things, made reference to dirty movies, the sexual revolution," he recalls. "My father belonged to the Playboy Club in the 1960s, and we had *Playboy* magazines around the house. I remember one time my parents put on a *Playboy*-themed party where my mother pulled out all the centerfolds and pinned them to the walls, then stuck little doilies over the naughty parts, so when everybody got drunk, they'd pull the doilies off and go 'ha-ha-ha.'" He clearly inherited his unapologetic love of nude women from his dad. Vraney recalls that when he told his father in the late 1980s of his plans to become king of the sexploitation movies, "all he said was, 'sex sells.' So I got a free pass from my dad to do this."

Mature-looking for his age, Vraney snuck into his first porn film, Alex de Renzy's *A History of the Blue Movie*, in the early 1970s, when he was barely in his teens. "I was tall with a light mustache, so nobody questioned me," Vraney says. But his first love wasn't nudie films, but comic books, which he began selling as a business while still in high school. Soon he became friends with a collector of Bela Lugosi films, Michael Copner (later publisher of *Cult Movies* magazine), who worked as a projectionist at several porn theaters in Seattle, including the New Paris Follies and the Mecca Twin. Copner would sneak him into the movies for free, and he started attending porn shows "religiously," as he says. I ask if he remembers any of the titles he saw in those long-gone days of adult cinema, and he nods, mentioning *Behind the Green Door* and a wildly obscene film called *Long Jeanne Silver* (1977), starring an amputee sex actress who used her stump to penetrate her partners.[52] "It was like going to the freak show," Vraney admits about his early exposure to porn. Soon after, he bought his first 16mm projector and his first batch of movies, a box of ten-minute "girlie loops" at an auction from a closed-down Washington theater. Almost inevitably, he started working as a porn-theater projectionist himself. "I begged the owner of the porno theaters for a job," he says frankly. "I was underage, and he put me in Seattle's only 16mm storefront house, called the Sultan Theatre. I remember the first movie I ran was *Centurians of Rome*. So here I am in this porno theater, a gay house. I was thrilled because I was running film; that's all I cared about." Around the same time he took over the lease on a 1,500-seat Seattle venue, the Showbox theater, and began staging rock shows, including Iggy Pop and the Police. Soon he began booking and managing punk bands, including TSOL, Flipper, Bad Brains, and the Dead Kennedys, and would often screen his collection of girlie loops between bands. "I learned if you showed a film in between sets, there'd be no fights. Because everybody'd be staring at the film," he says with a shrug.

In the mid-1980s he continued collecting, mostly 16mm prints of old AIP and Universal horror and sci-fi flicks, but he found himself increasingly fascinated by the forgotten sexploitation films of the 1940s to 1970s, in part inspired by books like V. Vale's *Incredibly Strange Films* (1985) and Michael Wheldon's *The Psychotronic Encyclopedia of Film* (1987). After getting out of the punk rock scene booking bands, he made a life-changing decision in 1988: "I decided I was going to be a video bootlegger, because it was obvious to me that the major studios were not putting out what us collectors wanted to see." Through *The Big Reel* magazine, he contacted a Texas dealer named J. G. Nelson who was advertising 16mm and 35mm prints of mondo-obscure sexploitation features for sale. Vraney bought ten features from him, including *Naughty Dallas*, *The Weird Lovemakers*, *Kitten in a Cage*, and *Hotter After Dark*, and after finding someone in L.A. to do film-to-tape transfers for him, he set himself up in the video business. Inspired by a 1967 Herschell Gordon Lewis movie of the same name, he decided to call his bootleg tape operation "Something Weird."

In 1989 he made the kind of discovery that collectors only dream about: "I got a phone call from a friend. He told me about an antique shop about thirty miles from my house, and in the back were boxes and boxes, all girlie material, from nudies to burlesque, women's wrestling, bondage." The back room of the Everett, Washington, antique store was filled with hundreds of original negatives for lost sexploitation films from the 1930s to the 1950s, with titles like *Nautical Nudes*, *Saucy Sue*, and *Tea for Two*. Vraney paid the owner two hundred dollars for the treasure trove, filled a van and drove off. Soon, the newly launched Something Weird Video label was releasing these strange and forgotten movies in packages like "Wrasslin' She Babes," "Grindhouse Follies," and "Bizarre-O Sex Loops." Although Vraney obviously loved the nudie content, it was the fact that these movies had been abandoned and neglected that truly appealed to him: "I was fanatical on finding lost films," he says emphatically.

Of all the carny-like showmen and grindhouse auteurs that Vraney has come across, the one he's fondest of is David F. Friedman. Friedman (who passed away in 2011) is best known today as producer of Herschell Gordon Lewis's seminal, gore-filled *Blood Feast* (1963) and *Two Thousand Maniacs!* (1964), along with later drive-in gems like *The Defilers* (1965) and *Ilsa: She Wolf of the SS* (1975).[53] His work was larely unseen and ignored when he called Vraney in the early 1990s to complain that Something Weird was illegally bootlegging his 1969 erotic flick *The Ribald Adventures of Robin Hood*. He and Vraney soon became close friends, the forgotten exploitation guru and the young punk-rock bootlegger, and Friedman kept dropping tantalizing hints about his secret cache of original negatives. "He kept telling me about his film vault on Cordova Street. It's old Film Row in downtown Los Angeles, where all the exploitation guys were in the 1940s, 1950s, 1960s into the 1970s," Vraney remembers. "I said, 'I want to put out your movies." He said, 'Kid, nobody wants to see my movies, because they're not hardcore.' I said, 'There's collectors who want to see them.'" Friedman finally relented and opened his vault to Vraney, telling him he could pick out ten movies he wanted to rerelease. "I picked out *The Defilers, Mr. Peters' Pets*. The last movie I asked about was *Space Thing*—I said, 'What's this *Space Thing*?' Friedman said, 'Oh, that's the worst science fiction movie ever made. If Ed Wood hadn't made *Plan 9 from Outer Space*, I'd be more famous than Ed Wood because it's so awful.' I said to him, 'I have to have that movie.'" He managed to land a deal with the two largest comic book distributors in the country at the time, Capitol and Diamond, figuring his Something Weird videos would appeal to comic book fans. "A few months went by, and I sent Dave Friedman his first check. He called me up and said, 'How the hell did you do that?'" Vraney says, grinning.

Through Friedman he soon met other aging exploitation producers with film libraries, like Dan Sonney (*The Flesh Merchant*) and Harry Novak, a canny but good-hearted character who habitually carried a .38 snub-nosed revolver in his baggy pants. "The first thing Dave said to me is, 'When you shake Harry's hand, make sure you count your fingers after,'" Vraney recalls. "A producer like Dave Friedman or Harry Novak would make a movie for anywhere between $5,000 and $15,000. They'd have the one negative, and they'd strike no more than fifteen prints. They'd give those prints to states' rights men," he says about the long-gone practice of selling films state-by-state. "Dan Sonney had the thirteen western states. There'd be a guy in Atlanta who'd have three or four states; then there was the guy in North or South Carolina, where they had more drive-ins than anywhere in the country. There was a very small print count off of the negative; that's why these movies are so rare." Friedman also helped educate Vraney on the importance of researching and clearing rights for the films he was releasing. Many sexploitation films weren't originally copyrighted, because the producers didn't want to pay the extra cost of making two 35mm prints for the copyright office—and also because of the questionable content of the movies. To this day, Vraney prefers the term "unregistered" to the more common "public domain" when talking about movies with lost or unknown provenance.

Among the many grindhouse treasures he discovered through his friendship with Friedman, one score stands out above all. In 1994 Friedman took Vraney to the abandoned East Coast Movielab, once one of the busiest film labs in New York City. "I end up going to this building and into the basement. It's the size of a football field, floor to ceiling, with racks and racks of negatives," Vraney says, eyes still shining with wonder. I fly back home and toss and turn in bed, thinking to myself, 'I just hit the jackpot. I just saw the largest cache of abandoned films that's ever been around.'" He returned two weeks later, and with the help of his friend, director Frank Henenlotter (*Basket Case*), he started desperately pulling lost negatives off the shelves. "Frank is screaming, 'Do you want *The Monster of Camp Sunshine?*' And I scream back, 'I've never heard of it, but it has "Monster" in it. It must be a nudist movie. I want it!!'" I ask if *The Monster of Camp Sunshine*, a 1964 nudist colony/horror mash-up, turned out to be any good. "It's so awful, there's a reason it was never released. But it's fantastic," Vraney replies. All in all, he and Henenlotter rescued over 130 abandoned negatives from Movielab, including *Way Out Topless*, *Olga's House of Shame*, and a number of director Barry Mahon's films, such as *Crazy Wild and Crazy*, *The Adventures of Busty Brown*, and *Forbidden Flesh*. "Every single one, because it was not available on video, it was considered lost," he says of the once-in-a-lifetime score. "In my mind, every single one was a gem."

Although he talks about sexploitation with a fanboy's enthusiasm, he has in fact spent a great deal of time studying the history and etymology of his favorite genre. "Sexploitation started with guys drinking coffee, Brigitte Bardot, all that crap. They'd be watching these French movies with a little tits and ass. Then Russ Meyer came along with *The Immoral Mr. Teas*, which is just a nudie cutie," he observes. "In 1965 the Supreme Court ruled that full-front nudity was not obscene. Prior to that you could just show tits and ass and guys in their underwear. The term the sexploitation guys had [for full-frontal nudity] was 'pickles and beavers,'" he says, chuckling. "By 1965–1966, with nudist colony films, nudie cuties that held women up on a pedestal, they had gimmicks like 'magic spectacles,' where you put them on and could see a woman nude. That was a gimmick in a lot of movies: a guy would turn invisible and walk into a woman's room to see her naked, or put on X-ray specs. But after 1967 the next genre of movies were nudie roughies that involved nudity but had a lot of violence." The nudie roughies, epitomized by films like Friedman's stark, still-disturbing *The Defilers* and *A Smell of Honey, a Swallow of Brine*, are among Vraney's personal favorites: "Most of these are shot MOS [i.e., without sound], silent with narration, in a very disjointed, surrealist, almost dreamlike way. They're also very forbidden—that's what I love about them," he admits about this most un-PC of subgenres. "The last piece of the puzzle before legal pornography was a group of movies in 1970–1971 called 'white coaters.' They had titles like *Man and Wife, He and She, Black Is Beautiful*. Basically what they were was, a phony doctor in a white coat would be behind a desk, and he'd tell you you're about to see the sixty-nine positions of love." Although Vraney soaked up more than his share of pornography as a teenage projectionist, it's clear that his real interest—at least as far as Something Weird goes—ends with the advent of hardcore films like *Deep Throat* and *Behind the Green Door* in the early 1970s and the death of the strange, sleazy sexploitation genre.

Although he has slowed down buying movies in recent years, he'll still leap at a good deal, most recently twenty titles from a man who'd worked for Alfred Sack of Sack Amusements in Texas, whom Vraney describes as the "cheapest distributor in the whole country—if you made a sexploitation movie and couldn't sell it to anybody else, you could sell it to Alfred Sack." Among the prints he bought were *Strange Confessions*—"a Peeping Tom psychological-sexual movie, which was considered lost"—and *Wild Hippie Orgy*, which Vraney confesses he had to have just based on the title. In 2005, realizing he had acquired literally mountains of film spread out over several warehouses, he began selling some of his prints on eBay. But by his own admission, he barely made a dent in his vast archive. He also, it turns out, had a hard time dealing with his fellow film collectors. "I stopped because film collectors are worse than comic book collectors. They're horrible. 'What kind of film stock is it on? Is it IB Tech, blah blah?'" he says with exasperation.

"I paid royalties regardless of the copyright status. I paid royalties to everybody," he notes about his evolution from video bootlegger to (almost) respectable businessman and, yes, film preservationist and champion of a long-forgotten genre. "Dave Friedman always said to me, 'If you do this legit and honest, you never have to look over your shoulder.'" He pauses for a moment, considering his own place in film history. "I figure years to come from now, I get that little niche in history: there was this joker, and he really loved sexploitation, and he saved literally hundreds and hundreds of movies that would've been destroyed if it wasn't for his passion."

16.

The Theory of Creative Destruction

Although most of the collectors and dealers that Jeff and I interviewed focused on film prints—meaning feature films, shorts, and trailers—in fact, there was and still is a vast quantity of 16mm and sometimes 35mm prints of vintage TV shows out there. One of the most remarkable and little-known collections in the United States has been assembled over several decades by a man in Orange County, California, named Ronnie James, whose specialty is vintage TV, including rare kinescopes of live TV broadcasts from the late 1940s and early 1950s, unsold pilots, paper research materials, and more. By his own estimate he has over ten thousand prints, making it arguably the largest private archive of rare TV materials anywhere in the world—and one of the largest private film collections, period.

Prior to the introduction of videotape, most of the television that America watched—including episodes of *I Love Lucy, Gilligan's Island, Big Valley, Gomer Pyle,* and *F Troop,* as well as feature films and commercials—was broadcast off of prints at the local TV station. Anyone of a certain age will remember those "Please Wait: We Are Experiencing Technical Difficulties" messages that sometimes popped up on-screen. That's what happened when the print broke or tore a splice, and the underpaid operator running it slapped that sign up while he was frantically trying to fix the print and get it on-air again. When TV stations across the country converted to videotape in the 1980s and 1990s, a vast quantity of used 16mm prints of old TV episodes and features flooded the underground collectors market. Middlemen were actually paid by the stations to haul these prints away for salvage or destruction; many were sold instead to dealers, who in turn sold them to collectors.[54]

Ronnie's enormous collection is all the more remarkable for being so imperiled: the prints are rarely rented or loaned out these days and sit, unused and unseen, in Ronnie's home, to which he rarely allows visitors. It's an invaluable and literally irreplaceable treasure trove of material that desperately needs to be preserved, but who will buy it? When I mention Ronnie's collection to the head of a major film and TV archive, he shoots back, "Who's going to pay us to store a collection of that size? Is *he* going to pay for the storage?" That attitude, of course, isn't going to convince many collectors to part with their precious materials.

"I'd rather have some other poor fool have the expense and the anchor, the burden of a large collection," Ronnie sighs early in our conversation. Of all the people Jeff and I interviewed, he is perhaps the most thoughtful about the grander implications of being a collector in the digital age, and also the most despondent. "I've found it to be depressing that what was once a viable, large, and important collection has been rendered obsolete. I do not feel any of the joy or excitement that used to come with the collection. It's a dead collection," he says flatly. Several times he repeats a kind of perverse fantasy, that he could travel back in time and warn his five-year-old self *not to start collecting*: "My advice to the five-year-old or six-year-old is, 'Own as little as possible. Own just as much as you can pack into two suitcases.' Much more liberating." The adult Ronnie is now in his mid-sixties, with glasses, a floppy beach hat that hangs down low, and a striped short-sleeve shirt. When he speaks, his voice has a deliberate tone with more than a hint of melancholy. It is, of course, his experiences as a five-year-old that set him on this path. He was born in 1951 and has lived in the same house all his life. As a young boy he'd get home from school, turn on the TV, and sit there enthralled by series like *The Adventures of Superman*, *The Adventures of Kit Carson*, the still-controversial *The Amos 'n Andy Show*, and *The Mickey Mouse Club*.[55] I ask jokingly if he was in love as a boy with Annette Funicello, like the rest of America. "The prettiest Mouseketeer was probably Cheryl Holdridge," he replies.

"That kind of planted the seed for me to become a film collector later on," he observes about his early love for 1950s television. "Because I wanted to see things that I had heard about but could not see." His funds for buying prints were limited, but after discovering magazines like *The Big Reel* and *Movie Collector's World*, he soon realized there was a huge quantity of TV prints being offered for sale at relatively cheap prices, and also that there were few others specializing in this field. "I always tried to acquire things that I recognized as not easily viewable, and that meant old television shows: kinescopes of network TV shows, an odd cartoon or feature or short, but mostly television." Among the rarities in his collection are a 1948 closed-circuit pilot of the *Arthur Godfrey and His Friends* show and the unsold pilot for *The Dick Van Dyke Show,* which was originally titled *Head of the Family*, starring comedian Carl Reiner. "Reiner wrote it and starred in it. It didn't sell; then they reshot it later with Dick Van Dyke," he says about the genesis of the famous sitcom.

"As far as I know, I have the only original 35mm answer print of the pilot for *The Adventures of Superboy*," he says of another rarity, a 1961 prequel series to the famed *The Adventures of Superman*. "The pilot is awful. They commissioned and had thirteen complete shooting scripts for the *Superboy* series. This is the cheapness of DC Comics at the time: they selected the one that would be cheapest to produce."

Although vintage TV isn't normally thought of in terms of stunning cinematography, since many shows were produced on sound stages with limited budgets, I ask if there are any prints in his collection that really stand out in terms of their photography. He pauses for a moment. "I think by a wide margin the best-filmed show on a weekly basis in terms of the quality of the imagery was *Four Star Playhouse*," he says, referring to the excellent and still-underrated anthology series that ran from 1952 through 1956 and featured a rotation of stars, including Dick Powell, David Niven, Ida Lupino, and Charles Boyer, and writers like the young Blake Edwards. "One need only look at the film noir titles, like the *Dante's Inferno* titles starring Dick Powell," Ronnie continues. "The number of set-ups, the lighting look just as good as any noir from the 1940s." Of all the unseen treasures sitting on shelves in Ronnie's garage, the one that arouses my curiosity the most is an unsold pilot from 1956 called *The Ethan Allen Sto-*

ry, starring TV stalwart Rhodes Reason, based on the Revolutionary War hero. It's not the subject or cast that interests me, though. It's the fact that the score was written by the great Bernard Herrmann, who would soon compose the score to Hitchcock's *Vertigo*. I ask what he plans to do with the pilot. "It just sits here. I ran it at a film party a few years ago. That's pretty much it," he shrugs.

As Ronnie's TV collection grew and grew, it started providing a steady income stream for him, licensing footage for documentaries and specials on golden age Hollywood celebrities. (He also supplemented his income for years by making quasi-legal 16mm dupes of Beatles concert footage until the growth of VHS killed that market.) Up until the mid-2000s, he estimates, one 16mm print a day was arriving at his house. Do some simple math, and it's easy to see how he wound up with ten thousand prints in his garage. "I relied on reputation and word of mouth, and I had more business than I could handle at one time," he says. "At one time most of the people who wanted stuff knew that this was one of the best archival TV collections, and they always called." Even when they called, though, it wasn't easy to get Ronnie on the phone. I remember trying to reach him several times in the mid-1990s about renting vintage TV prints for Cinematheque shows, with little luck. Even when Ronnie answered, he could be, to put it mildly, a bit prickly. His reputation doesn't seem to bother him: "One of the biggest dangers to film are film collectors. Film collectors destroy and damage a ton of film, because they're unwilling to do the basics before they do something. Unwilling, lazy, stupid, cheap," he says about his brothers-in-arms.

"In 1995 none of us would have foreseen that film would have been dead in ten years. But film essentially died in 2005. I mean, now we're just going through the motions of burying it altogether," he says about the cataclysmic changes that have nearly overwhelmed him and many other collectors. I ask why he picked the date of 2005. "It just seemed to me that that's pretty much when DVDs and Blu-rays overtook VHS completely. Film collectors were really bailing on their collections," he replies. "A lot of the people that I used to deal with vanished. The demand really started to fall off for film that I had at an accelerating rate." Although almost all the collectors Jeff and I spoke with addressed these changes, Ronnie has what I would call a unique *philosophical* grasp of the death of film collecting.

"Are you familiar with the term *creative destruction*?" he asks. I shake my head no. "*Creative destruction* is a term that was coined in 1942 in a work entitled *Capitalism, Socialism, and Democracy*, by a man named Joseph Schumpeter," he replies. "You can refer to creative destruction either as a paradox, or paradoxical term, an absurd term, a self-contradictory term, or an oxymoron. The theory of Schumpeter's tale of creative destruction is that society creates new things that have an adverse and usually very destructive effect on older things. This is something that's not new, but Schumpeter was the person who actually came up with this theory and coined it. Just as an example, do you know what the number-one primary industry was on the northeast coast of the United States during the 1800s?" Jeff hazards a guess that it was either whaling or clothing. "It was whaling," Ronnie responds. "And the whales were processed—a euphemism for butchered—aboard the whaling ship, and all the different parts of the whale, from the oil to bone, were sold. This is a business that just does not exist anymore. The horse and carriage have been replaced by the automobile. What I didn't realize is, the one part of creative destruction I was blind to—and this is very important—is that creative destruction continually works on at an accelerating basis. Technology keeps developing at a more and more accelerated pace. Look at cell phones: whatever cell phone comes out today is going to be obsolete in a year. But creative destruction has, in more recent years with the development of the computer, more or less destroyed the book industry, the newspaper industry, and changed the way people make phone calls. It has leveled almost all of the used book stores in the United States, brick-and-mortar book stores. You still have people selling books, but you no longer have the brick-and-mortar stores. The computer has by virtue of creative destruction also hurt true research, and the quality of research, and the quality of reporting. It leveled the playing field, so that people without qualification now can be seen on the same level as qualified reporters who have certain standards. It's also hurt *my* research and *my* reference library, because now people just go online and find out things. It's not a question of whether the information is correct or incorrect or supported by any kind of proof. The general public will support anything that is cheapest, fastest, and easiest.

"Creative destruction has destroyed film collecting. It's hurt film preservation and hurt research," he says with a profound sense of hopelessness. In many ways I understand and empathize with his despair. How can you argue with history? I ask if he continues to buy prints, and he responds with a bitter chuckle. "I don't have any more room. The cost. And I'm burned out." Jeff asks if he'd be willing to sell his collection, and Ronnie responds yes, if he could find the right buyer—or any buyer. "I don't want necessarily a lot of money. I just want *some* money. What else am I going to do? I'm over sixty years old."

The obsolescence of Ronnie's 10,000+ print collection is one thing, but there's also the loss of the knowledge that he's built up during fifty years of studying and researching vintage television shows. There is what he calls an "archaeology" to handling old TV prints. "When you have a TV show, is it first-run, is it syndication, has it been reworked in some way? A print of a television show is much more likely to have different versions than a theatrical feature," he points out, then launches into a dizzyingly complicated discussion of A-wind/B-wind TV prints from the 1950s, John D. Maurer soundtracks ("It's kind of a weird cross between a variable-density and area track," he explains), and other minutiae that soon has my head spinning. "It's like a dead language," he says quietly about the obscure facts swimming around his head. "Who can I talk to about the configuration of Ziv production numbers? Ziv was one of the most prominent producers of filmed television programming in the 1950s. It's the last name of the man who founded the company. You'd see the Ziv logo in big letters at the end of *Highway Patrol* and *Sea Hunt*." Ziv production numbers may not mean much to you and me—but it doesn't make them any less important. "You cannot know the history of U.S. television without knowing Ziv," Ronnie insists. "If you don't know the most famous, most productive company from the late 1950s, then you just don't know anything, really."

I ask how Ronnie spends his time these days, and he responds that he does a little research to keep busy, more out of routine than anything else. He recently had his first film rental in many months, licensing a print of an early 1950s show called *Rocket to the Stars* that featured visits to celebrities' houses, in this case the home of Charles Laughton and Elsa Lanchester. He earned seven hundred dollars from the rental. "I'm kind of resigned to the fact that it's going to sit here until I die," he says when I ask if he's considered selling off his vast print and research collection piece by piece on eBay. "I'm just afraid that people would look at my collection and think it's a hoarder's. It's really not a hoarder's collection per se, but that is a fear of mine, that someone will take it for being someone who's collected every soda bottle they could find. That is a sad possibility. I just don't know what to do."

17.

A Thousand Cuts

In 2011 director Michael Bay sent a well-publicized letter to the nation's theater projectionists, imploring them to run his then-current *Transformers: Dark of the Moon* in digital 3-D at "the brightness levels specified for the best results." He went on to add, in a spirit of camaraderie, "We are all in this together. . . . Projectionists are of ultimate importance because your expertise defines the audience's experience." In reality, Bay was pleading with a nearly empty projection booth. Part of the collateral damage of the transition to the digital age is that it's essentially wiped out the job of projectionist. As *Time Out London* observed in a recent article, "Projectionists as we imagine them are on the verge of extinction. This is down to big changes in the world of exhibition: hulking hard drives—to which films are sent digitally—are being installed in cinemas, while tactile, scratchy, buzzing celluloid film prints are being tossed on the scrapheap."[56] Theaters equipped for modern digital projection don't even require a professional projectionist: theater managers can easily "ingest" a Digital Cinema Package onto the server and push "play." No experience required.

"The mantra here, as far as I can tell, is that we'll continue to show film as long as the studios make it available to us," says Paul Rayton, film collector and head projectionist for the Egyptian Theatre in Hollywood, originally built by impresario Sid Grauman in 1922 and reopened by the nonprofit American Cinematheque as their permanent home in 1998. Paul has gray-white hair, glasses, and the spry, excitable temperament of a wizard out of a J.R.R. Tolkien novel. When Jeff and I arrive, he's in his usual semiflustered state, dealing with plugs for a Powerbook presentation for something called "Social Media Week." He's wearing, ironically, a gray T-shirt that says, "Never Forget," with icons of a film reel, unspooled film, and a Goldberg can, although the message may be lost on most of the Social Media Week attendees.

With him is his friend, fellow projectionist, and film collector Michael Schleiger, who has the rangy good looks and deeply lined face of an older Richard Widmark. Together, the two men have projected at nearly every surviving movie palace in the L.A. area (and a good number that are gone), including the famed Chinese Theatre down the block, where Mike was projecting for *Star Wars* in 1977. "When they would go into hyperspace the first time—whoosh!!—I'd turn the sound all the way up," he recalls. "When the Death Star exploded, same thing. During the ending credits, on the original '77 run, I'd change the side lights, very subtly, a little green, a little blue, a little purple. Purple was my favorite." Although most audience members wouldn't consciously notice the changes, these are beautiful examples of how a good projectionist could influence the movie experience. It's an art that is now sadly lost with the change to digital. Both men are past retirement age—"I hit seventy last month. It's a miracle I'm still here," Paul sighs—but continue to practice their craft at the Egyptian because, well, there is almost no one around qualified to replace them. "In 1969 when I came into the Projectionists' Union, there were 650 members of Local 150," observes Mike. "And now there's maybe forty. And of those forty, I'd say only ten, and I'd be really exaggerating if I pushed it up to fifteen, that could come in here and run film."

Lest anyone think that Paul and Mike are film-only Luddites, both men accept that digital is here to stay, and that it may be a good thing in some ways. "This is what did it for Michael: *The Good, the Bad and the Ugly*. You've got to see it on DCP," Paul says enthusiastically. "That's one of the things that made me a convert. It never looked as good on film as it did on digital," Mike nods in agreement. In many ways it's reassuring to hear these two expert projectionists—who've seen enough to know— embracing the new technology. Paul is the older of the two by five years. He was born in 1942 in Hanover, New Hampshire, the son of a physics professor and an elementary school teacher, and raised in the shadow of Ivy League school Dartmouth College. His father was an amateur ham-radio buff, who passed along his love of gears and gadgets to his son but who died when Paul was still in his teens. He came out to Los Angeles to attend the University of Southern California (USC) Film School, where he did second unit photography in 1966 on classmate George Lucas's seminal short *1:42:08*, which later formed the basis for the feature *THX 1138*. "I had a girlfriend back East who I wanted to see over Easter, and I had no idea George was going to the desert to shoot the race car stuff for *1:42:08*. Had I gone with George to the desert and spent time more actively working with him, my career path might have been significantly different," Paul says with a wry grin.

While studying at USC, Paul discovered that hundreds of vintage prints were being dumped in the trash at the nearby Gilboy film depot. "I went there and there's all this film in barrels and barrels and barrels," he remembers. "And I thought, 'That's interesting.' So I started going back. They left the gates open on a Saturday, and I just went in and helped myself." Among the treasures he rescued from the garbage heap were 35mm four-track mag prints of *Oklahoma!* and *The Sound of Music*, *An American in Paris*, and a rare print of Michelangelo Antonioni's *L'Avventura*. According to Paul, it's also most likely where he salvaged a 35mm mag print of James Dean's *Rebel Without a Cause*, which he loaned to Warner Bros. years later when it turned out the studio had lost all of the original stereo elements on the film. "Every single stereo element that is in existence now on *Rebel Without a Cause* came from Paul's print," Mike points out proudly, to which Paul gives a self-conscious little shrug. When I ask if he still owns this invaluable print, Paul turns to his friend: "Do I still have it?" he asks. Mike nods yes, confirming it's still in Paul's collection at UCLA Archive.

Mike was born in Omaha, Nebraska, the son of a movie theater manager and a cashier, who met at the theater where she worked. His mother died when he was four years old, and his father moved the family out to L.A., where he took a job with Fox West Coast Theaters. At one of the cinemas his father managed, the long-gone Picfair at Pico and Fairfax, he met the saxophone-playing projectionist, George Roth, who took a paternal liking to the young Mike. "So I gradually learned to be a projectionist. He'd teach me how to splice film: he'd take the splices after I'd made them and pop them—he'd go *bam bam bam!!* like that, to see if they held. And he'd charge me fifty cents for every splice that came apart, and twenty-five cents for every misframe." As Mike became more experienced, he discovered he could steal his father's keys and ride his bike to the theater after it closed, where it became his own private screening room. "I wouldn't run the whole movie. I'd just run a couple reels and then ride back home. I just loved the opening of *West Side Story*," he remembers. To make sure Roth didn't catch on to his midnight movie forays, he was careful enough to remove the used carbon stubs from the projectors and slip them in his pocket.[57] I ask Mike when he last saw his mentor Roth, and he rubs his face sadly. "At the Four Star Theatre in Los Angeles sometime in the 1970s," he replies. "He was the projectionist when the Mitchell Brothers were running *Behind the Green Door* when the Four Star was a porno house for a while."

As a collector, Mike has a fondness for 35mm four-track mag stereo prints and has rare copies of *Prince Valiant*, *The Brave One*, *Mr. Roberts*, and *Picnic* in his collection, featuring the now-obsolete sound format. "One of the rarest things I had, though, were the outtakes from *Spartacus* in 70mm, which I eventually gave to Robert Harris when he did the restoration," he says. These included the burying-of-the-baby sequence and a more explicit scene of Jean Simmons bathing in the pool. I ask where he found these, and he says from "an old sound guy from Universal that a friend of mine knew. He had a bunch of stuff in his garage and wanted to get rid of it." Like most collectors, he and Paul still mourn the ones that got away or, worse, went vinegar. His most painful loss to vinegar syndrome? "That would be my two-hundred-minute four-track mag version of *Lawrence of Arabia*," he says, wincing. "One night I got very drunk and took all fourteen reels out to the dumpster behind the Chinese." Paul nods in agreement—one of the rare *Oklahoma!* IB Tech prints he salvaged from Gilroy in the mid-1960s finally went vinegar a few years ago. Although he threw the print out, he couldn't bear to part with the film cans. After the interview he takes me out to his car and shows me where they sit, empty, nestled right behind the driver's seat.

The two men are philosophical about the changes that have swept the industry and made projectionists an endangered species. "Most of the people who come to see these movies are not coming necessarily to see something that's on a piece of a celluloid that's rattling through a projector," observes Paul. "They're coming to see the content: Fred Astaire and Ginger Rogers, *Gone With the Wind*, Clark Gable and Olivia de Havilland, the glorious cinematography." Mike agrees but worries that a younger audience is growing accustomed to seeing a pristine viewing experience. "In the 1950s and the 1960s when we were watching movies on television, we were watching scratchy and beat-up prints that were run off 16mm. That's what our generation was used to seeing," he says. "But now, this generation won't accept imperfections." One thing they agree on is that the movies have changed, permanently, with what they both call the "seismic shift" from film to digital. "This is as big as the one from silent to sound. Probably bigger," Paul says thoughtfully. Mike draws in a deep breath: "At least with silent to sound, you were using the same physical element to project shadows on the screen. But now . . . " His voice trails off for a moment. "Is it still shadows now, Paul?"

"I love film, I love touching it," says retired projectionist and collector Matt Spero as he leads us through his dark, curtained house in Hollywood. "You can't touch a digital file, you can't physically manipulate it and hold it in your hands. There's a tactile experience to running film, to being with film." In person Matt is a big, bearlike man with a handlebar mustache and an infectious, raspy voice. His house sits in a dodgy neighborhood near Melrose and Normandie with the concrete walls of the 101 freeway looming overhead. Inside, the place is either a fascinating paradise of movie memorabilia or something of a cluttered nightmare, depending on your point of view. The most remarkable feature is a jewel-box-like screening room immediately to the left as you enter, with its own theater marquee over the entry and a poster case sporting a one-sheet for Brian De Palma's *Phantom of the Paradise*, a personal favorite of Matt's. The screening room itself is like a grand old movie palace, just in miniature. He's decorated it with faded but still beautiful architectural elements salvaged from various old theaters that were being demolished. Overhead, the ceiling is decorated with a glorious abstract sunburst pattern, with a carved wooden emblem from the Whittier Theatre hanging above the red velvet curtains. He points to an ornate bronze-and-frosted-glass wall sconce next to an assemblage of gilded mythological sea-horses riding foaming waves: "These came from the Imperial Theater in Long Beach. At one time there were eighty different theaters in Long Beach. Now there's one, the Art Theatre, which has been restored," he says. Standing here I realize this is something like a theater graveyard, with the ghosts of bygone movie palaces still gathered here waiting for the show to begin.

"You found my booth!" he exclaims, as I poke my head into the cramped, dusty space at the back of the theater, reached by a narrow set of steps. "I can screen 35mm, including four-track mag, 16mm, and now video," he notes proudly. Although I don't say it out loud, my heart sinks looking at the state of the booth. It's filled with haphazard piles of loose film leader, plastic cores, and trailer reels. Can he even still show film in here? At one point he certainly did, and it must have been magnificent to sit in this tiny movie palace with its crystal chandelier overhead and its glass ticket booth by the door. "We had a sneak preview of *The Hand*, with Michael Caine. It hadn't even been released yet. I knew somebody who worked on the film, and they got me a print. *The Great Race* in IB Tech, my own personal print. We ran a four-track mag Tech print of *The Guns of Navarone*," he gushes. One night he had to hold the start of the show thirty minutes so that members of disco group the Village People could arrive to watch the sci-fi flick *Saturn 3*, starring Kirk Douglas and Farrah Fawcett.

Born in Berkeley, California, in 1945, Matt moved with his parents to Santa Rosa (the setting for Hitchcock's classic *Shadow of a Doubt*) when they opened a truck stop and café there. He caught the projecting bug running 16mm films in junior high school and began work professionally as a projectionist in 1970 in the L.A. area. Among the well-known theaters he worked at were the Vagabond and the Tiffany rep houses, and the downtown Orpheum, where he fondly remembers running a double bill in floor-rattling Sensurround of *Earthquake* and *Midway*. He is, of course, most proud of his own little cinema. I ask if he has a single favorite experience as a projectionist. He thinks for a moment, then recalls screening a print of *Mary Poppins* at home one day. "I'm sitting here watching this movie all by myself, and I said, 'You are the luckiest fucker in the world.' I'm watching this beautiful Tech print with stereo sound in my own home . . . I actually got tears in my eyes. I was so happy. How many people could say this?"

For him, the writing was on the wall for projectionists' jobs as early as the 1980s, when giant mechanical platter systems were quickly replacing the old dual-projector set-ups. "At the time I was getting paid about eight or nine dollars an hour. It was all going downhill by that point," he says in frustration. "By then I knew that being a projectionist was dead. They were beginning to make us teach the candy-counter people how to thread." He still maintains a small film vault at his home just off his back bedroom. It's barely big enough to squeeze into sideways and is stuffed to the ceiling with reels of 35mm trailers and odds-and-ends, like test footage of Mae West in her final film, *Sextette* (1978), that he plucked from a dumpster.

When I ask if he still runs his prints at home for friends like he used to do, he shakes his head and gestures to a digital projector perched in the back row of the theater. Even here, in this jewel-box-like theater literally made of movie memories, film is dead. Nowadays he runs prints only if he needs to check the condition to sell them on eBay. "Here's the absolute reality of digital versus film. I absolutely *love* film," says the man who talks passionately about the tactile feeling of holding film, almost breathing it in. "However—there comes the big one—show me a print directly out of a lab of a movie. Then show me the digital version that's been cleaned up, with all the scratches removed and the jiggle removed, and the digital version looks pretty damn good."

"I have a habit of going to movies every night. They're doing an Ernst Lubitsch series at the Aero, and I went to see *Trouble in Paradise*, the best film of its kind," says projectionist, union officer, and film collector Lee Sanders when he arrives at my house. A thoughtful, soft-spoken guy, Lee is tall and slim, with a gray-black nub of a mustache and an Ichabod Crane–like quality. In keeping with his personality, he's kept a low profile among L.A. area film collectors, but over the years he's quietly assembled a superb collection of 35mm and 16mm prints, including rare titles like Anthony Mann's bleak antiwar masterpiece *Men in War* (1957), which he freely loaned for a Mann retrospective at the American Cinematheque I organized in the mid-1990s. "I personally would be happy to see a terrible IB Technicolor print over almost anything else," he says about his love for film on film. "I think IB prints are like oil paintings." This story of Lee's sums up his passion for film best, and how he's shared it with others over the years: "One of my favorite memories was [journalist] Todd McCarthy borrowed one of my films to show to Jean Renoir. It was John Ford's *The Rising of the Moon*. Todd reported that Renoir said afterwards, '*Magnifique!*'"

Born in Evanston, Illinois, in 1943 and raised in Pasadena, Lee was a self-described "film freak" in the 1960s. Eventually he abandoned a career as an aerospace engineer at Jet Propulsion Laboratory to work as a projectionist. He started projecting in 1972 at theaters like the Vagabond and the downtown Arcade, where he recalls undercover cops would hang out with him in the projection booth because they were too afraid to sit with the audience. "I want to explain why I became a projectionist. It's not because I wanted a job—it's because *I wanted to preserve film*. I was a collector first," he notes with emphasis. Of all the projectionist-collectors Jeff and I spoke with, the soft-spoken Lee has been arguably the most vocal in fighting for the jobs of his brother workers: for twenty-five years he was an officer at Projectionists' Union Local 150 as well as a delegate to the county Federation of Labor.

There's a bitter irony to the fact that Lee's own job as a projectionist has been wiped out by the transition to digital. For a number of years he's worked on the private Bel Air circuit. It's one of the most exclusive perks in a town that prides itself on perks: millionaire producers, financiers, and studio executives would set up plush screening rooms in their Bel Air and Beverly Hills mansions and screen the latest films, often loaned by rival studios. "What I remember most is how incredibly clean and beautiful the houses are," marvels Lee, who makes three hundred dollars a night for his projecting services. "They're really beautiful places, and they're so pristine that you don't have to clean the projectors. There's no dust in the entire house." You might assume that Lee would eventually become resentful, surrounded by so much conspicuous wealth, but it's just the opposite. "Although politically a socialist, I still have great love for a lot of capitalists—I'm not prejudiced," he says. "It's not their fault that they have a capitalist system and know what to do with it. I might do the same things they do, although I might be happy to pay more for the projectionists," he adds with a wink.

When the end came for him on the Bel Air circuit, it came quickly and without a word. "That ended in December 2012. No more prints," he says quietly. "In December I did a lot of screenings, but nothing since then. I worked at three different places, but they're all finished. These were private homes, and they spent twenty-five thousand dollars per projector for beautiful Kinoton machines, which are the best and the most expensive."

With the transition to digital, there is simply no need for a projectionist like Lee any longer.

"I can agree with everything in the digital transition. Everything is okay with me, including losing my career, although of course I don't think it was actually necessary," he says toward the end of our talk. "But the one thing that is of greatest importance is losing the archival quality of film. Film is cheap to store. You can just 'store it and ignore it,' as they say. Set it aside for several hundred years, if it's stored properly by a good archive, and then you can come back and still use it."

Among collectors we interviewed, former New York City projectionist Michael McKay may have been the youngest to own a 35mm projector, at the tender age of fifteen. "I was just dicking around with it," he says now with a laugh. "Any trailers I got in 35mm, I'd just cut the trailer up and make slides out of them. I was a kid, you didn't know. I realized later when I started seriously collecting that I'd cut up some really great trailers: *Horror of Dracula*, *Forbidden Planet*, *The Time Machine*." The son of a New York City policeman, Michael was born in 1951 in Queens. His life changed overnight at the age of twelve when his mother committed suicide. "Because my mother died when I was very young, and the circumstances of her death, my father became very overindulgent and never said no to me," he recalls now about the first feature he ever got, a print of *Godzilla vs. Mothra* (1964) that his dad purchased for him at a local camera store.

"New York was a very small group of people who all knew each other," he says referring to the late-1960s East Coast subculture, then rattles off a list of names, including *Spartacus* restorationist Robert Harris, collector Wes Shank, producer Jon Davison, and director Joe Dante. As a teenager he fell in with *Castle of Frankenstein* magazine editor Calvin Beck, who was hosting screenings of classic horror and sci-fi films like *Metropolis* at the McBurney YMCA in New York City. He began tagging along with Beck and his mother, who took him to other film-buff screenings, like the legendary Theodore Huff Memorial Film Society events hosted by William K. Everson and attended by a young Leonard Maltin and Susan Sontag, among others. He mentions the famed connection between Beck and Hitchcock's *Psycho*: "They say that the character for Norman Bates was based partially on the relationship between Calvin Beck and his mother. Calvin was no murderer, but it was a weird, sick relationship that he had with his mother," he recalls. "He couldn't go anywhere without her. Very rare that they would ever be separated." He still has real admiration and affection for Beck: "Calvin was a great guy, deep love of movies. It showed in his magazine, which was not like *Famous Monsters*. I mean, I love Forry Ackerman and everything, but his magazine treated movies like a joke. Calvin was much more respectful of the genre: science fiction, horror, fantasy." I ask him for his impression of this underground group of New York cinephiles, and he pauses for a moment. "There was a group of older collectors, and I look back now and think a lot of them might have been either perverts or dysfunctional socially and sexually," he replies. "If they weren't just mama's boys in general, they probably had a lot of issues with their sexuality. They were either closeted or out-and-out gay people. It's probably part of why they had you hanging out with them, why they allowed young boys to hang out with the group. But nobody ever made any advances to me or my friends," he notes.

Michael was pretty much indulged by his father until the age of twenty-eight: "I had done nothing with my life," he admits. "I never developed like most people, get a job. I was locked in this drug and movie and sex thing." One day his father sat him down for a heart-to-heart talk. "He asked me, 'What is it you like to do, what do you enjoy doing?' I said, 'I like to get high and watch movies,' and I laughed. My father very seriously said, 'OK, let's start with that. You have a lot of knowledge; there's gotta be some way to turn your hobby into a job." Michael found it difficult to break into the Motion Picture Projectionists Local 306, but after befriending a projectionist at the local Haven Theatre named Angelo, he was finally able to get his union card. He says the union was rife with corruption at the time, tightly controlling who worked where and even stealing hundreds of prints of films like *The Graduate* from a company called In Flight that provided screenings on airplanes. Catching on to how things worked, he freely admits that he began routinely stealing prints himself: "As a projectionist, every time I'd go to a different theater, if I wanted a print I'd just take it. If the manager would say, 'Where's the print?' I'd say, 'They picked that up last week.'"

He also picked up a particularly notorious habit of projectionists: cutting his favorite scenes out of a movie, then shipping it on to the next theater.[58] "I had the European print of *Vault of Horror* with the scene where the vampire puts a spigot in the guy's neck and turns it on to fill a glass full of blood," he remembers, then adds: "I cut that out." There is a long silence. "You didn't ask the reason: why would I do this? I felt the movie business had treated me so poorly, the theater chains. I felt at that point I owed them nothing and had free hand to do whatever I wanted to them." According to Michael, the theater owners were constantly trying to bust the unions and refused to pay him and the other projectionists the agreed overtime rate. "So the next Bond film that would come in, I'd grab a couple prints and sell them and put a couple thousand bucks in my pocket."

"Most collectors are nuts. An awful lot of them are really disturbed," he says about his fellow film buffs. "I hate to say someone's a crook—here I am stealing films. I like to think I have some kind of integrity, but a lot of people did not. Is there such a thing as being an honest thief? Is that hypocritical?" he asks to no one in particular. He shares a bizarre and unsettling story about a collector who was, as he puts it, "famous for fucking with prints." After buying a copy of *It's a Mad, Mad, Mad, Mad World* from Michael for three hundred dollars that he planned to resell to someone else, the collector "starts going through the print taking out scenes for himself. Then he starts rewinding it and holding a razor blade to scratch up the whole print on the emulsion side." When I ask, slightly appalled, why he'd mutilate a perfectly good print, Michael just shrugs. "He was crazy. He was nuts."

When the end came for Michael as theaters transitioned to digital, it was a slow, painful process of erosion. "First I went from working 60 hours a week to 50 hours a week to 40 to 30, to 25, to 20," he says with barely disguised bitterness. The last film he projected was Rudolph Valentino's 1925 silent drama *The Eagle* in 2011 at the Library for the Performing Arts at Lincoln Center, before he was able to get an early pension at age sixty. "That was horrible, going digital. Very bad scene. It's death by a thousand cuts."

18.

The Score

In almost every field of obsessive collecting, whether it's comic books or rare coins or baseball cards, there exists a powerful fantasy of an untouched treasure trove, an elephants' graveyard that has somehow escaped the hungry claws of other collectors. There's an almost irresistible pull to it, the thought that someday you'll stumble onto an estate sale or thrift store or abandoned building filled with the forgotten objects of your dreams, whatever they may be. Movies themselves have eagerly fed this fantasy, from the literal elephants' graveyard sought by poachers in the 1930s Johnny Weissmuller *Tarzan* films to the vast government warehouse that swallows up the ark at the end of *Raiders of the Lost Ark*. Occasionally the fantasy becomes reality, as it did in 1977 for twenty-one-year-old Boulder, Colorado–area comic book collector Chuck Rozanski when he stumbled on a cache of over sixteen thousand golden age comics in near-mint condition—the legendary Edgar Church/Mile High Collection. I had a brief taste of it myself in 2001 on the outskirts of Tokyo late one evening. I was led by my friend Yoshiki past the sleepy front-gate guard at Daiei Studios and into the studio's movie print and poster archive, where for several hours I was allowed to purchase (illegally, of course) dozens of unused posters for 1960s *Zatoichi* and *Gamera* films, still in their original brown paper rolls. Even at the time, I knew this moment was something special, the glimpse of a poster collector's nirvana that would never come again.

On November 7, 1997, the entertainment industry trade paper *Variety* ran an article by Rex Weiner with the headline "Discarded Prints Prompt Probe: Film Shipper's Move Leaves Prints Behind." It was about a film depot named Gilboy Inc., in the bleak, industrial Southern California neighborhood of Pico Rivera. Gilboy was for a number of collectors and dealers the ultimate score: a vast warehouse of film prints abandoned by their owners. Jeff describes it as "truly a treasure hunt in every way," and dealer Al Beardsley says simply that it was "the best you've ever seen." But like every dream of Shangri-La, there's a price to be paid for a glimpse of heaven.

The Gilboy depot itself was—and still is—an enormous warehouse taking up an entire block in a nondescript neighborhood of indoor swap meets and welding supply places. Inside, enormous steel girders support the roof overhead, and UFO-shaped lights illuminate the cavernous interior, looking like something from a 1950s sci-fi flick hovering in mid-air. The best way to get around is probably by forklift or golf cart, given the warehouse's huge size.

At the time of the *Variety* article in 1997, Gilboy Inc. was operating as a franchise of National Film Service (NFS), a fifty-year old company that handled transportation of tens of thousands of prints for over thirty major studios and independent distributors, including such big names as Sony/Columbia, Paramount, and New Line. But all was not well with parent company NFS. A private letter dated September 8, 1997, from Rodger Hunter of Gilboy Inc. to Irv Rosen of Samuel Rosen & Sons, landlords of the Pico Rivera warehouse, indicated that Gilboy and NFS were seriously behind in rent to Rosen & Sons, and that NFS appeared to be on the brink of bankruptcy. "At a recent stockholders' meeting, the hat was passed in an attempt to improve the cash flow situation that is threatening a bank foreclosure," Hunter admitted. He confirmed that Gilboy Inc. could no longer expect payments from its parent company to cover the more than $23,000 in rent and taxes still owed to Rosen & Sons, or any future rent. In essence, Gilboy was out of the film business. In a paragraph that would have serious repercussions in what was to come, Hunter stated: "*As for the remaining film and fixtures in the Pico Rivera building, please feel free to dispose of them as you see fit.* Unfortunately, Gilboy does not have the resources or the manpower to deal with it. NFS was supposed to assist in the cleanup, but won't respond to my faxes or phone calls" (italics mine). In the November 7 *Variety* article, Don Trivette, general manager of NFS, defended his firm's actions, claiming that it had "moved all of its customers' films from Pico Rivera to its new depot in Glendale during one week in July." Despite his assurances, a vast mountain of film was left behind at the Gilboy depot: over five thousand prints, according to a later accounting.[59]

With a building literally stuffed to the rafters with prints abandoned by its former tenant Gilboy and parent company NFS, landlord Samuel Rosen & Sons decided they were well within their legal rights to sell them off. There is no surviving inventory of everything that was left sitting at Gilboy in 1997, but among the five thousand prints were rare 35mm copies of classics like Charlie Chaplin's *Modern Times*, the Marx Brothers' *A Night at the Opera*, and the Basil Rathbone–starring *The Hound of the Baskervilles*, along with more recent titles, including *Platoon* (Hemdale), *Predator* (20th Century Fox), *Dead Poets Society* (Disney/Touchstone), *Hook* and *Cliffhanger* (Sony), *A Few Good Men* and *The Princess Bride* (Castle Rock), *Black Beauty* (Warner Bros.), *Jason Goes to Hell: The Final Friday* (New Line), and many others. Nearly every major studio and independent distributor was represented there.

The first collector that Rosen & Sons let walk through the vast loading dock was a man named Randy "Cochise" Miller, whose daytime job was producing on-air promo spots for CBS and NBC on shows like *Magnum P.I.* and *The Equalizer*. He explains his unusual nickname: "The smog was really bad in 1973 [when I came out to L.A.], and I wore contact lenses. So to keep the hair out of my eyes, I wore headbands, and people would say, 'You look like an Indian.' I came up with the nickname 'Cochise,' and it stuck." Like many collectors, Randy sold prints on the side through *The Big Reel* to fund his hobby. He found out about Gilboy through a friend named David who collected movie projectors and who knew the building's owners. "I had never even heard of Gilboy before I went there with my friend," he confesses. "It was rundown. The skylights were leaking, so there were water puddles everywhere, and stacks of film everywhere." In one room hundreds of cans were thrown in a pile, forming a literal mountain of film. Another was filled with hundreds of Warner Bros. and MGM cartoon shorts from the 1930s, 1940s, and 1950s. "It was kind of sad to be a film collector and see the prints were abandoned here. It was a graveyard for film," he says. Randy, ironically, collected mostly 16mm himself, and since Gilboy contained almost exclusively 35mm prints, he wound up selling almost everything he bought. I ask if he remembers any of the prints he purchased: "The jewel of the crown that we found was a 3-D print of the 1950s film *The Maze*. I also found two 35mm prints of *We the Living*, the 1940s Ayn Rand film," he says. "That 3-D movie *The Maze* sold for about $3,500 to Germany to a 3-D archive there."

Jeff was second in line to get a crack at the ultimate film score. When I ask him to describe his impressions of the Gilboy depot, he shakes his head. "Oh my goodness. It was huge, I don't know how big—in my mind it was acres and acres," he replies. "No air conditioning, the middle of summer, so it was hot as hell in there. The building was abandoned at that point, so there were no people. It was just me. No lights, no electricity. I had to use a flashlight." Jeff spent several weeks digging in the darkness, grabbing whatever he could. By his count he purchased between three hundred and four hundred prints, still barely a scratch on the vast trove. "Originally the prices were something like fifty dollars a print, then it went down to ten dollars a print, then it was a few hundred dollars a palette by the end," he says. "I kept going back—I wanted to make sure I got everything that was good." When I ask if he had any fears that the studios might come after him for purchasing the prints, he shakes his head again: "The owner was selling abandoned material in his building. It's hard to imagine how anything could be more legal than that." Although he dismisses everything remaining as "junk" after he combed through it all, that still left over four thousand 35mm prints to dispose of. And, as we've seen, one man's junk is often another man's treasure. In retrospect, the first two dealers/collectors, Randy and Jeff, had it easy: they grabbed the cream of the crop and split.

The next man to walk in the door was dealer Alfred "Al" Beardsley, who had been busted seven years earlier in the MPAA-orchestrated L.A. County Sheriff's Department sting operation for selling illegally obtained prints of *Rocky V* and *Home Alone*. If the MPAA thought he would take the warning and disappear from the underground film market, they apparently didn't know Al. He swooped in on Gilboy and apparently made a deal with the landlord to clear out the remaining film. Soon he began making deals with other collectors and dealers to pick through the depot. "I got to the point where I got everything I wanted, my friends got everything they wanted," Al recalls today from his hospital bed. "Then I said, 'I want one hundred bucks a person for everything you can carry,' and we still didn't make a dent in it." He pauses for a moment, remembering the huge haul of film that was slowly being whittled down, like ants picking away at summer picnic leftovers. "You couldn't kill that frigging place," he sighs. "I used to go home and my hands were black from the dirt. I didn't know you could make dirt that black."

With thousands of prints still sitting in the sweltering, electricity-less warehouse, and the landlord increasingly anxious to empty it, Al turned to another contact of his, a collector named Brian LeGrady. Today, Brian is in his late fifties, with long, stringy gray-brown hair that hangs past his shoulders, and torn jeans; when he walks in the room he brings a distinct smell of incense with him. He carries himself with the laidback hippie air of a true film believer, with occasional startling bursts of excited temper. A former animation cameraman for Disney who worked on *Tron* and *The Black Cauldron*, he also helped build the motion-control cameras for the sci-fi epic *The Black Hole*. These days he works as a first assistant camera/focus puller for film shoots, and as a digital imaging technician, doing quality control and overseeing digital workflow. When I mention Al Beardsley's name, he nearly jumps out of his seat: "Fucking great! That guy almost single-handedly destroyed my love for film collecting and my marriage," he swears, face turning red. "I gave him four thousand dollars for all the prints in National Film Service. There were racks and racks and racks of prints in a football-sized warehouse, and a room of shorts and cartoons, Dave Clark Five, and all this stuff." It takes a few seconds for him to calm down before he continues: "I got three 25-foot-long trucks, all my friends and family, palettes, forklifts, laborers, to transport the film to a warehouse in Woodland Hills that I'd acquired. Sight unseen, not knowing what the prints were. Just imagining walking into a dark and dusty warehouse not knowing what was there. But I figured four thousand dollars was a small price to pay." He pauses for another moment. "But I paid for it in other ways. Because of Al."

Unbeknownst to Brian, Al had made what seems like a very odd move: he reached out to a friend at *Variety* and leaked news of Gilboy. Why? Keeping in mind Al's previous run-in with the MPAA in 1990, for which he was fined $300,000 and eventually lost his business, the Sunset Screening Room, why on earth would he want to alert them that he was buying a mountain of studio prints? When I mention this strange maneuver to Jeff, he rolls his eyes: "I'm sure Al had a big mouth about it like he normally does," he says dismissively. I put it to Al directly, and he simply shrugs: "To shake up National Film," he replies. Apparently, Al was hoping to light a fire under National Film Service to buy out the rest of the warehouse, or else Al would be in default with the building's owner, Rosen & Sons, for not clearing it out. My guess, though, is that Al leaked the story to *Variety* as a kind of sweet public revenge on his former tormentors, the MPAA, by pointing out how lax their security measures were if they could allow thousands of studio prints to slip into collectors' hands.

Whatever the reason, the press bit. The *Variety* article on November 7 caused a mini-firestorm in Hollywood, with worried studio execs alarmed at the safety of their films. Into this firestorm walked Brian LeGrady: "The next morning I show up with all these trucks, and the MPAA shows up. They're flashing their badges and saying, 'We're taking control of this situation.'" Appalled and frightened, Brian stood by with several family members—including his nephew, brother-in-law, and father-in-law—waiting to see if they'd all be arrested as film pirates. "Al Beardsley, and this is to his credit, he jumps up and says, 'This is all my contents. We bought this fair and square from the landlords. You do not own any of this material,'" he notes. After an uncertain hour or so, Brian and his family members started to tentatively pile up film prints while the MPAA agents looked on. What happened next is, well, truly bizarre: "They sent one of their guys out to get several cases of beer, and they gave it to us," he recalls. I ask him why the MPAA agents would buy beer for the men they were ostensibly sent to arrest. "I think they felt bad, because basically what they walked away with was some odd reels from *Top Gun* and *Men in Black*," he shrugs.

"Once they got in their cars and drove away, we felt empowered and proceeded to clear out the warehouse within a week's time. During that time, Al Beardsley was selling films at night from the warehouse to other collectors, which was a complete violation of our agreement," Brian says. Although he grudgingly admits that Al defused the situation with the MPAA agents, he still seems to blame Al personally for all the woes that followed. "I never knew whether to trust him or not. He also destroyed the deal by becoming shamelessly self-promoting through the *Variety* article," Brian replies. "And Al couldn't drive; I had to drive him everywhere.

I became his chauffeur. I felt like I'd just partnered myself with the devil." He pauses for another long moment. "At one point it got so crazy—it was three in the morning, as the rats were scurrying around in the warehouse. My nephew pulled a knife on Al and said, 'I'm going to kill you.'

"Part of my love for film died in that week," Brian says now. "It took so long to get the material out of Pico Rivera and over to Woodland Hills. Unloading them, palette after palette, shrink wrap not being properly tied, film reels falling out—just the dynamics of trying to deal with moving truckload after truckload of film to Woodland Hills." All in all, Brian estimates that he hauled over three thousand prints out of the Gilboy depot. "You can lose a leg from the weight of this. It's not a beautiful, glorified image when you're dealing with five hundred pounds of steel with celluloid that can crush you if it falls over." I know what he means. During the course of writing this book, I helped move several tons of film from a collector's house in Inglewood with two screenwriter friends, Steven Peros and Dan Madigan. After a back-breaking day of hauling heavy Goldberg film cans, literally caked head-to-toe with filth, I turned to Dan and flashed an exhausted smile. "Film is dead," he said, looking around at the pile of rusted cans. "And good riddance."

"The deal was to take every single scrap of film out of there, good or bad, but there was no way in hell I could take everything out of there," Brian recalls of the Gilboy deal, which was quickly threatening to overwhelm him. "Especially when I realized there were like fifty prints of *Halloween 3* and 4, and all these romantic comedies. Multiple prints of the same awful title that I had to scrap because nobody wanted to buy them." He confirms that he did get some real treasures out of the warehouse, including rare prints of grindhouse gems like Dario Argento's *Deep Red* and Herschell Gordon Lewis's *Blood Feast* and *Two Thousand Maniacs!*—which he was forced to sell as quickly as possible to cover his mounting costs for storing the film. "I was creating tension with my family, because we broke it down as a business deal. We said, 'If we sell each of these prints, we're still gonna make out like a bandit. Even if you sold each print for ten dollars, we'd still do very well.' But it just turned into a nightmare of inventorying," he says. "To come up with the four thousand dollars to pay Al for the warehouse of film, I had to take some of that out of the college fund for the kids, and I promised my wife it would be paid back as quickly as possible. I told her,

'Look at all these prints. Look at what a goldmine—it's even in the paper!' But if you amortize it over the years it took to sell them . . . I'm still paying storage costs on some of these things." Listening to him now, describing how his dream of an endless warehouse of film treasures turned into a nightmare that ate into his children's bank account and his marriage, it's clear there can be too much of a good thing, even film prints. "You're supposed to be home taking care of the kids, or getting a job, and you wind up playing with film," observes the now-divorced Brian.

There were other repercussions from the Gilboy affair. On January 9, 1998, two months after the news about Gilboy broke, *Variety* announced that National Film Service was shutting down operations and preparing to liquidate its assets. Although it's clear the fifty-year-old company was already on the brink of bankruptcy before Gilboy, the highly publicized scandal—which prompted several of its remaining clients, like Sony, to quickly terminate their contracts—pushed NFS over the brink. "A rival source claimed the company's decline was due to the studios' loss of faith in its security measures, following an incident at one of its locations last year. NFS denied the accusations," *Variety* reported.

The Gilboy depot, site of the ultimate film score, still sits on an industrial stretch of buildings in Pico Rivera. When Jeff and I drive down there on a hot summer morning, it looks forlorn and uncared-for, with trash blowing around the stumps of dead palm trees. A sign outside reads "Ros Electric"—and then below it, "For Lease: Available." We walk around to the rear of the building, and Jeff smiles in recognition. "We'd pull up right here to the loading dock," he says, pointing. "The film was all stacked inside on big metal shelves." Ironically, the building is being vacated once again on the day we visit, with workers busily emptying it of used electrical equipment. They ignore us as we wander inside, gazing up at the crisscross metal beams and the eerily beautiful UFO-like light fixtures. I look around, trying to imagine this vast space filled with thousands and thousands of film prints. Being a collector and walking inside, trying to take it all in. We blink hard as we walk back out into the glaring L.A. sun. I glance to the right: there are two faded signs looming over the building, one that reads "Kodak Cameras—Film" and another for a camera store called Fox Photo, showing a giant leaping fox in mid-air. Kodak film is now almost gone, and Fox Photo and Gilboy have completely vanished, but the signs are still here, and the massive building itself, waiting for another tenant.

I ask Brian if he broke even on the Gilboy deal in the end. "What's the end?" he responds with a bitter laugh. "The amount of time I had to spend on it took me away from my family. I had to go down to this warehouse in Woodland Hills and spend night after night after night there, piecing together all these incomplete pieces of the puzzle, trying to make complete prints out of them. I had to advertise it and try to sell it—and then come up with some disappointing figures at the end of the month." He has held on to a print of Tony Gatlif's 1993 documentary on the Romani people, *Latcho Drom*, which he calls "my little gift to me out of that collection." When I mention that his onetime partner and nemesis Al Beardsley is now semi-paralyzed in a hospital and may never leave under his own power, Brian breathes in sharply. "Everybody on this earth I have no ill feeling against," he finally says. "Except one, and that's Al Beardsley. What a crook. But if he's dying, I'll let go. I'll let go as of now."

19.

A Younger Generation of Collectors

If film collecting is quickly disappearing—and all the interviews and research that Jeff and I conducted indicate that it is—then one glaring question remains: Where are all the prints? The reality is that they're still around, sitting silently in collectors' garages and closets; in temperature-controlled film archive vaults; on metal shelves for the increasingly few distributors who still service them. Yes, there are still tens of thousands of 16mm and 35mm prints out there, along with 8mm, Super 8mm, 70mm, and all the gauges in between. They just aren't moving around much anymore.

Every day that goes by means that more prints are, slowly, inevitably, lost to vinegar syndrome, to fading, to obsolescence, and to neglect. Ironically, while film itself has been phased out almost completely by the major studios for production and distribution, it is still by far the most stable means of preserving a movie for the future. Making 35mm black-and-white separation masters for a film, whether shot on digital or on celluloid, is still highly recommended by archivists and should ensure a film survives for at least 150 years if properly stored. A century and a half isn't very long compared with, say, most oil paintings at the Metropolitan Museum or a papyrus scroll, but it's a lot longer than the life expectancy for current digital film formats, which are changing every few years at an alarming rate.

So, if the prints are still out there, what are collectors doing with them?

While some we spoke with, like Joe Dante and Jon Davison, have already looked ahead and put them on deposit with institutions like the Academy Film Archive and the UCLA Film & Television Archive, many are simply ignoring what will happen after they die and are passing the buck to their heirs. Film collecting doesn't seem to be genetically inherited, though, and very few collectors we interviewed have children eager to take on their hundreds of smelly 16mm and 35mm prints of *Bambi*, *The Beast from 20,000 Fathoms*, and *Thunderball*. Likewise, many collectors don't have children, and it's easy to picture what will happen then: their prized collections sold in bulk to the lowest bidder or, just as likely, thrown in the dumpster. A strange kind of apathy has set in with many older collectors who've held on to their precious prints. They aren't emotionally or physically able to deal with selling them off one at a time on eBay or one of the few online print forums, and yet they're not willing to part with their film treasures just yet. The plummeting value of prints adds to the problem. While the prints are still aesthetically and culturally valuable, they're not nearly as financially valuable as they once were, and many collectors balk at the thought of donating their collections without compensation to nonprofit film archives that simply don't have the resources to pay for them. It is, in many ways, a perfect storm that's leaving private collections increasingly imperiled and the collectors themselves, well, increasingly depressed and nostalgic for the good old days of the 1970s and 1980s, when a film was still a film.

Before you give up all hope, there is a younger generation of collectors out there, men and women who are actively buying and selling prints, and keeping the hobby alive despite the fact that technology and the film industry are passing them by. It's not easy being a film collector these days, but it should be apparent from the previous chapters that it never was.

"I was not a popular child," confesses L.A.-based collector and record store manager Phil Blankenship. "I watched a lot of movies with Mom or by myself." Although he specializes in grindhouse horror, sci-fi, and exploitation films, and has an astonishing collection of over seven hundred prints—all in 35mm—he's surprisingly mild-mannered, of medium height and soft-spoken, with a black beard and mustache. When I arrive to interview him at the Hollywood apartment he shares with his girlfriend and two cats, he meets me at the door wearing a T-shirt that reads "Terror Tuesdays." "I'm sorry if my stories aren't as colorful as some of the other film collectors you've talked to. Our apartment is also a bit of a mess," he says apologetically. Inside, the place is indeed packed floor to ceiling with an entire wall of rare VHS videos to the right and stacks and stacks of DVDs and Blu-rays in the small living room, but it's refreshingly neat and well ordered, especially compared to some of the collectors I've interviewed. While we talk, Phil's cats Buster and Samantha jump into his lap, and by the end of the interview his "Terror Tuesdays" shirt is covered with their hair.

Phil was born in 1978 in Los Angeles but grew up in the lonely central California farm country of Salinas, most famous as the home of writer John Steinbeck. "I would say I lived your average 1980s middle-class life. Not super exciting," he observes about his childhood. "My dad was largely just a workaholic. My mom was very dedicated to her children." He describes his family growing up as "dedicated video fanatics" and happily admits to soaking up 1980s multiplex hits like *Top Gun*, *Predator*, *Ghostbusters*, and *Gremlins*. In his teens he was exposed to more offbeat arthouse and midnight-movie fare at a reopened Salinas theater, the Fox (which still survives as a concert hall), and the beautifully named Dream Theater in nearby Monterey, which inspired the 1980s progressive metal band of the same name. "Movies to a fourteen- or fifteen-year-old are the most exciting badass thing you could ever imagine but now seem so average to see on the screen," he recalls of his early love for genre cinema.

After graduating college, Phil went to work for the famed Amoeba Record store in the San Francisco area and moved back to L.A. in 2001 to open their branch in Hollywood, on Sunset Boulevard. He started religiously attending screenings at the American Cinematheque's Egyptian Theatre and the New Beverly rep house but soon realized they weren't showing the kind of exploitation and horror films he loved as often as he'd like. He proposed doing a midnight movies series to the New Beverly's longtime owner Sherman Torgan (who died in 2007) and soon found himself becoming a film collector by default, buying prints he wanted to screen for other fans. "The first print I bought may have just been *Night of the Comet*," he says of the gonzo, postapocalyptic 1984 sci-fi film (whose female hero ironically works at, yes, a movie theater in Southern California). "At the time the movie wasn't available on DVD, but the VHS was collectible," he recalls about the print, which he paid one hundred dollars for.

Operating mostly off the radar, even among other collectors, he began voraciously snapping up 35mm prints of neglected straight-to-video and exploitation titles that had slipped through the cracks of film history. I ask what's the most he's ever paid for a single print. He grimaces slightly and draws a deep breath. "The most I ever paid was $2,500," he finally admits. "It was for an uncut international print of Dario Argento's *Tenebrae*." A graphic and disturbing Italian *giallo* horror film from the director of *Suspiria* and *Deep Red*, *Tenebrae* was released in the United States in 1984 in a badly butchered version under the title *Unsane*. I can immediately sympathize with Phil's love for the film. I once tracked down the only available U.K. copy of *Tenebrae* in 35mm to an obscure British distributor who was about to leave for a month's vacation when I rang him up, desperate to find it for an Argento retrospective I was presenting in L.A. "That is the most expensive thing I've ever bought in my life," Phil says about his prized print, which, like several of his rarest treasures, came from Australia. "All my cars previously have been less than $2,500, which is probably why I don't currently have a car. I felt, 'That's so much damn money,' but being able to see it on screen was worth any price basically. We screened it with Claudio Simonetti from Goblin last year at Cinefamily."

Ironically, Phil doesn't have a 35mm projection system at his apartment, which means that he's able to watch his own prints only when he shows them at the nonprofit Cinefamily, where he programs an ongoing series. Among his other rare finds are the 1982 cult sci-fi film *Liquid Sky* and his self-professed all-time favorite, George Romero's 1978 zombie classic *Dawn of the Dead*. I ask if his *Dawn of the Dead* print is an original, and he nods yes but then qualifies that statement: "It is an original U.K. copy. It's printed in Agfa or whatever, so the color is still perfect, but it has some of the gore removed. So it's kind of a sad story because it's not complete, but the color and condition look fantastic." He waits a beat, then shrugs. "The bad news is I can never screen it in public anyway," he says, pointing out that the film's producer has a reputation for seizing collector prints. Not every one of his prints is as rare or sought after as *Dawn of the Dead*. He admits to paying twenty dollars recently for a film that perhaps only he would know and love: "A couple weeks ago I screened *The Face with*

Two Left Feet. Have you seen that movie? It is a late '70s Italian Travolta-sploitation feature. The Italians found an impersonator who looks almost identical to Travolta and built a movie around him," he gushes about the 1979 oddity.

"I feel definitely like the collector circle is shrinking rapidly, which is both good and bad," he responds when I ask how many other younger film collectors he encounters these days. "Good because a lot of the people are selling off their collections, so I've been able to make a lot of acquisitions, and bad because there's fewer people supporting something that I love." He does most of his buying through the online 35mm Film Forum that was started by my writing partner Jeff and continued now by younger collector and programmer Jack Theakston. Phil's recent purchases include prints of the obscure Spanish horror flick *House of Psychotic Women* (aka *Blue Eyes of the Broken Doll*, 1974) and the deranged 1971 gore comedy, *The Mad Butcher*, both from video exploitation label Sinister Cinema, which has been selling off its print collection. "I love seeing film projected. It looks perfect to me when it's projected properly," he says about his intertwined efforts as a collector and repertory film programmer, then adds, "If your son is ready for midnight movies, we actually have parents bring their kids to the movies, like ten-year-olds, presumably to pass on the idea of going to see late-night shows."

"It's sort of a really stressful hobby, because practically every day you have to deal with some negotiation or transaction: someone isn't happy with a print you sold them, or you got a lousy print and you have to try to get your money back," says Chicago-based collector Julian Antos, echoing the sentiments of many collectors we spoke with. "Do you really think of it as a *hobby*?" his roommate and collecting partner Rebecca "Becca" Hall shoots back at him. Julian thinks for a moment, then responds: "No, it's not a hobby; it's a thing I do. I wake up in the morning, I eat, and I do my film stuff. I go to work and come back and do my film stuff, and I eat at night." Among the youngest collectors I've spoken to—Becca was born in 1987, Julian in 1992—they've managed to assemble in a few short years an impressive collection of over 175 16mm and 35mm features in what Julian optimistically refers to as their "vault," actually a former maid's room in a large apartment they share with several other roommates. "Whatever, we can call it a vault if we want to," Becca laughs. Among her recent purchases is a print of the 1970 religious drama *The Cross and the Switchblade*, based on the best-selling novel by pastor David Wilkerson and John and Elizabeth Sherrill. "My undergraduate thesis was about American evangelicals and their relationships to different kinds of media," she replies when I ask why she picked that particular print. "I didn't even check if it was available [on DVD]. I own, like, four DVDs—I don't even care about video. Well, it's not like I don't care, but that wouldn't have affected why I bought it. Part of why I really wanted to get it is it was a Technicolor print."

Julian was born and raised in Chicago, his father a proofreader of medical journals, and his mother in charge of raising him and three siblings. "My parents both volunteered at Facets [cinematheque] in Chicago, and I got to spend a lot of time around the projectionist there, who had a habit of smoking in the booth," he says about his early exposure to movies. "That was my first experience in a projection booth with clouds of smoke and art-house movies that I wasn't exactly interested in at a young age." Later on he discovered that his grandfather on his dad's side was an engineer of farming equipment who assembled an astonishing private archive of over fifty thousand photographs as well as 16mm footage of the equipment he worked on. "These home movies are amazing, because it's like he's shooting movies of his children, except they're *tractors*," Becca observes about the amateur footage that she and Julian are hoping to preserve in the near future. She was born in New Haven, Connecticut, her mother a psychiatrist, and her father "at the time . . . sort of a non-tenure-track professor, so he moved around a bit at Wesleyan, Yale, and Harvard throughout my childhood," she recalls. "At Wesleyan he was in the history department, at Yale in the divinity school, and business at Harvard. I like to say that it's in between those three is how philanthropy works."

By far their most ambitious project as collectors and preservationists has been rescuing an obscure 1956 musical comedy called *Corn's-a-Poppin'*, shot in Kansas City, Missouri, and cofinanced by the heads of a local movie theater chain and the Popcorn Institute to promote, yes, that great American institution, popcorn. The film might be justifiably forgotten save for the presence of a then-unknown screenwriter named Robert Altman in the credits. As critic J. R. Jones points out in a recent review in the *Chicago Reader*, "For Altman aficionados, it's essential viewing: his sarcasm and jaundiced view of the business world are already much in evidence, and the live country-western show at the center of the story makes the movie a fascinating precursor to two of his most beloved films, *Nashville* and *A Prairie Home Companion*."[60] "It's just fantastic. The first time I saw it, it was running at Doc Films at the University of Chicago. There was a totally packed house, and I couldn't wrap my head around it," says Julian today. Together with their friend and former University of Chicago alumnus Kyle Westphal, the three became increasingly obsessed with preserving this early Altman rarity and in 2011 formed the nonprofit Northwest Chicago Film Society to save the movie. At the time, the only available print was a copy at the Wisconsin Film Center that suffered from a projector arc burn and wasn't ideal for preservation. But in 2011 Julian spotted a 35mm print of the film for sale on eBay. "A few of us pitched in to get it. It went for around six hundred dollars," he says about their find. "It's probably the nicest print out there. It came from someone who was selling off the estate of a collector in Kansas. It's 35mm, black-and-white. There's a couple newspaper articles that say it was shot in Ansco Color or was going to be shot that way, and if you look at the print, it sort of has the look of a black-and-white TV print that was originally in color. My suspicion, at least, is that it was shot in color, and for whatever reason all the prints were printed black-and-white, either because it didn't look great or for financial reasons." Working with Westphal, Julian and Becca applied for and received a twelve-thousand-dollar grant from the National Film Preservation Foundation, which allowed them to make a preservation negative from their print and the Wisconsin Center copy and to strike two 35mm copies for repertory screenings. The restored film recently screened to enthusiastic audiences at the Music Box Theatre in Chicago and the Billy Wilder Theater at the UCLA Film & Television Archive in L.A. "Pretty much everyone that sees it loves it," Julian says about this strange and forgotten slice of pure Americana filmmaking.

I ask the pair how they feel about being younger collectors in a vanishing field. There's a long pause. "I think we get depressed a lot," Julian finally responds. "But not that depressed," Becca quickly adds. He nods, then adds: "But, you know, it's depressing. You sort of have to, you know, cheer yourself up. The thing that's most rewarding for me is being able to show a print, whether it's my print or the studio print, and to hear people say, 'That looked really good.' That sort of makes up for everything else." His partner Becca chimes in: "I think one advantage to being a younger person in this world is that we don't have to worry about the FBI, as far as we know. I don't want to speak for Julian—I try really desperately hard to avoid collecting things. But for me one of the pleasures of film collecting for us is public exhibition, and this has been part of film collecting forever, I guess."

"I'm afraid a little prank of mine has gotten a little out of control," confesses collector and film programmer Jack Theakston when I ask him about a startling image he recently posted on his Facebook page: a single frame from Tod Browning's *London After Midnight*. For those who aren't familiar with it, *London After Midnight* is possibly the most famous and sought-after lost movie in film history, a 1927 horror/mystery from Browning, who later directed *Dracula* and *Freaks*. It is perhaps best known today for the ghastly, spectral images of star Lon Chaney Sr. in horrifically gruesome makeup with piranha-like teeth. Even today, ninety years after the movie was made, Chaney looks like he could peel the meat off your bones. The film was remade in 1935 by Browning himself as *Mark of the Vampire*, costarring Bela Lugosi. Then, in 1967, a disastrous fire at the MGM Studios vault destroyed the original *London After Midnight* negative and all surviving prints. While production stills survive from the movie, to date not a single frame of footage has been found, not even a trailer. Among missing films there is lost—and there is *London After Midnight*. So you can imagine the flash of excitement a film buff would experience when seeing what looks like an authentic 35mm frame showing the title card of the movie with sprocket holes and the word "Eastman" printed across the left side of the frame.

Except it's not authentic. "No footage has been found from the film— it's a joke I concocted for some friends," Jack admits. "I was going to say something about it when people were starting to think it was legitimate. For a little image, I put a lot of work into it, to the point of anal-retentive detail. I threw some things into the frame that people who were truly experts would know it wasn't real, but I was shocked how many people thought it *was* real." Being one of those people who was fooled, at least for a few moments, I have to ask what clues would give it away. "I knew the fonts MGM used in the 1920s, things they were using on their title cards, like Cheltenham and Bodoni," Jack replies. "I took a real piece of 1927 nitrate I had and did a scan of that. That's what I used for the surrounding perforations. I had a lot of people saying it's not for real because it says 'Eastman' on the side rather than 'Kodak.' They didn't realize that Eastman really *was* printing that on the side of nitrate film. I left the copyright date on the title card that says 1928 instead of 1927. . . . I'll leave it in my will that I made it all up. Of course the biggest thing is I used a tinted piece of film, and MGM stopped tinting their films in 1926." Now that we're deep into the subject of the movie, I can't help asking if he thinks it will ever be found. "I think in all likelihood you may see some footage turn up from the film. It's not the film if somebody asked me, 'Which lost film would you most like to find?' *London After Midnight* is probably the most famous but the most uninteresting at the same time. The mythos surrounding it is Chaney in his makeup, but there are plenty of other more tantalizing films," he says, then continues: "If you find *London After Midnight*, the biggest part of the story would be the glory of finding it, rather than the fact it's a good film, because it's probably terrible by all accounts. I've never seen it. It's the only film from 1927 I can see anyone giving a shit about anymore. It's famously lost."

It should be apparent by now that the man who could convincingly fake a frame of *London After Midnight* is not your average film collector, and yet Jack is barely thirty years old. He was born in New York City in 1986. "I only know of a handful of collectors who are about my age or younger," he observes. "Part of the reason is good luck finding anyone interested in classic film in general. Part of it, too, is that both my parents were for all intents and purposes pretty hip, and were interested in turning me on to good art at a young age." His father had been an on-again/off-again collector of 16mm prints for several decades, but the real turning point for Jack came when a friend of his father's tipped them off to a dumpster outside his Manhattan window filled with discarded film prints from a distributor called Worldvision. "So my father and I spent the rest of the night dumpster diving through this dumpster of film," he says. He admits that a lot of what they found was "crap," but among the discarded prints were numerous episodes of television shows like *One Step Beyond*, *The Many Loves of Dobie Gillis*, *Hanna-Barbera's World of Super Adventure*, and *Bourbon Street*

Beat, plus oddities like a rare kinescope of a Nat King Cole performance from 1959. "That's incidentally one of the first times I encountered vinegar syndrome," he says about the find. "My father didn't know about it either. Still photographers knew about vinegar syndrome before people in motion pictures did: it's what happens when you don't wash the fixer off the negative properly."

Jack's current job is assistant manager at the Rome Capitol Theatre in New York where he programs Capitolfest, their annual classic movie festival; he is also cohead of the 3-D Film Archive (with collector Bob Furmanek) and maintains the 35mm Film Forum online, the main marketplace for buying and selling 35mm prints since the demise of *The Big Reel* magazine in the early 2000s. Amazingly, well into the twenty-first century, he is still making serendipitous discoveries of nitrate prints from nearly a century earlier. "I was at a flea market in New York—this is probably about 2004 or 2005—right around the time I started collecting 35mm, and I bought some tin cans that had come from a toy projector. There was a print of probably about two hundred feet of a hand-colored Pathé short from the late aughts in there. I thought, 'Hmm, that's neat and I never knew about that,'" he recalls. "In the early days, I'd find a lot of that stuff. There was one short in particular I bought called *An Elephant's Nightmare*, which was a French comedy short from around 1916, and I ended up trading it to [French preservationist] Serge Bromberg for some stuff, and Serge did well by it. He got the better end of the deal. . . . I don't mind Serge getting the better end of the deal, because he's actually going to do something with that." Another rare find was a single reel from the camera negative of an early Zionist propaganda film called *Springtime in Palestine* (1928), directed by pioneering Jewish filmmaker and photographer Ya'acov Ben-Dov. I ask where he located the reel. "It was through a friend of mine whose father had been a serviceman for 16mm projectors. He had this vault, and my friend didn't know what to do with it. He said, 'Hey I've got these films, they're in various states of decay.'"

Even for a younger collector like Jack, there are still the ones that got away. Several years ago he was visiting the derelict site of WRS Labs in Pittsburgh, perhaps most famous for its use in exterior shots in local filmmaker George Romero's *Night of the Living Dead*. "The place was amazing, I think it was something like ten acres," he recalls. "One was an office complex, one was set up for video duplication, and the last was set up for film processing. You went into the video duplication, and all you saw were rows and rows of VCR dubbers. Totally useless even at that point. Think of an airplane hangar filled with VCRs." The deal Jack and fellow collector Bob Furmanek had made with the owners of the site was that they could take away prints only from a list they'd submitted before the visit. "We went to the film section. The place was very eerie—the lights had been off, the electricity was only on one circuit at that time." Sitting unnoticed on one of the metal racks was the original camera negative to a classic cartoon short called *Rhapsody of Steel* from 1959. Directed by animator Carl Urbano and produced by the Sutherland Studios, who were responsible for much-loved educational films like *A Is for Atom* (1953), which played for decades in American public schools, *Rhapsody of Steel* traced the origins of steel in gorgeous Technicolor animation. Wandering through this massive, barely lit Pittsburgh film lab, most collectors wouldn't give *Rhapsody of Steel* a second thought, but Jack knew immediately what a rare find it was: "The score was by Dimitri Tiomkin, and they made an album of it, but they never printed the short in stereo. What was at WRS were the successive-exposure negatives and the full-coat of the final mix of the left-center-right." I ask if he snatched it up, and there's a long pause. Finally he answers with a heavy heart: "I wasn't able to get it, because it wasn't on the list of things I was allowed to take. There's an Arabian nights tale of Aladdin and his lamp—and he's only allowed to take one thing or he'll die."

"Anyone can buy a DVD and passively put it on a shelf, maybe never even open it. But to collect film, it's an ordeal," says editor, filmmaker, and collector Mike Williamson. "It's an ordeal as a film lover you're able to validate, because the reward is greater than the pain that collecting film also brings." When he greets me at the door of his Burbank-area house, he's clutching a huge kitchen knife—perhaps appropriate for a collector of vintage horror prints. But it turns out I've caught him in the middle of chopping salad during his lunch break from work.

Mike is tall and gregarious, with curly brown hair and a big grin usually plastered across his broad face. An enthusiastic and unrepentant fan of 1980s slasher films like the *Friday the 13th* and *Nightmare on Elm Street* series, he talks about print collecting with a surprisingly sophisticated and subtle aesthetic perspective. "I think it's an undebatable fact that film looks better than digital. Any digital medium—music, whatever—is like the Robot Boy—it's trying to look human. It's trying to seem analog while being acceptable to consumers," he observes. "For me, it can get pretty deep, because storytelling is what makes humans unique. It's part of our DNA, and it's how we learn. For me, motion pictures are the most representative of humanity as far as storytelling goes, because movies represent the technology of the period and what people can do at the time. They acknowledge the atmosphere of the era; almost every era has defining tones to its movies. And as far as storytelling medium goes, it's the most communal. It's really an important human experience to watch a movie, and since movies are my favorite form of storytelling, it's important to me to experience that as deeply as I can. Watching a movie that I love on a TV set with compressed picture and the phone is ringing—there's so many distractions. It's not like having a giant screen and a rich film print twelve feet wide, letting you get transported into the movie's universe."

Mike was born in Austin, Texas, in 1977. His mother was a schoolteacher who segued into real estate; his father was a wine salesman who passed away when Mike was ten. "None of them were movie lovers in particular. I would say they're just sort of general enthusiasts of entertainment; they liked to listen to a Celine Dion record here and there," he says of his parents. "I remember my biological father and movies that he loved from when I was around. I don't know the movies he loved when he was a kid. I know he loved *Stand by Me*. I know he loved *Top Gun*, which he took me to, and I was too embarrassed to tell him I didn't like it, because he loved it so much." As a kid he started to discover the subversive gore-filled horror films that would become a lifelong fascination.

"I would go to my friend's house who had a more lenient mother," he recalls. "My mom was a very strict Catholic, very frightened of dark entertainment, rock music, horror movies. I don't want to make it sound like she's a nun, but she definitely thought there's some Satanism going on in that kind of stuff. So I would go across the street to my friend Daniel's house and secretly watch *Nightmare on Elm Street* movies that we'd rent from the video store up the street that I'd eventually work at in high school and college."

As a collector he specializes in genre films and collects only 16mm. Among the prints he's most proud of are his IB Technicolor copies of *Blood and Black Lace*, *Rosemary's Baby*, *The Birds*, *The Skull*, and *Dr. Terror's House of Horrors*. He's quick to point out that original prints can preserve the artistic intention of the filmmaker better than new digital transfers, where a colorist can sometimes misinterpret a scene. "I can think of two films in my collection where someone turns a light off," he says, citing his prints of *Darkman* and *Friday the 13th Pt. 4*. "On the DVDs of those movies, the colorist corrected for that, and so in the scenes on the DVD, the lights are never turned off. The colorist 'corrected,' and they stay on—and it's just flat out a mistake."

Perhaps the best thing about Mike's collecting is that he continues the tradition of backyard screenings for friends and family, setting up a big screen and elaborate sound system, and then blasts away with prints of guilty pleasures like *Wolfen*, *Child's Play 2*, *Poltergeist III*, and *Nightmare on Elm Street 4: The Dream Master*. He and his wife, Terry, now have two infant sons to take care of, which has put a bit of a damper on his hobby, at least until the boys are a little older. Since he's a relative rarity as both a younger collector and a married collector, I ask if it's difficult balancing his obsession with being a husband. He thinks for a moment, then replies: "With film collectors, the OCD nature of it is heightened, because there might be only three of [a certain print] in the world, and if you don't get it, you're fucked. It can create a lot of obsessive behavior that might be repulsive to a woman. I've had episodes where I'm trying to catch this collection, and you might ignore your wife for a day or two. When you sit back and look at it later, it's shameful—that you care so much about chasing a print that you didn't go to dinner with your wife." There's a pause and then he shrugs as if admitting he can't help it. "But that's part of the deal. If you want to have a collection that you're proud of, there's that element of aggressiveness that comes with it."

20.

The Man Who Went to Jail for the Movies

It's a long and fairly pleasant drive up the Antelope Valley Freeway, climbing higher and higher through the San Gabriel Mountains as you leave the Los Angeles sprawl behind. The farther you go, the more sparsely populated the terrain becomes, and soon it feels as if you're in the lonesome deserts of New Mexico, even though you're still technically in Los Angeles County. The remoteness of these rocky hills has always attracted film companies looking for a southwestern feel. In fact, the freeway runs right past the area's most famous feature, Vasquez Rocks—named after the infamous 1870s Mexican-Californian bandit, Tiburcio Vásquez, and a familiar location from episodes of the original *Star Trek* TV series. (The most prominent outcropping has even been dubbed "Kirk's Rock" in the series' honor.)

They're entirely appropriate associations—California bandits and the entertainment industry—for the man I'm driving up to see: Jeff Joseph, for many years one of the most successful and knowledgeable film dealers in the United States, and my writing partner on this book. In May 1975 he was one of the sixteen dealers and collectors indicted by the U.S. Justice Department, charged with "federal criminal violations related to the piracy of feature motion picture films and television programs," as announced in the *Hollywood Reporter*.[61] "When the FBI busts finally happened and we all congregated at the court, I knew almost none of the other people there. That shows how minor I was," he says of the arrests that defined the collecting subculture for decades after, and his own career in many ways. Of the sixteen men charged, only Jeff—who was twenty-two years old at the time—would do jail time.

This is a drive I've made several times before, to visit Jeff's sizable film warehouse and private screening room in Palmdale. I met him in the early 1990s when I came to work at the American Cinematheque in L.A., and over the years we'd organized several retrospectives together showcasing rare dye-transfer Technicolor and four-track mag stereo prints. But this time there's a difference: recently Jeff has gotten out of the business of selling prints altogether. He's sold his entire inventory of over fifty thousand original trailers for classic Hollywood films, including the sole surviving nitrate copy of the original *Citizen Kane* trailer, newsreels, and rare outtakes, such as two unique reels of 1949 Greta Garbo screen tests for a never-made project, her last appearance on film. In addition to the trailers, he sold his irreplaceable collection of original dual-interlock prints of 3-D features and shorts, including one-of-a-kind 35mm copies of *I, The Jury* and *Gog,* and the earliest surviving true stereoscopic footage, from 1922 and showing New York City and Washington, D.C.[62] It was by far the best and most complete 3-D print collection anywhere in the world, which Jeff drew on to present three editions of the World 3-D Film Expo at the Egyptian Theatre between 2003 and 2013, described as "a Woodstock for movie geeks" by Leonard Maltin. The purchaser of Jeff's massive private archive is the nonprofit Packard Humanities Institute, run by enigmatic film benefactor David Packard, which has divided the collection between the UCLA Film & Television Archive and the Academy Film Archive. It's a remarkable turn of events for the man who, four decades earlier, was branded a film pirate and led away from an L.A. federal courthouse in handcuffs.

The change is immediately apparent as Jeff greets me outside the padlocked gates of the now-empty warehouse on a dusty road where the only interruption is locals roaring past at 70 mph in their Chevy pickups. "I tried to keep my company running, but I was on the brink of foreclosure three times in the past few years," he shrugs as he fiddles for his keys. "I was hoping I could keep the screening room and warehouse intact and sell it to someone who loves film, but there were no takers. I even offered the building to the city of Palmdale to use for a couple years until I could find a buyer, but they didn't need it." (Subsequent to this interview, Jeff finally managed to rent the warehouse, to a local church.) Inside are dust-covered desks and empty shelves where there were once stacks of film that Jeff had acquired and then resold. Even his crown jewel—a spacious screening room with a dazzling curved silver screen and dual-interlock projectors for showing 3-D—is gone. Nothing remains but gaping holes in the ceiling for ventilation in the projection booth. Although I can't guess it at the time, this conversation in a forlorn Palmdale warehouse—far from the "great muted chromium studios," in Graham Greene's beautiful turn of phrase—will stretch out over many months and eventually lead to this book.[63]

"In terms of 35mm out there, I'm responsible for at least a third of it. We dealt a lot of fucking film," he says. When I ask how much "a lot" is, he does some quick calculations. "When we were really boogieing stuff out the door, I'd say at least 1,000 prints a month, over 10,000 a year. About 100,000 prints over that ten-year-period; about 70 percent of it 16mm, and the rest 35mm." One of the major differences between Jeff and his peers in the collecting world is that he was a dealer, first and foremost. "As a dealer I wouldn't keep stuff except for a few trailers. Everything else would go," he says. This empty building is proof there's nothing he won't part with. After the sale, this man who was once synonymous with 35mm and 16mm will literally have no film to his name. "I became a kind of bartender to collectors, and I got tired of hearing their stories. 'Well my wife is going to divorce me if I buy this print . . .' 'Well, don't buy the print, then!' But that's not want they want to hear."

Jeff is medium height, dressed in black T-shirt and slacks, with a bit of a potbelly and an occasional wild, anarchic gleam in his eyes, as if he's about to hatch some devilish prank. His graying hair and beard are practically the only difference between now and photos of him in the 1970s, when he famously kept two exotic cats as pets, an ocelot named King and a margay named Sabu, whose name and likeness became the logo for his film company, SabuCat. "We used to take Sabu the margay with us everywhere," he recalls, smiling. "We took her out once on a leash, walking her through Westwood Village." He pauses, then recounts that when he was sent to jail in 1976, he didn't have time to say good-bye to his wife, Lauren, or his cats. "When I came back from jail after two months to this grungy little apartment, King saw me and he ran to me. I swear to you, Dennis, he grabbed me around the leg with his front paws and wouldn't let go. It was the damnedest thing. I'm tearing up just thinking about it.

"I was born at Kaiser Sunset Hospital when it was still evil socialized medicine. My parents were both members of the Communist Party, although they'd resigned from it by the time I was born," he says, recalling his childhood in L.A. in the early 1950s. "[My father] was an organizer for the Social Workers Union in the late 1940s. He told me that he used to have an apartment in Silver Lake, and he let women stay there overnight to recover from illegal abortions." Jeff's father was brought up in a progressive Jewish orphanage in Cleveland, where he was trained to become a printer; his mother was a nurse. "Politics was always in the house," he remembers. "Tom Lehrer had a song called 'The Vatican Rag.' I was always instructed by my parents, 'Never play this for a Catholic; you'll insult them.' So, of course, I went out of my way to do just that," he adds, grinning.

"The first movie I ever fell in love with was with Laurel and Hardy. Then, when I was eleven or twelve, I discovered Blackhawk. I realized you could buy Laurel and Hardy movies and own them." It's somehow fitting that one of Jeff's projects postretirement is helping to finance UCLA Film Archive's restoration of the Laurel and Hardy catalogue, but as a boy he could barely afford a single film. "I found a projector and bought *Another Fine Mess* by Laurel and Hardy on 16mm. You could send them five dollars a month—it probably cost sixty or seventy dollars total—and would take about a year to pay it off. I didn't get it until I paid it off, of course." It's hard to imagine someone working a newspaper route for a year to pay off *a single film*, but that's the dedication of collectors in the pre-home-video and pre-internet days. Jeff started out running prints in his garage for his neighborhood friends, and later at a nearby recreation center run by a rabbi. Ironically, his first encounter with the FBI was as a senior in high school and had nothing to do with film. "I was blue-boxing at the time, making illegal phone calls," he admits. "It was a way of hacking the phone company."[64] Jeff sold one of his homemade phone-hacking kits to another student. "So I got a call from the FBI, and they said, 'We know you built this blue box.' I was scared out of my wits," Jeff says. "They told me, 'Just don't do that anymore.' At some point later I got the blue box back, I don't know how, and I destroyed it." When he graduated from high school in 1971 he took a cross-country trip with a friend but insisted on making a special detour.

"I insisted on stopping in Davenport, Iowa, to see Blackhawk Films. It was better than the Empire State Building any day," he recalls of the legendary, century-old structure that was shut down in 1987.

"I met Ken in 1971. He was the first quote-unquote 'film pirate' I ever met," Jeff says of his initial meeting with Ken Kramer. He couldn't imagine at the time how their personal and professional lives would become intertwined over the next four and a half decades. "We met because I heard he had *Star Treks* to sell. He had a great connection down at the lab." At the time Jeff was working a two-dollar-an-hour job as a movie theater usher. After acquiring 16mm prints of *The Graduate* and *Bonnie and Clyde* from the theater manager and trading them to Ken for a profit—"He got by far the better of the deal, because I didn't know anything," Jeff quips—he decided to quit his job and become a film dealer, working with his mentor/partner. Ken was able to use the teenage Jeff as something of a front. "Ken couldn't put his name on things, because he had a bad reputation, and he couldn't rent things at Budget Films or Films Inc. Labs wouldn't deal with him. So he used my name to do that sort of thing. I also discovered that he utterly hated doing any actual work, so I wound up schlepping all the film," Jeff recounts with a wry grin. "I got something out of it, because I learned to hustle. I didn't bitch about it at the time, and I still don't."

Those were heady days. He was barely out of high school, and he was suddenly thrust into the black-market Hollywood film trade, dealing with the rich and famous. "One time we got a call from one of Hugh Hefner's guys," Jeff recalls. "Hefner wanted to run *The Godfather*. Well, they hadn't even made 16mm prints of it yet. So we asked if he'd be interested in 35mm, and he said yes. He was set up for it, and he'd pay three thousand dollars for it, which was a lot of money. And we knew we'd get it cheap, since no one was dealing 35mm at the time. So we called Larry Goldberg," Jeff continues.[65] "He knew other drivers, so he made some calls. A week later Larry shows up with a new print of *The Godfather*. It still had the labels on it from the drive-in it'd been stolen from. So we put it in the trunk of Ken's car, drive it over to the Playboy Mansion, and get paid. Fast forward a month: I'm reading *Time* magazine. In this article, it very casually mentions Hugh Hefner ran *The Godfather* for a few people the other day. I was terrified we'd get in hot water for that, but nothing ever came of it. In the 1970s I was willing to play games like that, dealing in stolen merchandise, but I didn't do that in the 1980s," he confides.

He soon moved into a new apartment, right above Ken, his young wife, Lauren, and their son, Jay. "There were no hours there, that is to say, movies were being run 24/7. You could call at three in the morning or three in the afternoon; time didn't matter at Ken's house," he says. He and Lauren had an immediate aversion to each other. "She couldn't stand me, and I couldn't stand her," he says simply. "From my point of view, she was this horrible woman yelling at this guy I wanted to be friends with. From her point of view, I was another punk kid who wanted to just get film from Ken." Over the next year he and Lauren gradually became closer. "We'd gotten to the point where we were good friends, and we'd lie in bed and just chat, fully clothed," Jeff says. One of his personality quirks is his unnerving ability to pinpoint the exact date of events in his life—in this case, he pulls out his iPad and, after a quick search, startles me by telling me the date he and Lauren first slept together: "September 26, 1972, was our first time together. I was a virgin, and she definitely was *not*. She and Ken had been into the swinging lifestyle for a while at that point."

After being caught together a second time by Ken in 1973, Lauren took off and moved in with Jeff. They were together for the next thirty-four years, except for his two months in jail, until her death in 2007. "Look, Lauren and I should have never been a couple. We had so much going against us. She was seven years older, she had two kids, two ex-husbands. She had lots of health issues even then. There were a lot of reasons we should've never gotten together," he says of his late wife, who, by his own admission, was much more of a movie buff than he. For her sixtieth birthday, while she was seriously ill and battling for her life against cancer, he organized a screening of her favorite film, *The King and I*, for friends and family at SabuCat. It was a tremendously moving afternoon, and sitting here now with Jeff in the empty screening room, it's hard not to think of the emotion of that day.

Although he and Ken split as partners in 1973, Jeff continued working some of their lucrative contacts, most notably the illicit film trade to South Africa. It would have serious repercussions for Jeff. "Because of apartheid, they didn't have deals with any of the studios," he recalls. "So people like Peter Theologo would acquire prints of TV shows from people like me. I'd pay ten dollars for a *Mod Squad* and sell it to him for two hundred. I was making great money."⁶⁶ He even socialized with his South African counterparts, taking Theologo and his wife to that classic Southern California destination, Disneyland. "They almost wouldn't let Lauren in; she had a real low-cut dress exposing her breasts," Jeff laughs. "They made her pull it up. As soon as she got in, she let it down again." The South African film pirates were not so different from Jeff and Ken. "They were operators, hustle artists trying to make a buck like you'd find in Hollywood. Peter was an average-looking bald guy in his sixties," he says with a shrug. Things could get nasty, though. "The only time I had anybody physically threaten me in my life was over a film deal. A guy stuck a knife right here." Jeff points to his lower gut. "He was one of the South Africans. He was a crook—they were all crooks to a point, but he was a real crook." Jeff had sold him a 16mm print of the 1973 Michael Crichton sci-fi film *Westworld*. "He calls me, furious, saying the print had a scratch on it. I never said it was mint—it was a good print. Turns out he needed a mint print so he could bootleg it." The South African dealer insisted on meeting Jeff to get his money back. "We met at a bar, and he pulled a knife on me. Scared the fuck out of me. He took my wallet; only had a few bucks in it."

Although he didn't realize it at the time, the FBI was zeroing in on him because of his illicit dealings with Theologo and other South African film pirates. When the feds finally sprang into action, it caught Jeff totally by surprise. "Lauren and I were living at an apartment on Hollywood Beach near Oxnard. It's a beach nobody's heard of. They started pounding on the door, so we flushed the pot down the toilet—which was unnecessary, because their search warrant was only for the garage and our storage locker," he says. "I wasn't arrested that day. Later on, I went down and turned myself in." He shakes his head, remembering the wave of arrests that stunned the underground network of dealers and collectors. "There'd always been rumors they were investigating film dealers—stories you tell at night when the lights are out—but nothing ever came of it. But in 1974, they busted Roddy McDowall. It was in the *Los Angeles Times*, front page, part two. McDowall was their name bust.

"I was randomly assigned a judge named Lawrence Lydick," he continues. "When we found out, my lawyer said, 'Uh oh.' Lydick was a Nixon appointee and did not believe in suspended sentences. The deal my lawyer worked out with for me with the prosecutor was a six-month suspended sentence and a $500 fine. I was originally charged with ten misdemeanors and one felony, the felony being receiving stolen property, and the misdemeanors were copyright infringement. In retrospect, I was not guilty of copyright infringement, but I didn't know that. I pleaded guilty randomly to one of the misdemeanor counts, and it happened to be for selling prints of *It Takes a Thief*, the old Robert Wagner TV show, to South Africa." On January 6, 1976, Jeff appeared in an L.A. courtroom, expecting to receive a suspended sentence and pay a fine, but instead the judge ignored the deal prosecutors had worked out and sentenced Jeff to six months in jail. He was led away in handcuffs by federal marshals. (In a strange disparity, several of the other indicted dealers were convicted of charges similar to Jeff's but received suspended sentences and fines.) "My dad was in court the day I was sentenced, and the look on his face was not good," Jeff recalls quietly. "I'd forgotten about that actually. He was pretty devastated about that. Of course he didn't expect it either. We all thought I was going home."

Jeff spent a month in the L.A. county jail, waiting to be transferred to a federal prison at Lompoc. "One guy was a murderer. He told us this lovely story about killing someone," Jeff recalls, grimacing. "I remember hearing a guy getting raped. That wasn't a fun thing to hear." Did any of his fellow prisoners ask why he was in jail? He nods with a broad grin. "I assume you are familiar with the song 'Alice's Restaurant' by Arlo Guthrie? In the song, they send him over to the Group W bench, where murderers and rapists and father killers and all these horrible people are there. The song goes, "What were you arrested for, kid?" And I said, "Littering." And they all moved away from me on the bench.' And that's how it was for me in jail: 'You're in for what, murder? You're in for what, rape? You're in for what, *copyright infringement?!*'" After another month at Lompoc, Jeff was startled to find out that Judge Lydick had agreed to commute his sentence as a result of Jeff's father's relentless legal work on his son's behalf. Jeff was released and ordered to serve three years' probation.

It spelled the immediate end of his career as a film dealer. "I didn't want to mess with film anyway. I was terrified," he admits. "First, I didn't have any film, because the FBI got it all. Thinking about this in retrospect, I don't think anyone would've dealt with me, because they knew I'd gone to jail. It was a moot point—I didn't even try it. I did electronics work for the next dozen years." I ask how his wife, Lauren, reacted to his jail time, and he responds, "She was probably more devastated than I was." In a truly bizarre coda to his arrest and jail time, in the early 1980s he received a call from the FBI agent who'd been in charge of his case. Jeff was initially panicked by the thought they'd come up with new charges against him. "I'm an electronics technician. Why does the FBI want me now? So I call them back. The FBI says, 'We have all this film—do you want it back?'" There's a long pause as Jeff shakes his head, still stunned by the strange turn of events. "I said, 'This is the film you busted me for? The same film? *Now you want to give it back to me?!*' The guy said yes. So I rented a truck, went and picked it all up, and sold it to someone for two grand, which I really needed. Unbelievable."

Thirteen years had passed since he essentially walked away from film, but in 1989 he decided to get back into dealing. "I was doing electronics and hated it," he says bluntly. I ask him what had changed since he'd been away from the business. "There was certainly more 35mm," he replies. Once considered an exclusive "rich man's hobby," 35mm collecting was suddenly in vogue because of the falling prices of used projectors and a younger wave of collectors entering the market, men like Joe Dante and Jon Davison who had the financial means and knowledge to collect the larger format. Ironically, for a former convicted "film pirate," one of Jeff's first deals on reentering the fray was with a major studio, Disney. In 1940, when *Fantasia* was originally released, it contained several brief and highly offensive scenes with a black centaur named Sunflower, presented as a grossly racist caricature. Starting in the 1950s, the character had been cut out of reissues of the film, but when Disney archivists wanted to restore the original version of the film in the late 1980s, they discovered the stereo soundtrack elements to those censored scenes had been lost. Jeff located a four-track mag stereo print of the film that was going vinegar, but the sound was still usable, and that's what mattered.

Within a few years Jeff's company SabuCat became the go-to source for 35mm prints in the United States and even worldwide. When I came to Los Angeles in the early 1990s to work for the American Cinematheque, I remember opening issues of *The Big Reel* and seeing enormous double-page SabuCat ads listing literally hundreds of prints each issue, at astonishing prices. Jeff likes to joke that when he returned to dealing, he added a zero to the price of 35mm prints, and it's not far from the truth. "I used to tell collectors, and I wasn't kidding, 'If you want to get a divorce, start collecting 35mm,'" he says with a sigh. "The wife is gonna roll her eyes at 16mm, but 35mm she'll throw you out the door. It takes up a lot of room, it's stinky, it's expensive. Collecting 35mm becomes a lifestyle." A lot of collectors were willing to take on that lifestyle, and in many ways, the decade between the early 1990s and the early 2000s was the golden age of film collecting. The major studios and MPAA increasingly looked the other way as they found themselves occupied with video, and soon digital, piracy; and as TV stations switched from film to video, and nontheatrical distributors like Films Inc. shut down, a vast quantity of prints flooded the market. Prices for in-demand 35mm prints shot up from the hundreds to the thousands. At some point Jeff drew up a joking list describing the typical collector, and while it trades in stereotypes, it also hits perilously close to the truth:

REAL FILM COLLECTORS

1. Real film collectors live with mom.
2. Real film collectors don't live with mom, 'cause mom is stuffed and mounted in the closet.
3. Real film collectors don't have jobs.
4. Real film collectors do have jobs, but at film labs, film rental companies, junking facilities, or other places that they can "rescue" film from.
5. Real film collectors don't drive.
6. Real film collectors do drive, but they only have a "limited" license that allows driving to film conventions, screenings, film depots, etc. This is known as a "class IB" license.
7. Real film collectors don't do drugs.
8. Yeah, but isn't the bouquet of Kodak Film Cement just wonderful?
9. The sexual orientation of most film collectors is unknown.
10. "My son is NOT gay!"
11. Real film collectors would never "swap" footage without permission.
12. Sure they would.
13. Real film collectors never marry.

14. Real film collectors do get married, but get quick divorces when their spouses discover that the 70mm pink and smelly print of *Circus World* is taking up all the closet space.
15. Real film collectors have no life.
16. Real film collectors *do* have a life, but it stopped around 1956 or so.
17. Real film collectors will buy a print before they pay the rent or buy food for the kids.
18. Real film collectors never put oil and vinegar on their salad.
19. Real film collectors are named Bill, Alan, Mike, Bob, Jim, or Tom.
20. Real film collectors will sell their soul for a print.
21. Film collectors have souls?

The number of rarities that passed through Jeff's hands during that decade is hard to fathom. It could be something ephemeral, like a long-forgotten promotional short from the 1930s that mysteriously turned up in a reel of 1970s-era trailers he was projecting: "Suddenly I look up and see a two-color Technicolor piece; somebody just stuck it on the end of the reel. It was called *Race Night*. Remember in the 1930s they had things like 'Dish Night,' where they'd do giveaways to get people in the theater? They had a prefilmed race: you'd look at your ticket, and there was a number on the end, and if it came up, you were a winner." *Race Night* may not be an essential piece of cinema history, but it's fascinating in part because it was meant to be disposable, like a nineteenth-century handbill that gives us a clue as to how ordinary people thought and felt back then. Other discoveries were more significant, like a virtually mint 35mm nitrate print from France of Michael Curtiz's 1933 horror film *Mystery of the Wax Museum*, starring Lionel Atwill and Fay Wray, one of the earliest two-color Technicolor movies. "The Warner logo fades in . . . it had the original leaders on it, just stunning. I didn't have the balls to run it, but it was just beautiful," Jeff says admiringly of the print, which is now part of the Packard Humanities Institute collection at UCLA Film & Television Archive. He began acquiring 35mm trailers, a formerly overlooked area of "film ephemera," and discovered that not only were certain trailers exceedingly rare or even lost (the original 1939 *The Wizard of Oz* trailer remains missing to this day; existing versions are from later reissues), but a number of trailers featured alternate takes or one-of-a-kind footage not included in the actual feature film. "The most I ever paid for a trailer was five hundred dollars for the *Citizen Kane* trailer," he says. "To the best of my knowledge, it is the only original element of the original trailer." By the time he closed SabuCat and sold his collection, his trailer archive had grown to over fifty thousand items—the largest private trailer archive in the world.

Jeff is often identified with classic 3-D cinema, especially after purchasing the collection of Bob Furmanek of the 3-D Film Archive (which included a number of one-of-a-kind 35mm dual-system 3-D prints from the early 1950s) and essentially doubling its size.[67] "I was never a 3-D nut," Jeff admits candidly. "To me, the appeal of it was the 'orphan aspect'— just like trailers, nobody was taking care of it." His favorite 3-D discovery involves a mysterious short titled *A Day in the Country* from 1953 that was released by entrepreneur Robert L. Lippert in the brief period between the first 3-D feature release in the United States, *Bwana Devil*, and *House of Wax*. "Nobody had seen *A Day in the Country* in fifty-plus years, it was a lost film. This guy on the East Coast reads me a list: 'I've got this and this and this and *A Day in the Country* . . .' I said, 'Back up; what did you say?' He said, '*A Day in the Country*—and it's in 3-D.' He wanted five hundred dollars, which was insanely expensive, but I agreed." Jeff sent him the money for the short—and the man promptly disappeared. A year went by with no news from him. Jeff even enlisted a private detective to find him, with no results. Finally, Jeff managed to get the elusive dealer on the phone. He admitted he no longer had *A Day in the Country*; the print had been sitting in the back of his truck when it was towed. But Jeff refused to give up: "So I tracked down the towing company and gave her the long spiel on the phone. She said, 'Let me look that up . . . well, we still have that truck here.' I said, 'Would you go look for it?' She says, 'Okay.' She puts the phone down for five minutes and comes back: 'I have this reel of film, and it says *A Day in the Country* on it.'" Incredibly, the reel had been sitting forgotten in the back of the dealer's impounded pickup truck for over a year, but Jeff got his hands on it and, with the help of 3-D expert Dan Symmes, managed to extract usable 3-D images. After examining the film, Jeff realized the release date of 1953 was misleading. "What we found out is that in 1941 a guy named Jack Rieger, a minor B-producer of mostly boxing shorts, produced this little 3-D short called *Stereo Laffs* on his own, with his own camera. And nothing happened with it. And then in 1953 he sold it to Lippert, and that's why it looks like the late 1930s," he says of the short, which he screened during the 2006 World 3-D Film Expo at the Egyptian.

In addition to selling prints directly to dealers, Jeff soon learned he could license footage from trailers in the public domain to cable networks like A&E doing biographies on Hollywood celebrities, a business that became a lucrative sideline (and eventually overtook his print dealing.) I ask him what rare footage was most in demand, and he immediately answers Audrey Hepburn's screen test for *Roman Holiday*, from an early 1950s series called *You Asked for It*, which he bought from a fellow collector. "It was an early reality show is what it boils down to. People would send in, 'I want to see skydiving or how cookies are made,' and they'd show them," he explains. "Somebody suggested, 'I want to see screen tests,' so they got screen tests from Paramount for *Roman Holiday*; the whole thing is, like, seven minutes total." Equally in demand was lost footage of Greta Garbo shot in 1949 for a never-made film project. "Don't forget Garbo retired in 1941 or so. The only professional films of her shot after that time were these makeup and costume tests," he says. "Producer Walter Wanger was gonna do this movie. If you read biographies of Garbo, they talk about these screen tests, but they were considered lost." I ask Jeff where he found the footage, and he hems and haws for a moment. "Basically I stole it—I'm just thinking of a polite way to put it. It was being thrown away in the trash, and I took it," he finally admits. "It said on the two cans 'Garbo Tests.' I was at the storage facility for a perfectly legitimate reason, and this was kind of off to the side.

"You think collectors were paranoid? It's because of the film busts. I mean collectors are paranoid in general. Collectors are nutty to begin with—and film collectors on top of that," Jeff says about the fear that persists in the subculture to this day. "The busts tainted a lot of stuff, it really did, and ultimately it hurt the studios, because the collectors wouldn't deal with them. To this day, there's a fellow in Chicago who claims to have the missing stereo tracks to the Vincent Price 3-D *House of Wax*. And the collector refuses to deal with the studio. I tend to think he's telling the truth, that he really has it. What's really a shame is that *House of Wax* is probably the first stereo film most people saw. The studio has the surrounds but not the front three tracks." For Jeff, the Laurel and Hardy fanatic, perhaps the most frustrating one that got away is *The Rogue Song*, a 1930 musical directed by actor Lionel Barrymore and starring the duo in supporting roles. "It was two-color Technicolor—it was an operetta starring Lawrence Tibbett, the famous opera star. It was too slow, so Louis B. Mayer asked Hal Roach to loan Laurel and Hardy," he explains. "Richard May [former Turner archivist] found paperwork in the old MGM files, a note from Technicolor to MGM in 1937, that 'since we can no longer print two-color Technicolor anymore, you might as well junk your negatives.' And they did. There was an original nitrate print that survived into the 1950s, but it went up in a lab fire. There are a few bits and pieces that've survived. A collector has one scene, but it's set inside a cave, so you can't see much. He found it in a box in a used bookstore," Jeff says. "An entire reel turned up in Europe; unfortunately, it's a reel without Laurel and Hardy! It's the holy grail of Laurel and Hardy films." In 1989 Jeff was contacted by a collector named Randy in San Diego who'd seen one of his ads in *The Big Reel* and claimed he had a nitrate print of the long-sought-after *Rogue Song*, missing one reel but otherwise complete. "I said, 'Come on, anyone can say that. This is one of the most famous missing films.' But who knows, maybe he has it? I ask how much he wants. He says, 'One thousand dollars,' which is very reasonable." Being a little cautious, Jeff agreed to forward him $200 as a down payment. On the day they'd agreed Jeff would see the famous missing print, he drove down to San Diego to meet the collector but found only his girlfriend at his apartment. "'Are you waiting for Randy?' she asks. I say yes. She says, 'He's gone out of town. Somebody sent him two hundred dollars, and he bought a plane ticket to Chicago.'" Jeff throws his hands up in despair, remembering the frustration of that day and sensing *The Rogue Song* slipping through his fingers. He finally continues: "What eventually happened is he died in Chicago. I assume it was a scam, but to this day, I don't know for sure. What makes me wonder is that I asked him to prove he had it. I picked a random reel, say reel four, and said, 'Describe it to me'—*and he did*. And I knew someone who had a cutting continuity for the film. I called him, and he said, 'That's the correct scene.' So to this day I'm not sure if he had it or not."

"God, those were the days of some great lists," he sighs, thinking back on the hand-typed lists of prints that dealers and collectors zealously fought over. He shows me one of them that he's kept for some reason, from a former engineer at ABC Television who was selling his 35mm collection. It is, quite frankly, an astonishing line-up: *American Graffiti*, *Bringing Up Baby*, *City Lights*, *The Conversation*, *Dumbo*, *8 1/2*, *Gone with the Wind*, *The Great Dictator*, *The Innocents*. The collection is long since dispersed, but Jeff still has the list to muse over. Finally he shakes his head and throws it in a trash pile. By the early 2000s the writing was on the wall for the decline of film collecting and dealing: "I would say when we opened it was maybe 90 percent of our income from dealing film and 10 percent from licensing footage, and when we closed it'd completely flipped." In the final days he had trouble making payroll for his already dwindling SabuCat staff and freely admits if the Packard Humanities Institute hadn't purchased his vast archive, he'd be selling off his fifty thousand trailers one by one on eBay. "There's a lot of film floating around in people's houses, that's true, and probably most of it gets dumped when people die," he responds when I ask what happens to all the film he sold over the years. Although he claims he's out of the business of buying and selling film, subsequent to our interview he does confess to buying a 35mm print of Franco Zeffirelli's 1972 *Brother Sun, Sister Moon*: "I bought it for $500 and immediately resold it for $1,250 to somebody I knew who wanted it. It was an IB Tech print," he says with that old gleam in his eyes. "I haven't dealt film in five years, but this was low-hanging fruit." And as any film dealer knows, low-hanging fruit is hard to resist.

Epilogue

Since being interviewed for this book, collectors Alfred "Al" Beardsley, Bob DePietro, Evan H. Foreman, Ken Kramer, Lee Sanders, Tony Turano, Mike Vraney, and Steve Wachtel have, sadly, passed away.

Special Thanks

Jeff and I would like to acknowledge the very significant contributions to this book by his late wife, Lauren Jones-Joseph, who compiled a large amount of invaluable research into the film-collecting and dealing subcultures before her death in 2007. We owe an enormous debt of gratitude to fellow writers Sylvia Townsend and Vincent Lobrutto, who read drafts of this manuscript and generously offered their friendship, support, and guidance. Thanks to Susan Sedman, Jonathan Mersel, and Lisa Williams for their expert proofreading, and Sam Arnold-Boyd for her help preparing the index.

Many current and former film collectors and dealers willingly consented to be interviewed for this book, often sharing rare photos and news clippings of a bygone era. Although there wasn't room to include all of their reminiscences and observations, Jeff and I would like to acknowledge and thank everyone who participated. Whether or not they appear in or are quoted in the manuscript, this book could not have been written without their help. Each interview was unique and fascinating, and opened another window into a sadly disappearing world.

Adam Sargis	Bob DePietro	Dave Barnes
Al Beardsley	Bob Furmanek	David Bordwell
Alan Cylinder	Bob Krasnow	David Shepard
Allan Scott	Bob Leader	Denis Clark
Amanda Huntley	Boris Zmijewsky	Dominick Rubalcava
Andy MacDougall	Brian LeGrady	Don Furr
Andy Nixon	Bruce Calvert	Donald Key
Anthony Timpson	Carl Hallstrom	Eddie de Roo
Becca Hall	Carl Watkins	Evan Foreman
Bill Longen	Conrad Sprout	Gary Meyer
Bill Shurr	Craig Call	Gunther Jung

Hillary Hess	Mark Punswick	Richard Ducar
Jack Theakston	Marty Kearns	Richard Haines
James Bouras	Matt Spero	Richard Scott
Jayson Kramer	Michael Arick	Rick Fearns
Jerry Bryant	Michael McKay	Rik Lueras
Jerry Panza	Michael Schlesinger	Rob Buskop
Jim Reid	Mike Gaines	Robert Osborne
Jim Zippo	Mike Hyatt	Ron Roccia
Joe Dante	Mike Schleiger	Ronnie James
Jon Davison	Mike Smith	Roy Wagner
Julian Antos	Mike Vraney	Ryan Pettigrew
Karl Thiede	Mike Williamson	Serge Bromberg
Kathleen Karr	Mort Zarcoff	Steve Newton
Ken Kramer	Packy Smith	Steve Wachtel
Kevin Brownlow	Pat Rocco	Tag Gallagher
Kingsley Candler	Patrick Stansbury	Ted Newsom
Kit Parker	Paul Burt	Todd Tuckey
Lee Sanders	Paul Ivester	Tom Holland
Leonard Maltin	Paul Rayton	Tommy Cooper
Lowell Peterson	Paul Rutan	Tony Turano
Mark Cantor	Peter Dyck	Wade Williams
Mark Haggard	Phil Blankenship	Wes Shank
Mark Kausler	Ray Faiola	Woody Wise
Mark McGee	Richard Bann	

Notes

1. Dionne Searcey and James R. Hagerty, "Lawyerese Goes Galactic as Contracts Try to Master the Universe," *Wall Street Journal*, October 29, 2009.

2. One of the funnier sight gags in *Austin Powers: International Man of Mystery* (1997) has poor, thawed Austin trying to play a CD of the Byrds' "Mr. Tambourine Man" on his record player, with disastrous results.

3. Although cellulose acetate or "safety" film stock was developed in the 1930s, it didn't become industry standard until 1948, when the studios stopped using potentially flammable nitrate stock. Since then, nitrate has gotten something of a bad rep: although there were several disastrous nitrate-related fires, many prints were destroyed by the studios simply because they were on nitrate.

4. "Discontinuation of Motion Picture Film Production," FUJIFILM Corporation, April 2, 2013, http://www.fujifilm.com/news/n130402.html.

5. Although there were several magazines that catered to film collectors and advertised prints for sale, by far the most important was *The Big Reel*, which started publication in April 1974. Not only collectors read *The Big Reel*—FBI agents were apparently avid readers, too, and at one point interrogated publisher Key: "As a matter of fact I was contacted—they were asking questions about one of my advertisers," he recalls. "I went to a deposition, and I refused to answer any questions. I was found guilty for not answering the deposition by the federal people, and I went to a federal court, and the judge fined me $1,800 for not revealing the information." Key sold the magazine in 1993, and it struggled on for several more years before shutting down. Almost every collector I spoke with mourned the passing of *The Big Reel*.

6. In a highly publicized move, in July of 2014 Tarantino, Nolan, Apatow, and Abrams announced that they'd convinced the heads of the major studios to place enough advance orders with Kodak to ensure that motion picture film negative would still be manufactured and available to filmmakers who choose to shoot on film for the next several years. Ben Fritz, "Movie Film, at Death's Door, Gets a Reprieve," *Wall Street Journal,* July 29, 2014.

7. The heavy metal cans—named after the Goldberg Bros. of Denver, Colorado, manufacturers of motion picture equipment since 1897—are octagonally shaped and nearly indestructible. They, too, are quickly disappearing in the Digital Age.

8. Francis M. Nevins, Jr., "The Film Collector, the FBI, and the Copyright Act," 26 Clev. St. L. Rev. 547—558 (1977).

9. The decision involved a publisher, Bobbs-Merrill Co., suing retailer R. H. Macy & Co. (later just Macy's) for selling a now-forgotten book, *The Castaways*, at the retail price of eighty-nine cents. Bobbs-Merrill had insisted that selling it for less than a dollar was a violation of their copyright. The court disagreed, and first sale was born.

10. Making a "dupe" or copy involves creating a new 35mm or 16mm negative off of a release print, and then using this to strike more prints. This was perfectly legal with public domain films, but obviously less than legal with copyrighted movies. Because the source material—the release print—is already several generations away from the original camera negative, the subsequent dupes are usually fuzzier and grainer, depending on the care taken in making them. In general, original release prints were much more valuable and sought after than dupes, which were akin to making a bootleg copy of a VHS tape.

11. Robert Rawitch, "U.S. Indicts 16 in Movie, TV Film Pirating Case," *Los Angeles Times*, May 30, 1975.

12. In a follow-up interview, Foreman points out that his book "can be copied by anybody—I renounce any copyright interest in it."

13. In addition to 16mm Filmland, Foreman ran a small company that published business forms.

14. Nevins, "Film Collector, the FBI, and the Copyright Act."

15. Nevins, "Film Collector, the FBI, and the Copyright Act."

16. Atherton's other credits include producing the documentaries *Murderers, Mobsters & Madmen, Vols. 1 and 2*, and cowriting the 1977 grindhouse flick *Meatcleaver Massacre*, which inadvertently features legendary horror actor Christopher Lee—who shot footage for another movie entirely, which was sold without his knowledge to the *Meatcleaver Massacre* producers.

17. Robert Rawitch, "FBI Seizes Films from Actor," *Los Angeles Times*, January 17, 1975.

18. Although impossible to say for sure, this dealer from Chicago is in all likelihood Ray Atherton.

19. Jim Harwood, "Appeals Court, in Reversing Atherton Conviction, Lays Down Tough Evidence Guides," *Variety*, October 9, 1977.

20. Sadly, the *Guide* ceased publication in 2014, after forty-five years—another victim of the Digital Revolution.

21. In a move the studio has long regretted, in 1958 Paramount sold its *entire pre-1948 film library*—including screwball comedy classics by Preston Sturges and Mitchell Leisen, Billy Wilder's *Double Indemnity* and *The Lost Weekend*, and much more—for the then-substantial sum of $50 million to Jules Stein's Music Corporation of America (MCA) for TV broadcast. Eventually, the films wound up at rival studio Universal, which owns the Paramount treasure trove to this day.

22. For the home collectors market from the 1940s to 1960s, the two most important distributors were Castle Films and Blackhawk Films. Both specialized in 8mm, Super 8mm, and 16mm silent and sound shorts and cut-down versions of feature films. Castle, started by former newsreel cameraman Eugene W. Castle, began in 1924 but didn't focus on the home market until the late 1930s. In 1947 United World, a nontheatrical division of Universal Studios, bought into Castle, making a number of classic horror titles available to the monster-hungry, post–WWII audience, films such as *Abbott & Costello Meet Frankenstein*. Castle changed its name to "Universal 8" in 1977, but by then its day was done. Just as important was Blackhawk, started in 1927 by Kent D. Eastin. The company specialized in the protean giants of the silent and early sound era, including Charlie Chaplin, Laurel and Hardy, Hal Roach's Our Gang comedies, and Buster Keaton. Blackhawk's 16mm prints were especially prized by collectors. After several changes of ownership, Blackhawk was purchased by preservationist David Shepard, who now concentrates on restorations for the home video market.

23. The society was first started by Everson, Huff, film critic Seymour Stern, and *Variety* writer Herman G. Weinberg.

24. Although notorious serial killer and cannibal Ed Gein has often been cited as providing general inspiration to Robert Bloch, the author of *Psycho*, Calvin Beck and his mother apparently provided many of the physical and emotional details for the book. See Stacy Conradt, "A Boy's Best Friend Is His Mother: Everything You Need to Know about Norman Bates," *mental_floss*, March 18, 2013, http://mentalfloss.com/article/49524/boys-best-friend-his-mother-everything-you-need-know-about-norman-bates.

25. Home theater enthusiasts could argue convincingly about the increasing quality of large-screen HD TVs playing movies on Blu-ray and 4k (and soon 8k).

Realistically, though, home theaters are limited by the size of, well, your home. Even watching a film on a giant 65-inch TV is a very different experience from seeing it projected on a mammoth 27-foot x 53-foot screen like the Egyptian Theatre's in Hollywood, with a public audience. The scale of our cinema experience is one of the things that has changed, and generally gotten much smaller, in recent years.

26. Thirty-five millimeter four-track magnetic stereo sound (or simply "four-track mag") was introduced along with CinemaScope by 20th Century Fox in 1953 with *The Robe.* The edge of the film was striped with magnetic sound and read by special heads on the projector, much as with reel-to-reel or cassette tapes. Four-track mag stereo and later six-track mag (in 70mm) were the THX and Dolby Digital of their era, but as with so much else, *Star Wars* changed everything in 1977 when prints were released with an optical soundtrack. Four-track mag quickly became obsolete, with six-track mag hanging on for another decade or so before being replaced by digital sound formats. Although prized for their superb sound, four-track mag prints are also highly susceptible to vinegar syndrome, due to oxidation of their tracks. See Susan King, "Hollywood History Lesson, in Four-Track Stereo," *Los Angeles Times,* November 29, 2002.

27. Although it's far from Preminger's best film, *Porgy & Bess* is exceedingly rare. Because of rights issues, it's never been released on DVD or Blu-ray in the United States, and getting permission to screen it is very difficult. Worse, all original 70mm prints of the film are badly faded—meaning Ken's 35mm Technicolor print is one of the only screenable elements on the film, which was entered in 2011 into the Library of Congress National Film Registry.

28. The Cinecon Classic Film Festival, now approaching its fifty-second year, is one of the most popular gatherings for silent- and early-sound-cinema buffs.

29. The Tennessee Children's Home Society in the 1940s and 1950s was a front for a black-market adoption ring that involved, among other crimes, the kidnapping of children from unwed mothers, who were told their newborn babies had died; taking babies from state mental-hospital patients; and destroying birth records.

30. The very last feature printed in IB Technicolor in the United States was reportedly a reissue of Disney's *Swiss Family Robinson.* These prints were made in December 1974, but the dye-transfer Technicolor facility in Hollywood didn't officially close for business until early 1975. *The Godfather: Part II* (1974) is often cited as the final U.S. film released in IB Tech, although technically it was the last *new* feature.

31. "Court Report: O.J.'s dealer had history of mental illness," *N.Y. Daily News,* September 25, 2007, http://www.nydailynews.com/news/crime/court-report-o-s -dealer-history-mental-illness-article-1.243706.

32. Paul Grondahl, "O.J. Simpson Robbery Has Colonie Connection," *Times Union,* March 25, 2010.

33. Thanks to collector Bob Leader for sharing copies of these documents with me.

34. Will Rogers, online column, September 21, 2007, http://home.earthlink .net/~willrogershome/id24.html.

35. "The Felon behind O.J.'s Bust," *TheSmokingGun.com,* September 18, 2007, http://www.thesmokinggun.com/documents/crime/felon-behind-ojs-bust.

36. During my time in Hollywood, I've spoken to at least half a dozen people who claimed, with complete seriousness, that they were invited to the Tate house that same night.

37. Although *Daddy-O* is, admittedly, a turkey, it managed by some mysterious process of transubstantiation to inspire one of Ellroy's finest short stories, "Dick Contino's Blues" (1994).

38. Torme was one of the celebrity film collectors that Roddy McDowall identi-fied in his 1975 confession to the FBI. See separate chapter on McDowall.

39. There's no doubt that Tom Dunnahoo was an important figure in the film collector subculture of the early 1970s: a number of collectors Jeff and I spoke with bought prints of public domain (legal) or copyrighted movies (illegal) from Thunderbird, which was one of the best-known independent film labs in Holly-wood. (Jeff even worked, for all of a week, for Dunnahoo in the early 1970s.) Even the name of the lab can be interpreted several ways: while "Thunderbird" can refer to a mythological Native American creature or a classic American sports car, it's also the name for a brand of gutbucket wine—which is more appropriate in Dun-nahoo's case. "I was a pusher, selling fixes to film junkies," Dunnahoo bragged in a 1977 *Los Angeles Times* piece, titled "Confessions of a Hollywood Film Pirate." Maybe that's the way he liked to see himself, as a pirate, rogue, outlaw spitting in the face of the major studios. In reality Dunnahoo was a deeply troubled and predatory individual who was convicted of sexually molesting two young girls in 1980 and sentenced to prison. After his release he seems to have more or less vanished. His former Thunderbird employee Kingsley Candler recalls, "I heard he went back to Texas to take care of his father, and died down there. Some people

said he died in San Diego. I heard from somebody else he died in Mexico, and they brought his body across the border. The truth is a mystery to me."

40. "L.A. Film Piracy, Thousands Copied, Distributed," *Los Angeles Times*, January 11, 1975; and Robert Rawitch, "U.S. Indicts 16 in Movie, TV Film Pirating Case," *Los Angeles Times*, May 30, 1975.

41. Although "IB Technicolor" brings up images of eye-popping, color-saturated MGM musicals like *Singin' in the Rain*, IB Tech prints of *Star Wars* are in fact more muted and "realistic"-looking than current DVD and Blu-ray versions of the film. This is especially evident in the characters' flesh tones and scenes on the desert planet of Tatooine. Having seen one of these rare prints myself, I can only say it brought back a startling nostalgic jolt: it looked like the *Star Wars* I first saw in 1977.

42. See the separate chapter on Lueras.

43. Louis "Louie" Federici was an important art-house theater owner in Los Angeles.

44. Kevin later wrote a magnificent eight-hundred-page study of the director and his films, *David Lean: A Biography* (1996). Like father, like son.

45. Gance's project revisiting the film was eventually released as *Bonaparte et la Révolution* in 1971.

46. The Kinematograph Renters' Society of Great Britain & Ireland (KRS) was founded as a trade organization in December 1915, during WWI. Its ten founding members were: Advance Film Service, Butcher's Film Service, Gaumont Film Hire Service, Globe Film Co., Green & Co., Ideal Film Renting Co., International Cine, Jury's Imperial Pictures, Pioneer Film Agency, and Ruffell's Imperial Bioscope. It had a significant influence on the growth and structuring of the British film industry and continues to this day under the name of the Film Distributors' Association (FDA).

47. *Bob Monkhouse: The Million Joke Man*. Dir. Mark Wells. UKTV, 2015.

48. His remarkable life and career are well documented elsewhere, most entertainingly in Jacques Richard's delightful 2004 documentary *Henri Langlois: The Phantom of the Cinémathèque*, although—and here I digress into true film geekdom—the original 210-minute version screened at festivals is superior to the shortened, 128-minute version available on home video. In the true spirit of Langlois, the complete version of his own documentary is something of a lost film and in need of preservation.

49. In an almost inconceivable act of destruction, in 1923 Méliès burnt the neg-

atives to over five hundred of his films, enraged at the loss of his longtime home, the Théâtre Robert-Houdin, and the forced sale of his studio in Montreuil. To date, approximately three hundred of his films remain lost.

50. DCP stands for Digital Cinema Package, essentially a portable hard drive that contains a film. It's become the standard commercial format for presenting films digitally in recent years.

51. There have been two mini-series TV adaptations of *The Day of the Triffids*, in 1981 and 2009.

52. "Long Jeanne Silver," the amputee actress, was later busted with noted sex educator/performance artist Annie Sprinkle in a sting operation set up by Rhode Island police. Obscenity charges against them were later dropped.

53. Friedman is featured in two excellent documentaries about the exploitation era, Ted Bonnitt's and Eddie Muller's *Mau Mau Sex Sex* (2001) and Ray Greene's *Schlock! The Secret History of American Movies* (2001).

54. Years ago I spent a swelteringly hot L.A. morning helping my friend, dealer Bob DePietro, unload a large haul of used 16mm TV prints he'd purchased from a middleman. I remember seeing prints of several Hitchcock films and, for some reason, multiple copies of the 1940 wartime melodrama *Waterloo Bridge*, starring Vivien Leigh and Robert Taylor.

55. Although it has, perhaps thankfully, disappeared as the public's tastes changed, the early 1950s *The Amos 'n Andy Show* was mentioned by numerous collectors and dealers Jeff and I spoke with: at one point, it was one of the most heavily bootlegged shows in 16mm out there. Why? The series was controversial right from the start: based on the long-running radio series that had white actors playing the black main characters, the TV version *did* feature black actors in a number of lead roles but was the target of NAACP protests almost from the time it debuted in 1951; CBS-TV pulled the series in 1953 after seventy-eight episodes. For decades after, it was heavily copied by dealers for nostalgia-hungry fans. The show's legal status has long been in question: many dealers claim the first two seasons are in the public domain, although CBS in the late 1990s sent cease-and-desist letters to several distributors selling the show. Conrad Sprout, one of the largest public domain dealers in the country, told us, "I sold 100,000 VHS pieces of *Amos 'n Andy* in the first year at $9.99 retail." Needless to say, nearly one million dollars gross for a vintage TV show is good money. He later withdrew the title under threat from CBS. To date, *The Amos 'n Andy Show* has never been officially released on home video.

56. David Jenkins, *TimeoutLondon*, 2013, http://www.timeout.com/london/film/where-did-all-the-projectionists-go-1.

57. Before the introduction of xenon bulbs, movie projectors used two carbon rods—one positive, one negative—in the lamp-house that created a blinding arc of light between them. These rods had to be replaced every hour as they burned down. The switch from carbon arc to xenon bulbs was one of the small but very significant changes that reduced the number of projectionists needed at a cinema.

58. For years it was almost impossible to find a print of *The Seven Year Itch* that wasn't missing Marilyn Monroe's famous subway grate scene, and I once screened a print of Billy Wilder's *A Foreign Affair* that had all of Marlene Dietrich's musical numbers neatly snipped out.

59. *Daily Variety*, January 9, 1998.

60. J. R. Jones, "The Robert Altman Film Altman Never Wanted You to See," *Chicago Reader*, June 17, 2014.

61. "16 Indictments in Piracy Crackdown by Justice Dept.," *Hollywood Reporter*, May 30, 1975.

62. There are several earlier "accidental" 3-D shorts, such as the 1903 Georges Méliès films that French preservationist Serge Bromberg created over a century later when he discovered that Méliès had exposed two negatives side-by-side—thereby inadvertently creating a 3-D image.

63. "The great muted chromium studios wait . . ."—this marvelous passage was written in an essay by Graham Greene in 1937 and can be found in *The Graham Greene Film Reader: Essays, Interviews & Film Stories* (Hal Leonard Corp., 1994).

64. Blue boxing, aka phone phreaking, emerged as a subculture in the 1960s when pranksters discovered they could make free long-distance calls by reproducing the tone used by AT&T. Famous blue boxers included future Apple Computers founders Steve Jobs and Steve Wozniak.

65. Larry Goldberg of salvage/trucking service Film Transport Company (FTC) was mentioned several times as a well-known print source. On August 18, 1976, the trade paper *Variety* reported "Son of Trucker Nabbed for Theft of Major Films," noting that Lawrence J. Goldberg, employed by Film Transport of California, owned by his father Earl, had been charged with stealing and selling prints of movies, including *One Flew over the Cuckoo's Nest*, *The Exorcist*, and *Family Plot*. With stiff upper lip, Goldberg Senior said that "his son remains in the employ of Film Transport and noted the firm is 'completely insured for employee honesty.'"

The company eventually went out of business because of son Larry's illegal film activities.

66. In a sworn deposition from May 1975, FBI Special Agent William A. Mehrens testified that the Bureau had subpoenaed the records of Anglo African Shipping Company of New York, Inc., "a shipping agency utilized by several South African film importers including Peter Theologo, a known film pirate." In April 1975 Theologo voluntarily sat down for an interview with the FBI in Los Angeles and confirmed that he'd operated in South Africa under the names Thebis Films, Crest Films, Acquarius, and Marathon Film. He confirmed that he'd "done business with Jeff Joseph for several years" and that a "conservative estimate of the sale price of the television feature and television series that he has purchased from Joseph would be approximately $75,000." After being shown an export invoice from 1973, Theologo confirmed he'd received from Jeff prints of the TV series *It Takes a Thief, Ironside,* and *Marcus Welby.*

67. Although there are many different 3-D film formats, features from the so-called golden age of 3-D from the early 1950s, such as *House of Wax* (1953) and *Creature from the Black Lagoon* (1954), were released in dual-system 35mm prints, with one being the "right eye" and the other the "left eye." Projection was complicated: each print was built up on a six-thousand-foot reel (with an intermission to change reels); the projectors had to be synchronized with each other, and the prints shown through a polarized filter onto a special, highly reflective silver screen, with audience members wearing polarized glasses to experience the stereo image. It's no wonder the "golden age" lasted less than two years!

Glossary

8mm/Super8mm: Amateur format. Many collectors started with 8mm, then "traded up" to 16mm and/or 35mm. Companies like the defunct Castle Films are still fondly remembered for their 8mm and Super8mm reductions of classic comedies and Universal horror films.

16mm: A "prosumer" format, mostly used for homes, hospitals, schools, and other institutions, film clubs, TV broadcasting, and nontheatrical rental libraries. Historically, this was the format of choice for most collectors: 16mm prints were more readily available, projectors were much easier (and cheaper) to own and operate, and prints easier to store.

35mm: Standard commercial theatrical format for film projection for most of cinema history. A minority of film collectors collect 35mm, mainly due to the increased cost and complexity of owning and operating 35mm projectors, and the much larger "footprint" it takes out of one's home.

70mm: Visually spectacular, high-resolution large format commercially introduced with the release of *Oklahoma!* in 1955. Expensive to make and develop, 70mm was reserved for event movies like *West Side Story* (1961), *Lawrence of Arabia* (1962), and *The Sound of Music* (1965). Very few collectors specialized in 70mm, because of the cost of projectors needed to screen properly, and the enormous size and weight of the prints. Seventy-millimeter prints were never struck in IB Technicolor, so almost all original prints from the 1950s to the 1970s have faded badly (although later 70mm prints from 1982 onward were struck on low-fade LPP stock).

Blue-track Technicolor (16mm only): Late 1940s/early 1950s method of printing soundtracks on 16mm film; contrasted with the normal "grey track" method, which was more expensive and used for 35mm. By the early fifties, Technicolor started doing 16mm in the "grey track" method as well. Blue-track prints frequently had fuzzy sound and would not play at all on some projectors.

CineColor/SuperCineColor: Another form of dye-transfer printing, not done by Technicolor. Holds its color, though can look a bit odd. Both 16mm and 35mm have blue soundtracks.

Dirty dupe (aka: Reversal dupe, auto-positive): Positive print made from another positive print without making a negative first. Such prints tend to have contrast issues.

Dupe: A copy; not an original print. Generally made by a "bootleg" film lab, using an existing positive 16mm print. A duplicate negative is made, from which positive prints ("dupes") are struck. The quality of these can vary widely, depending on a variety of factors. For example, some labs used positive film stock (which was cheaper) to make dupe negatives instead of regular negative stock. Some labs rerecorded the soundtrack; others did not.

Eastmancolor: Various color stocks that are NOT IB Technicolor are referred to by collectors as "Eastman prints," but not all are actually on Eastman Kodak Color stock. Eastman prints (or Fuji prints) printed before late 1982 are subject to film fade.

EK print (35mm): A print struck from the camera negative. Most prints are struck from duplicate negatives to save wear-and-tear on original camera negatives.

Film fading: Until late 1982 most non-Technicolor film prints were printed on "dye-coupler" stock (such as Eastmancolor, FujiColor, etc.). Colors that were printed "dye-coupler" can fade quite rapidly, sometimes in just a few years. In late 1982 the chemistry was updated, and dye-coupler films no longer fade (we hope). Prints done "dye-transfer" (such as

Technicolor, CineColor, and others) had much more stable color. Such prints are prized by film collectors for this reason.

Film rejuvenation: Used motion pictures are cleaned using various chemicals and other means to make them "project like new" again. Scratches and dirt are removed and "filled in" so that they don't show when projected. Unfortunately, many scratch-removal processes cause the film to "go vinegar" rather quickly; film collectors tend to avoid prints that have been "treated" for this reason.

Four-track magnetic sound (35mm) and six-track magnetic sound (70mm): Now-obsolete sound formats that in their prime offered superb multichannel stereophonic sound in theaters. Prints were striped with magnetic sound tracks to the side of the picture frame. Four-track offered left-right-center full range tracks with a monophonic surround. Six-track offered left, left extra, center, right extra, right, and surround.

LPP (Low-fade Positive Print): Kodak prints struck after late 1982 that are (at least theoretically) "non-fade." So far, that appears to be the case. Fuji released its own version: Fuji LP stock.

Nitrate film stock: Original nitrocellulose film stock, made until about 1950. Known to be quite flammable, especially when starting to decompose. Made only in 35mm.

Original print: A print made from the original printing elements (usually by the studios). Original prints have a much better "look" than copies made by bootleg film labs.

Projection booth terms:
—Carbon arc: Original method used in professional 35mm projection. Two carbons are spaced very slightly apart; then a very high voltage is applied, causing a very bright "arc" to form. The carbons are kept a specific distance from one another as they burn. The projectionist must replace the carbons after each twenty-minute reel is shown.
—Xenon bulb projection: The "modern" method of showing film. Al-

though they last much longer than carbons, the xenon bulb must still be replaced by a professional periodically, and they are *very* expensive bulbs.

—DCP projection: The new digital method (no more film!) of showing movies in theatres. DCP stands for "Digital Cinema Package."

Reduction dupe: The bootleg lab uses a 35mm release print (instead of a 16mm print) to make their duplicate negative. These generally look far better than dupes made from 16mm, but again, quality can vary widely.

Safety film stock: Triacetate film stock. Invented in the 1930s, but not in wide use until about 1950 (for 35mm). Was used in 16mm earlier, however. Safety stock can decompose but is not flammable.

Technicolor (or "Tech"): The gold standard for color prints. Generically called "IB Tech" (short for Imbibition Technicolor); also referred to as a "3-strip print" or "dye-transfer print." Technicolor prints are renowned for holding their bright vibrant colors and not fading. Dye-transfer printing has not been done in the United States since 1974 (with a very brief exception when Technicolor brought it back in the late 1990s).

Vinegar syndrome: When acetate safety stock starts to decompose, it starts to smell like vinegar (the smell is actually acetic acid). Film that's "going vinegar" starts to shrink and ultimately can turn to brown dust (which still smells like vinegar!). Vinegar syndrome will happen to all acetate safety film over time, but the two worst factors that accelerate this are heat and moisture. Film should therefore be kept in a cool, dry place for long-term storage.

Bibliography

Basbanes, Nicholas A. *A Gentle Madness: Bibliophiles, Bibliomanes and the Eternal Passion for Books*. New York: Henry Holt, 1995.

Basbanes, Nicholas A. *Patience and Fortitude: A Roving Chronicle of Book People, Book Places, and Book Culture*. New York: HarperCollins, 2001.

Brownlow, Kevin. *Napoleon: Abel Gance's Classic Film*. London: Jonathan Cape, 1983.

Brownlow, Kevin. *David Lean: A Biography*. London: Richard Cohen, 1996.

Brownlow, Kevin. *The Parade's Gone By . . .* London: Secker & Warburg, 1968.

Ellroy, James. *Hollywood Nocturnes*. Otto Penzler Books, 1994.

Everson, William K. *American Silent Film*. New York: Oxford University Press, 1978.

Everson, William K. *Classics of the Horror Film*. Diane Publishing, 1974.

Everson, William K. *The Detective in Film*. Secaucus, N.J.: Citadel Press, 1972.

Greene, Graham. *The Graham Greene Film Reader: Reviews, Essays, Interviews & Film Stories*. Hal Leonard Corp., 1994.

Harrington, Curtis. *An Index to the Films of Josef von Sternberg*. Sight & Sound, Special Supplement, 1949.

Harrington, Curtis. *Nice Guys Don't Work in Hollywood: The Adventures of an Aesthete in the Movie Business*. N.p.: Drag City, 2013.

Huff, Theodore. *Charlie Chaplin*. New York: Arno Press, 1951.

Kelly, Stuart. *The Book of Lost Books: An Incomplete History of All the Great Books You'll Never Read*. New York: Random House, 2006.

Maltin, Leonard. *The Great Movie Shorts*. Crown, 1972.

Maltin, Leonard. *Movie Comedy Teams*. NAL, 1970; revised editions, 1974, 1985.

Maltin, Leonard, and Jerry Beck. *Of Mice and Magic: A History of American Animated Cartoons*. NAL and McGraw Hill, 1980; rev. ed., 1987.

McDonagh, Maitland. *Broken Mirrors / Broken Minds: The Dark Dreams of Dario Argento.* London: Sun Tavern Fields, 1991; reissued New York: Citadel Press, 1994.

Muller, Eddie. *Dark City: The Lost World of Film Noir.* New York: Macmillan, 1998.

Muller, Eddie. *Dark City Dames: The Wicked Women of Film Noir.* New York: HarperCollins, 2002.

Muller, Eddie, and Daniel Faris. *Grindhouse: The Forbidden World of "Adults Only" Cinema.* New York: St. Martin's Griffin, 1996.

Osborne, Robert. *85 Years of the Oscar: The Official History of the Academy Awards.* New York: Abbeville Press, 2013.

Rubin, Samuel K. *Moving Pictures and Classic Images.* Jefferson, N.C.: McFarland, 2004.

Schumpeter, Joseph. *Capitalism, Socialism and Democracy.* New York: Harper & Row, 1942.

Segrave, Kerry. *Movies at Home: How Hollywood Came to Television.* Jefferson, N.C.: McFarland, 1999.

Segrave, Kerry. *Piracy in the Motion Picture Industry.* Jefferson, N.C.: McFarland, 2003.

Vale, V. *Incredibly Strange Films.* San Francisco: Re/Search Publications, 1985.

Weiss, Ken. *The Movie Collector's Catalog.* New Rochelle, NY: Cummington, 1977.

Wheldon, Michael. *The Psychotronic Encyclopedia of Film.* New York: Ballantine Books, 1987.

Wicking, Christopher, and Tise Vashimagi. *The American Vein: Directors and Directions in Television.* New York: E. P. Dutton, 1979.

Index

CPSIA information can be obtained
at www.ICGtesting.com
Printed in the USA
BVOW03*0313091116

467299BV00002B/5/P